THE

THEOCRATIC PHILOSOPHY OF FREEMASONRY,

IN TWELVE LECTURES,

ON ITS

SPECULATIVE, OPERATIVE, AND SPURIOUS BRANCHES.

BY

GEORGE OLIVER, D.D.,

INCUMBENT OF THE COLLEGIATE CHURCH, WOLVERHAMPTON; D.P.G.M. FOR LINCOLNSHIRE; DOMESTIC CHAPLAIN TO THE RIGHT HON. LORD KENSINGTON; CORRESPONDING MEMBER OF THE SOCIETY OF ANTIQUARIES, SCOTLAND.

NEW YORK:

MASONIC PUBLISHING AND MANUFACTURING CO.,

430 BROOME STREET.

1866.

TABLE OF CONTENTS

LECTURE VIII.

LECTURE IX.

LECTURE X.

LECTURE XI.

LECTURE XII.

PREFACE.

In the present extension of Freemasonry, when it flourishes abundantly in every quarter of the globe, and embraces many objects of research, which our brethren, even of the eighteenth century, did not entertain; and when spurious rituals have been offered to public notice, professing to contain a description of the entire secrets, pursuits, and machinery of the Craft, it becomes a duty of no inconsiderable moment, to place the Institution on its proper basis, as a society which blends science and morals, unites benevolence and philosophy, and displays an example of paternal union which is sought in vain amidst other scenes in these times of religious and political excitement.

The pure philosophy of Freemasonry is embodied in the legitimate Lectures of the Three Degrees. These form the Text on which the scientific Mason loves to expatiate. He draws from this fountain his materials for dissertation and research; and the improvement of his mind becomes commensurate with the extent to which he carries his investigations. To make a satisfactory progress in this sublime study, a previous knowledge of the routine business and Lectures of the Lodge is indispensable. The practical working Mason is best qualified to estimate the beauties of its theory, provided he have acquired also a competent knowledge of its history and antiquities, and possess the requisite zeal and industry to surmount the difficulties which impede his first attempts to explore the hidden stores of Freemasonry.

It is a matter of extreme regret to the well-informed portion of the fraternity, that Freemasonry, as it is practised in some of our Lodges, offers to the candidate few opportunities for satisfying his enquiries on the subject of its refined philosophy, and affords little aid towards the enlightenment of his mind on those abstruse subjects which none can understand without the labour and assiduity which are prompted by a zealous desire to excel. It is for the satisfaction of this class of enquirers that the Author has been induced to publish a consecutive series of Lectures, all of which are intended to contribute to the same end, viz., the honour of Masonry as a moral and scientific institution—the instruction of the brethren—and the glory of the MOST HIGH; in the anticipation that they may lead, at no very distant period, to the formation of Lodges in the metropolis, and the populous manufacturing and marine towns of England, in this age of literary improvement and refined taste, where the leisure of talented brethren may be exclusively devoted to a minute investigation of the genuine principles of the Order; that the true and valuable pursuits of science may be substituted for unimportant observances on the one hand, and on the other, an extended conviviality which may terminate in debauch.

It is in the pursuits of philosophy, blended with those great principles of the Order, active benevolence and universal charity, that Freemasonry claims our unmitigated esteem. *That* fills our bosoms with the undisguised love of our species; *this* shews our love to be sincere by its practical development in our commerce with the world and with each other. *That* stores the mind with a pure religious feeling, by tracing the works of nature, till they lead to reflections on the immensity of power—the triumphs of wisdom and goodness of Him, who constructed the vast machine of the universe for the advantage of his creatures;—*this* evinces our gratitude and reverence, by inciting us to "act on the square" with the worthy and the good, whatever may be the external circumstances in which they are placed by the just and equitable decree of Providence. In any other point of view Freemasonry is human—here it is divine. This consideration encircles it with the luminous rays that enlighten the "glory in the centre," and confer its real dignity and value. It is the THEOCRATIC PHILOSOPHY OF FREEMASONRY that commands our unqualified esteem, and seals in our heart that love for the Institution which will produce an active religious faith and practice; and lead, in the end, to "a building not made with hands, eternal in the heavens."

Such being the professed design of the following work, little need be said on the principle of its construction. A view of the Institution has been taken under every form which it has assumed throughout the long series of ages that have intervened from the creation to the days in which we live. It is admitted that ample justice has not been done to the diversity of subjects which presented themselves to the Author's attention; because, in a field so wide, twelve short Lectures is a space too limited to afford scope for all the important investigations to which they naturally give rise; but it is hoped that much important information has been communicated, which may direct the learned reader's view to subjects which his previous knowledge of the art may render interesting, and which the disquisitions suggested by his own ingenuity may illustrate and confirm. And if the fraternity should admit that the Author has succeeded in displaying a connected view of the science in all its principal divisions; if he have correctly traced its progress in the ancient world, until it assumed the form under which it now appears: if he have satisfactorily shewn that the great object of the Institution is to promote the glory of God and the good of mankind; the testimony will be highly gratifying to his feelings; and he will not regret the time and attention which have been bestowed on the composition of the Work.

A spirit of enquiry distinguishes all ranks of men in the present day. Every art and every science forms a subject of public disquisition in our literary societies and institutions; and it is unreasonable to expect that the pursuits of Freemasonry will escape enquiry amidst that universal curiosity which now animates mankind to search into the hidden secrets of nature, and to detect each process by which her various changes are produced and modified.. Our Institution pervades all classes of society, in every region of the globe; and it is not to be expected that the uninitiated will be satisfied with our pretensions, except they be borne out by an appearance, at the least, of superiority; and it cannot be denied that Freemasonry, previously to the present century, had not kept pace with the scientific improvement of the times. A dearth of masonic publications was acknowledged and lamented by our most worthy brethren; and, from this unpropitious circumstance, the Order was in evident danger of sinking in public estimation. From that period a new era has commenced; talented individuals no longer refuse to honour our Institution with their avowed patronage, as our philosophy becomes better understood; because it is defensible upon grounds that are equally honorable and just; and this accounts for its extension amongst the aristocracy both of talent and wealth; and the distinction with which the fraternity is favored in every country where superior civilization has elevated the dignity of man.

A decision on the manner in which the following Work is executed, must be submitted to the reader's judgment.

Various opinions may exist upon this point. The Author has consulted the taste of every reader, and flatters himself that he has not been altogether unsuccessful. The scholar may derive some gratification, if not instruction, from the manner in which the subject is treated in reference to the usages of a remote antiquity, about which written records afford little aid to enlighten the path; while the practical Mason may reap much information from the latter division of the subject; and a fair portion of general knowledge will result from a candid perusal of the whole course. The industrious Brother who takes up the volume with a view of assisting his recollection, or improving his mind, will not, it is presumed, bestow his time in vain; and while he may derive amusement from a view of the various forms which the Order has assumed in different countries, and under divers modes of organization, he will not fail to augment his masonic resources, and become more impressed with the beauty and moral usefulness of the Institution into which he has been admitted. Hæc studia adolescentiam alunt, senectutem oblectant, secundas res ornant, adversis solatium et perfugium præbent, delectant domi, non impediunt foris, pernoctant nobiscum, peregrinantur, rusticantur.—Cic.

THE THEOCRATIC

PHILOSPOHY OF FREEMASONRY.

LECTURE I.

SPECULATIVE MASONRY EXAMINED UNDER ITS DENOMINATION OF LUX.

O'er all were seen the Cherubims of LIGHT,
Like pillar'd flowers amidst the falling night;
So high it rose, so bright the mountains shone,
It seem'd the footstool of Jehovah's throne.
James Montgomery.

Hail, holy Light!
Milton.

FREEMASONRY, in its primitive and ineffable state, was an institution of pure, ethereal Light. But light was Heaven,[1] the eternal seat of the divinity, and a place of absolute perfection and happiness. It follows, therefore, that Freemasonry is synonymous with eternity, undefiled charity, or heaven. In conformity with this definition, we derive heaven *ουρανος* from the Hebrew AUR, Light; because it is above the mountains *ουρεα*.[2] And hence probably sprang the opinion of Eugubinus and others,

[1] Col. i. 12.
[2] Thus mountains and high places were considered throughout all antiquity, as being more eminently adapted to the purposes of devotion.

that Light was the supreme empyrean or local habitation of the Deity, which always shone with surpassing splendour; because the Eternal himself was believed to be the source and origin of Light. In all his communications with man, Light has been his constant attendant; or, in the felicitous language of David, "he clothed himself with Light as with a garment."

The Holy Book which constitutes the furniture of the Pedestal, is full of testimonies to this effect. God is termed by the prophet Isaiah, the Light of Israel. Daniel says, the Light dwelleth with him; and Habakkuk compares his brightness to the Light. Simeon calls him a Light to lighten the Gentiles. The glory of that Light appeared to Saul at his conversion, and to Peter at his miraculous deliverance from prison. St. John affirms that God is Light; and in another place, that he is the true Light; which is confirmed by the Saviour in these remarkable words, "I am the Light of the world."

On this view of the subject, primitive Freemasonry may be referred to the Light of Wisdom, which the Almighty Architect of the Universe possessed "in the beginning of his way before his works of old;"[3] which was "present when he made the heavens, and assisted in setting a compass on the face of the abyss;"[4] and having been communicated "at sundry times and in divers manners"[5] to mankind; it serves as "a lantern to the feet,"[6] and "a light that is never extinguished."[7] This Wisdom or Light is, indeed, "the breath of the power of God;"[8] a pure influence flowing from the eternal source of Light; compassing the whole circuit of heaven,[9] and forming the architrave of pure and holy religion. It is to be observed that Solomon, our Grand Master, speaking masonically, generally used the word Wisdom as a substitute for Light. And thus also it is asserted in the Book *de divinis hominibus*, ascribed to Dionysius the Areopagite, that "this is the most divine knowledge of God, according to the union that is above understanding, when the mind, getting at a distance from all things that are, and having dismissed itself, is united to those *superillustrious*

[3] Prov. viii. 22.
[4] Prov. viii. 27.
[5] Heb. i. 1.
[6] Ps. cxix. 105.
[7] Wisd. vii. 10.
[8] Ib. vi i. 25.
[9] Eccl. xxiv. 5.

ams, from whence and where it is enlightened in the unfathomable depths of *Wisdom*."

In all the divine manifestations which have been vouchsafed to man, it was necessary to accommodate the grossness of his nature, by the use of a visible and material Light. But it must be understood, throughout the present Lecture, that this was only a symbol, or a mild emanation of the glorious Light which illuminates the celestial regions. This is evident from the evangelist's description of the heavenly kingdom: "the glory of God doth lighten it, and the Lamb is the Light thereof." This Light, or Freemasonry, so to term it, was peculiarly intellectual. A Light adapted to spiritual faculties—the Light of God's word and spirit. It was enunciated with equal perspicuity by the Jewish prophets. Thus Isaiah says, that in those blessed mansions "the sun shall be no more their Light by day, neither for brightness shall the moon give Light; but the Lord shall be an everlasting Light." It is evident, therefore, that the Light of heaven is supernal and intellectual; and that a gross material Light will be unnecessary to its glorified inhabitants; of whose complete illumination we are at present unable to form any just or rational opinion. It has been correctly termed "a glorious lustre, filling all heaven—an abyss of Light, in which the imagination is lost."

This luminous principle is represented in our Lodges by the *First Great Light*, and symbolized by *Three Lesser Lights;* which, being material, point out palpably to the senses, a reference to the operation of Light on the mind, as held forth in the three true religious systems which will extend from the creation to the destruction of the globe which we inhabit; viz. the Patriarchal, the Mosaic, and the Christian dispensations. Again, the eyes of the Second person in the Trinity are represented as a flame of fire.[10] Now, "fire is a symbol of intellectuality, especially a flaming fire that implies Light. Thus we read of the *fiery intellect* in the Magic oracles, and of *shining fire* attributed to the soul, as being a certain divine and intellectual essence, as Plethon speaks. Wherefore the Logos is rightly said to have eyes like a flaming fire,

[10] Rev. xix. 12.

because he is not only intellectual, but that great and eternal Intellect from whence all intellectual beings are; as also their operations, exercised by virtue of the more pure, and ethereal, and igneous spirits."[11] The subject therefore, can be treated only as the Almighty himself has condescended to treat it, in pity to the weakness and incapacity of his creatures, viz. by a reference to material fire and Light, under which his personal appearance has been manifested amongst men.

These preliminary ideas naturally direct our attention to the divine SHEKINAH, or blaze of Light which usually accompanied the divine appearance on earth. It consisted of a visible splendour, or pure emanation of the Deity, and has been termed *splendor gloriæ Dei*, as St. Paul described the glory of Moses' countenance when he returned from the mount. This Light, in the form probably of a bright cloud, conversed with Adam in paradise.[12] After his unhappy Fall, Light guarded the entrance of this blissful abode, that no profane steps might penetrate to the tree of life. The same spiritual Light confirmed the piety of Abel, and probably conveyed Enoch to the eternal regions of Light, without tasting the bitterness of death. From this time to the Flood, it has been thought the Shekinah was withdrawn, on account of the increasing wickedness of men.[13] This, however, does not seem to be borne out by sufficient testimony; for it is certain that God conversed with Noah on the subject of the Earth's corruptions; destroyed the world by water united with *Fire*;[14] confounded the language at Babel,

[11] More. Apoc. p. 197.

[12] Gen. ii. 16. Dr. Lamb, (Hierogl. p. 82.) says that the image by which our first parent communicated his knowledge of the Creator to his descendants, was a picture of that vision of the cherubim which appeared to Ezekiel and St. John; and that the Hebrew letters or hieroglyphics for a man, an ox, a lion, and an eagle being put together, produces the phonetic word ELOHIM; and this he thinks was the origin of animal worship.

[13] Ovid's fable of Astræa fleeing to heaven in consequence of the world's impiety, appears to be a tradition of this probability.—Metam. i. 149.

[14] Pionus, who suffered martyrdom in the year 250, under the Emperor Decius, thus addressed his persecutors: "You yourselves, from your old traditions acknowledged that the deluge of Noah, whom you call Deucalion, *was mingled with fire*, &c."—Pont. Hist. Norw. p. 52. See also Whiston's Cause of the Deluge illustrated.

and on every occasion manifested his displeasure against sinners—for Speculative Masonry had its system of Justice as well as Mercy—and confirmed the faith of the righteous, by imparting a portion of that Light and Truth, which constitute the divine essence; *humiles per claritatem suæ ostensionis illuminat;* a striking evidence of His approval of that system of religion which was practised by the holy patriarchs.

This supernal Light protected Abraham in the fiery furnace of the Chaldees, as it did subsequently Shadrach, Mesech, and Abednego, in that of Nebuchadnezzar; shewing that while the divinity assumed the appearance of "a wall of fire"[15] for the protection of his people, he was "a consuming fire"[16] for the destruction of their enemies. Abraham enjoyed the advantage of frequent revelations of Light from on high; and the same Shekinah destroyed the cities of the plain. It was a gracious manifestation of Light that the Almighty vouchsafed to Jacob, when, benighted and weary on his journey to Padanaram, he saw the vision of that wonderful Ladder, with Seraphim ascending and descending, which was intended to increase his Faith, encourage his Hope, and animate his Charity, while the Great Architect of the Universe, in a flood of Light at its summit, gave him those cheering promises which were so amply fulfilled in his posterity.

Moses, at the Burning Bush, was favoured with the inspiration of Light, and received that holy and incommunicable name which still constitutes the awful Secret of Speculative Masonry. The Shekinah, manifested on this important occasion, was a very significant symbol. The Bush burned with fire but was not consumed; and Israel was subjected to the fiery oppression of Egypt, and was not destroyed; although possessing no greater power of resistance against Pharaoh and his people than the feeble bush to prevent the encroachments of the devouring element. The truth is, God was in the midst of both; and, therefore, fire and persecution were equally powerless. Moses was here instructed to approach the majesty of God with his feet bare, and his face covered; and it was not till the deliverance of Israel

15 Zech. ii. 5. 16 Heb. xii. 29.

from bondage that the Light shone permanently amongst them.

The preparations for this remarkable Deliverance were solemn and imposing; and the difference between the Darkness of idolatry and the Light of Truth, or, in other words, between the Spurious and the true Freemasonry, was specially manifested for the instruction of the Israelites, as well as the punishment of the Egyptians. A thick and tangible darkness was upon the latter for three days. All business ceased—no man moved from the place where this awful visitation overtook him—fields, houses, streets, and highways were peopled with living statues; food was not sought—rest unheeded; and terror and dread the only feelings which prevailed. There they stood, each as in a cell of darkness—monuments of the divine displeasure; wondering in silence and solitude what the result of such an unlooked for judgment might be. Visions, like the dramatic scenery of their Spurious Freemasonry, flitted before their imagination;[17] awful shapes, heart-rending lamentations, and gibbering noises, as if in mockery of the darkness, which was celebrated in those institutions by divine honours and loud acclamations.[18] But the Israelites had Light in their dwellings. They were illuminated by the true Shekinah, or Light of Heaven; which was a mystery to the Egyptians equally incomprehensible with the preternatural darkness in which they themselves were shrouded. The Light shone in darkness, but the darkness comprehended it not.

From this time the Light took the form of a pillar of Cloud and of Fire, which in the day time was bright, and perhaps transparent; and at night was like a fierce fire of ample dimensions to enlighten a camp of twelve miles square. It may be objected that the heat of such a fire would have consumed the tents, the tabernacle, and every thing within its focus. But this was no natural or elemental fire, for it existed without fuel; and, like the fire at the Burning Bush, its consuming properties were restrained, although it retained sufficient light for the most distant tribes. In a word, it was the cloudy Pillar,

[17] Wisd. xvii. 14. &c.
[18] Euseb. præp. evan. l. iii. 9. Damascius.

illuminated by the Shekinah of God. This divine Pillar took its station amongst the people, and formed the sublime object of Jewish Freemasonry. It continued with them during all the fluctuations of their history, till their renunciation of the true, and abandonment to the abominations of the Spurious Freemasonry, induced the Almighty to withdraw the Light of his presence, and give up their city and temple to the rage and fury of an idolatrous people.

Nothing could have been assumed to point out, in a more clear and explicit manner, the essential difference between Light and Darkness, than the divine Shekinah at the period when Israel passed through the Red Sea. It was a Light and a guide to them, but a darkness and a terror to their unhappy pursuers, who were annihilated by the junction of the waters, when Moses lifted up his rod as a signal that the power which restrained them had been withdrawn.

It was the Shekinah of God that appeared in clouds and fire on the holy mountain when the Law was delivered to Moses. The mountain was clothed in darkness, and nothing but the smoke or cloud was visible to the people; while the legislator at the summit was favoured with a view of the Shekinah as a lambent flame of Light, out of which Jehovah conversed with him on the religious and political government of the people whom he had redeemed, with signs and wonders, from the power of the Egyptians. The dark cloud has been thought to symbolize the law of Moses, which was a type of the Light of the Gospel. *Congruit*, says Borrhaius, *nubes in functionem legalem quæ tenebrarum est non Lucis;* intimating that the true Light would not be made perfect till the advent of the Messiah; and Christianity contains the most complete system of morals that ever was proposed to the mind of man.

It was an emanation of the Shekinah which illuminated the countenance of Moses when he descended from the mountain where he had conversed with the Almighty face to face.

——————————and we
Shall one day, if found worthy, so defin'd,
See our God face to face as he did then
His Holy of Holies, nor be blasted by his brow.

Byron.

This glory was imparted *ad honorem legis*, and as a special token of God's love and favour towards this meek and holy patriarch. It may likewise be considered as an unquestionable credential, whence the people might be assured of his divine commission, and hold him, as the vicegerent of God, in greater reverence and esteem. They were unable to endure the lustre proceeding from the reflected brightness of the Shekinah—a striking evidence that their minds were not sufficiently enlightened to bear the revelation of the mysterious system which was typified by the Law. Moses, therefore, drew a veil over his face as a token that "their minds were blinded;" and that though the true Light was shadowed forth, gloriously indeed, in the Jewish religion, it would not be fully developed till the veil was removed by the appearance of the Messiah, or Light personified. These emanations of the Deity form constituent parts of the system of Speculative Masonry, as it is practised at the present day.

In the wilderness, Korah, Dathan, Abiram, and their company, were punished by the Shekinah for endeavouring, illegally, to intrude themselves into the priest's office; and it was the same divine Light that manifested itself in mercy or indignation on various signal occasions. Gregory and others think that this mixture of mercy and justice was symbolized by the mild and bright cloud which led them by day, and the terrible fire by night.[19] And it was always accompanied by a subdued radiance of that holy Light which shone in heaven before the worlds were created.

I have already remarked that the Creator was called "the Father of Light." Iamblichus, in his Book of Mysteries, agrees with this interpretation; for he says that "Light is the simplicity, the penetration, and the ubiquity of God." And it is remarkable that the earliest inhabitants of Egypt, the source, probably, of Spurious Freemasonry, were called Auritæ, from the Hebrew or Chaldaic root AUR, LIGHT. If this be true, the Egyptians did not gather the above idea of Light from a tradition of the power of Moses, and the pillar of fire which destroyed the army of Pharaoh, because the probability is that they entertained some such notions before the

[19] Greg. Hom. 21. in Evan.

Israelites came into their land. The transactions of Moses might add strength to their previously conceived opinions, and invest the subject with a solemnity which might make it worthy of more special notice in their Spurious Freemasonry. Many of the natives accompanied Moses at the Exodus ; and some would probably return and repeat the wonders which they had seen in the wilderness ; all of which were accomplished by the agency of God's Shekinah—fire or Light. To such communications, the people, as well as the priests, would attach considerable importance, from the fact of their monarch and his whole army having disappeared in so mysterious a manner before an unarmed multitude of all sexes and ages, arranged without order, and ignorant of military discipline.[20]

I cannot but think that Lux was shadowed forth in the Urim and Thummim of the High Priest. Urim signified Light, and Thummim, Perfection. These appendages were invested with such an inpenetrable mystery, that, if their real signification was known to the High Priest, it was never revealed ; for the Jewish Rabbins differ materially in their conjectures respecting their use and application. The High Priest was certainly acquainted with their use as oracles ; for there does not appear to have been the least ambiguity about them, nor any difficulty in their interpretation. The supposition most to my present purpose is, that the Teraphim mentioned by the prophet Hosea, as being withdrawn from the Jewish nation, were the identical Urim. Now Teraphim[21] was

[20] The Druids of Britain, like the Egyptians, appear to have entertained some idea of the Supreme Being clothed in Light, as is evident from the following passage in an old British Poem :

The smallest, if compared with small,
Is the mighty Hu, in the world's judgment
And he is the greatest, and Lord over us,
And our God of mystery.
LIGHT *is his course*, and rapid.
A particle of lucid sunshine is his car.

[21] The Teraph has, by some authorities, been differently interpreted. Rabbi Eleazer holds, that it was made of the head of a male child, the first born, and that dead born, under whose tongue they applied a lamen of gold, whereon were engraved the characters and inscriptions of certain planets which the Jews superstitiously wandered up and down with, instead of the Urim and Thummim, or the Ephod of the High Priest. (Notes to Thalaba, B. X.) It will, however, be generally believed, that the opinion in the text is the most rational.

but another word for Seraphim, or angels of Light—the true Freemasons of the sky—ministering spirits, continually ascending and descending from earth to heaven, and from heaven to earth, to receive and disseminate divine commissions for the benefit of man; and serving on great occasions as the chariot of the Deity.

On Cherubim and Seraphim
Full royally he rode.
Sternhold.

These holy spirits were symbolized in the seven lamps, or inferior Shekinah, mentioned by Zechariah. They are denominated "the eyes of the Lord which run to and fro through the whole earth;" and St. John compares them to "a flame of fire." Urim and Thummim conjointly signified *the Light of Truth*, or divine inspiration. And this high quality of perfect judgment was vested in the High Priest, when clothed in his seven ceremonial garments as the representative and vicegerent of the Deity. Like the Urim, the Shekinah was a pure Light—a fire that burned not—Light and flame combined without heat;[22] a striking symbol of that intellectual Light which will impart its rays into our souls, if, with sincere and upright intentions, we seek the knowledge of God, and worship him in spirit and in truth. The Pectoral of the High Priest was enlightened by Urim in the same manner (only inferior, perhaps, in degree,) as the Shekinah illuminated the ark of the covenant in the Holy of Holies. It was Light—pure Light—that constituted the essence of both. Hence the High Priest was sometimes honoured with the title of THE DIVINE WORD. And truly, for he was the substitute and type of the Messiah; or, in other words, the Logos of the Logos.

King David was favoured with a glimpse of this divine Light, when the Almighty at Ephrata revealed to him the place which he had selected as the site of the intended temple, and he frequently celebrates the presence of God in his sanctuary. But to Solomon, the Grand

[22] Oppose to this description of supreme Light, the ever-burning fire of hell. It is represented as a flaming fire—a fire that never can be quenched; and yet *it is a place of absolute and profound darkness.* Thus, as the Shekinah was a flame that gave Light but did not burn —so the fire of hell burns, but gives no Light.

Master of Freemasonry, it was fully revealed at the dedication of the temple. At this period occurred the most awful display of the Light shining in Darkness. "The house was filled with a cloud, so that the Priests could not stand to minister by reason of the cloud. Then said Solomon—the Lord hath said that he would dwell in *the thick darkness.*" The solemnity of that darkness was enlightened by the Shekinah, and nothing else was visible, until this lucid appearance rested between the cherubim of the Mercy Seat.

Some theological writers conceive that darkness, when thus opposed to Light, was intended to represent the deplorable state of intellectual blindness in which those persons were unfortunately placed who had renounced their allegiance to the Most High, and practised the senseless idolatry that emanated from the unholy caverns where the rites and ceremonies of Spurious Freemasonry were celebrated. *Superbos per caliginan erroris obscurat.* Others refer it to the weakness of man's understanding; which, even under the influence of revelation, is unable to form any rational idea of the glory of God, who, as we are informed by St. Paul, "dwelleth in Light which no man can approach unto; whom no man hath seen or can see," in this frail state of imbecility and ignorance.

The Shekinah, or Light, was revealed to Elijah on Mount Horeb; and to Isaiah in the temple. Gloriously to Ezekiel, when "a whirlwind came out of the north, *a great cloud, and a fire* unfolding itself, and a brightness was about it; and out of the midst thereof, as the colour of amber, out of the midst of the fire." And still more gloriously to Daniel; for he himself says, "I beheld till the thrones were cast down, and the Ancient of Days did sit; whose garment was white as snow, and the hair of his head like pure wool; his throne was like a fiery flame, and his wheels as burning fire. *A fiery stream issued and came forth before him.*" In this vision Daniel not only beheld the Light illuminating the darkness, but also saw the Son of Man coming in a Shekinah of Clouds to take possession of his everlasting kingdom.

These favoured individuals had a very indistinct notion of the *mystery* to which such splendid revelations of Light referred. They had drank, it is true, of the living fountains of knowledge, although, when composing their prophecies "under the influence of that inspiration which dictated whatever was conducive to the promotion of God's designs, they delivered both sentiments and expressions of which they themselves understood not always the full importance and extent. Sensible of the predominating power, they communicated their divine intelligence as the spirit gave utterance; conveying prophecies of which neither they nor their hearers probably perceived the full scope, nor foresaw distinctly the spiritual accomplishment, writing for the advantage of those who were to come after, and to furnish evidence in support of a future dispensation."[23]

After the punishment of the Jewish nation for the neglect of their sabbatical years, by the captivity in Babylon, this branch of Speculative Masonry was withdrawn till the eve of a better dispensation; and its absence was lamented with tears and loud wailings. Darkness was finally cast, as a mantle, over the minds of that favoured race, whose ancestors had possessed, but misapplied, all the advantages of Lux, or Speculative Masonry; and that darkness will remain, until, in God's good time, the veil shall be removed, and the Shekinah of their forefathers be manifested with such lucid brightness, as to open their hearts for a reception of the glorious truths of revealed religion.

In process of time the divine Shekinah again appeared in the likeness of a miraculous Star, overshadowing the place where He abode in whom "dwelt the fulness of the Godhead bodily."[24] Isaiah had prophesied of the Messiah under the name of Light;[25] and accordingly when he came he denominated himself "the Light of the world;" and was described by his beloved disciple as "the true Light which lighteth every man that cometh into the world." He appeared on earth with the benevolent purpose of enlightening his benighted creatures with the rays of Light and Truth; and teaching them the way to heaven, the seat of eternal and universal Light, by the three principal steps of the Theological Ladder. The Light again shone in darkness, but the darkness comprehended it not. It was in reference to this mild and benig-

[23] Gray's Key to the Old Test. p. 338.

[24] Col. ii. 9. [25] Isai. ix. 2.

nant appearance of the Shekinah, that the Jewish prophet burst out into that magnificent strain of rejoicing at the prospect of salvation being offered to the Gentiles. "Arise, shine, for thy Light is come, and the glory of the Lord is risen upon thee. For, behold the darknes shall cover the earth, and gross darkness the people; bu the Lord shall arise upon thee, and his glory shall be seen upon thee. And the Gentiles shall come to thy Light, and kings to the brightness of thy rising."

The holy Shekinah of Light was visibly manifested at the baptism of Christ, and at his mysterious transfiguration. And as the presence of God in the cloudy pillar of the tabernacle was full of glory, so was the cloud which overshadowed Christ on these occasions much more glorious; for he was the brightness of God's glory, and the express image of his person; and in the latter instance his face is represented as shining like the sun, and his raiment as being white as the Light. He permitted the glory of the indwelling Deity to appear for a few seconds, to enlighten the eyes and irradiate the understanding of his ravishing beholders. They were, indeed, enraptured with the vision; but he restrained their transports, by desiring them to keep the event an inviolable secret until after his resurrection. At his crucifixion, darkness covered the whole face of nature, as a striking emblem that the Light of heaven had suffered a partial extinction upon earth; but, at his resurrection, the Light again appeared, and paralyzed the Roman soldiers who watched at the sepulchre; and was displayed at his public ascension into heaven.

From these appearances it has been thought that Christ was symbolized by the Urim and Thummim. Calvin, Marbuchius, and others, thus explain the Breastplate of Judgment: "The Urim, which is interpreted Light, shewed that in Christ are laid up all the treasures of wisdom and knowledge: and Thummim, which betokeneth Perfection, was a sign or symbol of perfect purity, which is to be sought only in Christ. And both signify, that as without Christ there is nothing but darkness and sin, so he is our illumination and perfection." Archbishop Tenison asserts that the Shekinah or Light was Christ. On this holy vessel of Christ's body, when he was baptised by John in Jordan, the Shekinah appeared; a mighty lustre, as Grotius hinteth, hovering, after the fashion of a dove, upon these waters of the second creation. On him the Holy Ghost dwelt, or rested, as God was said to do in the tabernacle. In him, as the law of God in the ark, and the will of God, known from the oracle of the Shekinah, were deposited all the treasures of wisdom and knowledge. He is the great oracle of God; whom by a voice from heaven, *out of a bright cloud*, or God's excellent glory, we are commanded to hear. The fathers will have it, that when in his childhood he went into Egypt, and was brought to Memphis, the Egyptian idols fell at his feet."[26]

This interpretation of the Shekinah or Light, appears to have been the *mystery* so frequently referred to in the New Testament. Thus Christ himself said: "I will utter things which have been *kept secret from the foundation of the world*." St. Paul repeatedly expresses himself to the same effect. To the Romans he speaks of *a mystery* which was *kept secret* since the world began." To the Ephesians he also refers to "*the mystery* which, from the beginning of the world, *hath been hidden*." And the expression in the original does not vary, when he reminds the Colossians of "*a mystery that hath been hid* from ages." The secret which so frequently constituted the subject of scripture prophecy, must have been of vast importance. It had been carefully concealed from all the world, except a select few in every age, and they were not favoured with a clear conception of its nature and end. Thus it continued an ineffable mystery which the angels of heaven desired to look into, from the beginning of time. The great exultation which was displayed amongst the hosts of heaven, is described in the Apocalypse, when Christ was declared worthy to open the Book of Secrets; into which neither angels, men, nor infernal spirits were thought worthy to look. This inviolable mystery was no other than the revelation of Light, or scripture morality, by the true Shekinah of God, during a visible and bodily appearance on earth. And to whom was this Light revealed? St. Paul tells us that it was first communicated to the Apostles, and from them it passed to all who should faithfully receive it. And thus

[26] Ten. Idol. p. 372, 374.

was fulfilled a series of remarkable predictions uttered by the prophet Isaiah. "*The people that walked in darkness have seen a great Light;* they that dwelt in the land of the shadow of death, upon them hath the Light shined," And again, "he will destroy the *covering* cast over all people; and *the veil* that is spread over all nations." For this reason the Messiah was termed *ανατολη*, the East;[27] because in the prophetical style the East signified Revelation, or the moral light of God. The prophet Zechariah, according to the Septuagint, says: "Behold the man whose name is the EAST;" and again: "I send my servant *the East*." The same phraseology is preserved by Zacharias, speaking under the influence of Light. "The day spring *(the East)* from on high hath visited us, to give Light to them that sit in darkness;" for the prophet Malachi had said that when the time was accomplished for the revelation of this ineffable secret, the Shekinah, or *Sun* of Righteousness "*should arise* (in the East) with healing on his wings."

We have no reason to believe that the Shekinah was withdrawn at the ascension of Christ; although, so far as regards the science of Speculative Masonry, it forms a subject of sublime speculation and unceasing interest. This beatific principle continued to enlighten saints and holy men until the temple was finally destroyed, and true religion so firmly established as to need no *visible* manifestation from on high. It appeared in a glorious Light to the first martyr Stephen, who "saw the glory of God, and Jesus Christ standing on the right hand of God." It was manifested to Saul in so vehement a Light as for a time to deprive him of his vision. And at Pentecost the Holy Ghost was commissioned to be, as it were, a substitute for the Shekinah, and appeared in the form of fire hovering over the Apostles. Bishop Andrews, citing Eusebius, says: "the glory of Christ is now much greater than it appeared on the mount of transfiguration; with which, if his apostles were then dazzled, how can it be now expressed?" And this glory is described by St. John as "the God Omnipotent; the King of Kings and Lord of Lords; appearing on his throne of Light crowned, and with eyes like flames of fire."

[27] This word signifies not only *the rising of the Sun*, but *the place* where it first appears.

The consecutive manifestations of the Deity, in the visible form of a Cloud, Fire, and Light, produced some very remarkable effects upon the nations of the earth. In their search after the true Light, which they had good reason to believe would contribute vitally to their spurious systems, the heathen fell into many grievous errors. The Light of Speculative Masonry was impalpable and intellectual; and hence, by the adoration of the sensible element of fire, the Gentiles forfeited the substance by cherishing the shadow. Their apprehensions being limited to material subjects of contemplation, they soon lost all vestiges of the true Light, and became incapable of comprehending mysteries which related exclusively to the immaterial world. And this may partly account for the introduction of polytheism; and for the very unimportant nature of the topics which pervaded their system of Spurious Freemasonry, on which Gentile philosophy was accustomed to exercise its ingenuity, or apply its reasoning powers.

It is remarkable that, after the advent of Christ, the Shekinah did not appear in a *thick cloud*, as under the Jewish dispensation; because the true Light was now come which should illuminate all mankind. Thus, at the baptism, transfiguration and ascension, the cloud is uniformly denominated "bright;" although, perhaps, containing some degree of opacity; and the Shekinah which inspired the Apostles assumed the form of small tongues of lambent flame, accompanied by an invisible wind which filled the house where they were assembled. And it is ever present in the believer's heart by the Holy Ghost. Still, however, the Light which we have the happiness to enjoy is not absolutely clear, nor can it be in our present imperfect position. The Lectures of Freemasonry contain many allusions and references to the holy and sublime appearances of the Deity in the form of Light; and to its eternal existence as the Wisdom, or intellect, or glory, which, surpassing our conceptions, forms the object of our Faith and Hope, and which, united with Charity, is coeval with the Great First Cause. But when the invisible world shall be fully disclosed, and the Grand Lodge above opened for eternal enjoyment, then shall we be able to appreciate that full communication of supreme Light and unbounded knowledge which constitute the perfection of Charity, and form the true Freemasonry of heaven. "Now we see through a glass darkly; but then shall we see face to face. Now we know in part, but then shall we know even as we are known."[28] And then shall the SECRET of the Lord be fully revealed to them that fear him.[29]

[28] 1 Cor. xiii 12. [29] Ps. xxv. 14.

LECTURE II.

VIEW OF SPECULATIVE MASONRY AS A SYSTEM OF CHARITY.

Each other gift which God on man bestows,
Its proper bound and due restriction knows;
To one fixed purpose dedicates its power,
And, finishing its act, exists no more.
Thus, in obedience to what heaven decrees,
Knowledge shall fail and prophecy shall cease;
But lasting CHARITY's more ample sway,
Nor bound by time, nor subject to decay,
In happy triumph shall for ever live,
And endless good diffuse, and endless praise receive.

Prior.

IN all public Institutions, some form of admission has ever been adopted, with an approach to sublimity, proportioned to the rank and importance which each society may sustain in public estimation. In most cases the ceremony is preceded by a ballot, to ascertain whether the proposed candidate may be acceptable to the community at large; that harmony may not be interrupted, nor discord fomented by the introduction of improper persons. This being satisfactorily arranged, admission is accompanied with various degrees of solemnity, from the simple signature of a name, to the imposing rite of initiation into Masonry, or the solemn ceremony of appropriating a candidate for the ministry to God's service, by episcopal ordination.

Such have been the usage of society from the earliest times; and I am persuaded that the pure Freemasonry of our antediluvian brethren was accompanied by a characteristic rite of initiation, which forcibly impressed upon the candidate's enquiring mind an historical legend or tradition, which it was of the utmost consequence should be preserved; and was hence transmitted through those ages when letters or alphabetical characters were unknown, and oral communication could alone be adopted as a method of recording past events. The length to which human life was extended, rendered such a course equally simple and effective; nor do any doubts exist that this Freemasonry (so to call it) was deteriorated in the slightest degree, either in its facts or ceremonies, while it remained in the custody of the pure and holy race who erected their superstructure on the firm and solid basis of Charity, or the love of God and man. I am restricted by obligations, the most sacred, from attempting to describe this ceremonial, or to name the legend on which it was founded; yet every brother, who is in the habit of investigating the true nature and tendency of the science into which he has been initiated, will be at no loss to discover, in the brief account which Moses has given of these early times, sufficient data for the foundation of a theory on this subject, which will approximate very nearly to the truth.

That the legend was varied, and the points of morality extended by the Noachidæ, there cannot exist the slightest question; for to record the course of events, and to justify the ways of God to man, historical recollections would be augmented; and additional incitements to virtuous actions, springing from the love of God, would be embodied in the patriarchal Lecture: thus would the holy science hold onward its progressive course, till the grand union of Speculative and Operative Masonry at the building of king Solomon's Temple; the most remarkable epochs being the Creation, the Deluge, the Offering of Isaac, the deliverance from Egyptian Bondage, and the erection of the Temple;—and the most striking events which were deemed worthy of being incorporated into the science, were the appearance of the Cherubic forms at the gate of Eden, the translation of Enoch, the mechanical excellence of Jubal and Tubal Cain, the grand Festival given by Abraham at the weaning of his son Isaac, the Vision of Jacob, the mission of Moses at Horeb, the building of the Tabernacle, the slaughter of the Ephraimites, the Offering of David on the threshing floor of Araunah the Jebusite, and the Dedication of the Temple.

This pure and primitive system was founded on Brotherly Love or Charity. I am aware that there exists in the world, and I am afraid also amongst the brethren, a mistaken opinion respecting this great principle of Freemasonry. The error arises from a superficial consideration of the true meaning of the word Charity. Taken in its literal and more obvious sense, it is supposed to be embodied in our benevolent institutions. We have, however, a different name for the sensible and material virtue which operates so beneficially for the advantage of our widows, orphans, and brethren in distress. And that is *Relief*, which constitutes one division of the principal Point of Freemasonry. Thus, if a person give profusely that his name may appear to advantage on a subscription list;—if self-love incite him to acts of liberality that he may receive the homage of those amongst whom he lives—would it be correct to attribute to such a man the practice of true Masonic or Christian Charity? Far from it. His benevolence is laudable, because it is beneficial. But it is not Charity—it is Relief. To speak masonically, it may be Faith, it may be Hope, but it cannot be Charity. These are distinct things. An inspired writer has enumerated them, and informed us which is the greatest.[1]

Again, the same quality may be exercised to establish a name, or to acquire a reputation. And I confess the applause of the world is one of its greatest comforts. That man's heart must be cold indeed which is insensible to it. The blessing of the poor—the glistening eye of the widow as she pours forth her gratitude for benefits received—the cheerful greeting of the orphan, are amongst the gratifications which it may be right to covet. But if our benevolence have only this end, we shall fall short of that beautiful—that masonic Charity which believeth all things, hopeth all things, endureth all things. And why? Because the principle of doing good, merely to enjoy the pleasure of being thanked for it, is selfish and unprofitable; because the praise of men is at best but an uncertain support—a broken reed. It will assuredly give way. And when this shall happen, all our imaginary honours, if they base their existence on this

[1] 1 Cor. xiii.

hope only, will be prostrated and scattered to the winds of heaven.

> And if we fall—we fall like Lucifer,
> Never to rise again.

But let bright-eyed Charity be practised in its pure disinterestedness;—let there be no alloy—no unworthy motives when you exercise liberality;—no secret wish for an equivalent, or covert desire to establish a reputation for benevolence; and you will never be disappointed of your reward—the unsullied pleasure of doing good. You will have chosen for your support the pillars of Wisdom, Strength, and Beauty, and they are based upon the eternal Rock of ages. Calumny, with envenomed tooth may attack—reproach may vilify—envy may exercise its cankerous cravings to afflict and wound—still, in the midst of all these pelting storms, you are at peace; conscious rectitude is your sheet anchor; your foundation is Freemasonry, which cannot be shaken; and all attempts to impeach your integrity will be impotent and unsuccessful.

In order to form a clear idea of this supereminent principle, it will be necessary to define the three Theological Virtues, and compare their respective merits and excellencies. By this process we shall, perhaps, discover what Freemasonry, under its designation of Charity, really is. Faith and Hope are essentially necessary to our happiness both here and hereafter. Without the former, it will be impossible to perform our duty to God with satisfaction to our own consciences; and the latter is the sure and steadfast anchor of the soul. Thus Faith and Hope are essentials both of Masonry and religion; and indispensably necessary to a successful progress, not merely through our masonic career, but, what is of greater importance, through the vicissitudes of a life of trial, if we wish to finish our course with joy. But greater than this is Charity. Faith in God, and Hope in futurity, are not enough; they must be animated by Charity, or the universal love of God and man; else they will be ineffectual to draw aside the veil which conceals the Holy of Holies from profane inspection; they will fail to exalt us to that superb Temple above, where the Great I AM eternally dwells amidst pure Light and undivided Charity.

This is the Charity which animates the system of Freemasonry; and reveals the Theological Ladder, by virtue of which we hope to ascend from earth to heaven. This Ladder dates its origin from the following historical fact: Jacob was the beloved son of Rebecca, the wife of Isaac; and she knowing that a blessing of a peculiar nature was vested in her husband, was resolved, at any risk, to obtain it for her favourite child, though it was the legitimate property of her first-born Esau. She succeeded, though by an unworthy stratagem, in her design; but Jacob was no sooner in possession of his aged father's blessing, than he was obliged to flee from the wrath of his brother, who threatened his life for having supplanted him alike in his birthright and his father's blessing. By the advice of his mother he went down to Padanaram, a distant country in the land of Mesopotamia, to seek refuge in the hospitality of her brother Laban. Being weary and benighted at the close of his first day's travel, he laid himself down to rest, with the cold earth for his bed, a stone for his pillow, and the cloudy canopy of heaven for his covering. Here he was favoured with a divine communication. In a vision of the night he saw a Ladder resting on the earth, its summit extending to the heavens, and angels ascending to the throne of grace for divine commissions, and returning to disseminate them over the face of the earth for the use and benefit of mankind. It was from his throne in heaven, at the summit of this Ladder, that Jehovah was pleased to make a solemn league and covenant with Jacob, that, if he walked in his ways and kept his statutes, he would not only bring him back in peace and plenty to his father's house, but would exalt his posterity to great temporal honour and pre-eminence. This promise was remarkably fulfilled. Jacob's favourite son became lord of all Egypt; and the children of Israel, in the days of Solomon, were the mightiest and the most powerful people under the sun. In our Lodges this Ladder contains three principal staves. It rests on the Holy Bible, and extends to the cloudy canopy. By the doctrines contained in that sacred volume, we are induced to believe in the dispensations of Providence; which Faith enables us to ascend the first step of the Ladder. A firm and well grounded Hope of being sharers in the promises therein recorded being thus created, enables us to ascend the second step. The third and sublime step is Charity; and the Mason who possesses this virtue in its most extended sense, may justly be said to have arrived at the summit of the science;—figuratively speaking, to an ethereal mansion veiled from mortal eye by the starry firmament; which is emblematically depicted in the Masons' Lodge by Seven Stars; without which number of regular Masons no Lodge can be perfect, neither can any candidate be legally initiated therein.

Let us, then, consider the distinctive properties of these three virtues. Faith is a firm and sincere assent to the fundamental truths of religion, viz., the being and attributes of God; the true nature of the worship which is most acceptable to him; the doctrine of universal redemption, and a future state of rewards and punishments. It includes also a free reception of the means which have been provided for avoiding the one and obtaining the other. This definition, which makes Faith the imperishable rock on which pure religion is founded, is perfectly consistent with revelation; for St. Paul expressly says: "Faith is the substance of things hoped for, the evidence of things not seen;" and it is, therefore, the first incentive to obedience; the *first step* towards Hope and Charity. Nothing can cast clouds and darkness over the prospect of eternity, but a consciousness of guilt, and a consequent apprehension of punishment. But Faith becomes our surety, and presents itself to calm our desponding fears. The doctrine of human redemption dispels the threatening cloud, and admits a glimmering of divine Light, that the dread of God's offended majesty may not completely overwhelm his creatures with darkness and despair. Thus the *second step* becomes attainable by the admission of Hope; which lends its assisting hand to cheer the faithful brother amidst all his troubles, sorrows, and adversities, with the prospect of everlasting peace in the mansions of glory.

Hope is an earnest desire, and a well assured expectation of escaping the dangers which threaten, and of obtaining the rewards which have been promised, by the means prescribed in the pages of divine revelation. The belief of future rewards and punishments, united with perfect ignorance of the means by which happiness may be attained and misery avoided, would be a state of suspense the most distressing that could be conceived. Hence arise the consolations of Hope. A firm reliance on the divine promises will enable us to circumscribe our wishes and desires within the limits of that most gracious covenant which God has established with us. An all-sufficient atonement has been made for sin; by the efficacy of which, Hope points the way to an inheritance amongst the blessed saints in Light.

Charity is the *third step* of the Masonic Ladder; its foot based on revelation, and its summit concealed amidst the brilliant clouds of heaven. It consists of an ardent love of God, united with an unfeigned affection for all his creatures. Possessed of Charity, the heart expands—the bosom warms—and a sensation of ineffable and unmixed kindness engrosses the whole man. Nor is this sublime virtue capable of a more restricted sense. If we exclude the divine love, and understand it simply of affection for our species, it becomes earthly; and we should find it difficult to assign a satisfactory reason why it should take the precedence of Faith and Hope. But if we consider Charity in its most extended sense, for the unfeigned love of God and man, the beauty of the principle immediately displays itself. The Mason who possesses a lively faith in God will endeavour to imitate the divine perfections on which the Hope of salvation is founded: and will be jealous to fulfill that precept which tests the purity of his Charity—"he who loveth God shall love his brother also."

Here, then, we find the joint and separate excellency of these three Theological Virtues clearly exemplified. Faith is the foundation and pedestal of the system. It points to duty, and displays the means of obtaining its reward. Hope is a polished *Shaft* raised on the Pedestal of Faith in the existence of a God, and of his superintending care over his creatures. This bright assurance adds vigour to our energies by the consoling promise of happiness, if sought in the ways of virtue and holiness. Charity is the beautiful *Capital* which crowns and completes the system. It constitutes the sublimity of Faith and Hope: because we have authority for saying that "Charity *believeth* all things; *hopeth* all things." Faith imprints a strong sense of responsibility on the mind, and opens to our view the prospect of a glorious recompense. Hope perseveres in a faithful discharge of its duty apprehending the reward to be attainable. But Charity surmounts all difficulties; turns duty to delight, and yields a tranquillity of mind which the world cannot bestow. This is the consideration which elevates Charity above all other graces and perfections.

Would you trace this sublime principle to its source? You must look beyond the bounds of time, you must penetrate the empyrean to the heaven of heavens; and there you will find it existing amongst the happy society of angels, before that black apostacy was introduced, which ended in the expulsion of the rebel spirits, and the restoration of this branch of Freemasonry, the bond of peace and of all virtues. And when the existence of this globe shall terminate; when the Great Architect of the Universe "shall descend from heaven with a shout, with the voice of the Archangel, and with the trump of God," masonic Charity will continue to illuminate those blessed abodes where the just exist to all eternity. This splendid branch of the Masonic science is the distinguishing characteristic of the Deity. All other virtues, whether cardinal or theological, are mortal—Charity alone is immortal. Like the central blazing star in the firmament of heaven, Charity shall shed its resplendent beams through ages of eternal glory.

St. Paul, in language purely masonic, speaking of this virtue, says: "Charity never faileth; but whether there be prophecies, they shall fail; whether there be tongues, they shall cease; whether there be knowledge, it shall vanish away." What were the reasons which induced the Apostle to make this assertion? It was because these gifts are transient, and adapted to an imperfect state, because they would be useless in a state of beatitude and Light. Even Faith and Hope, though essential to every one during his mortal pilgrimage, will have no place in the realms of bliss. There we shall see the things which are now unseen, and consequently we shall not want the evidence of Faith. The first step of the Masonic Ladder being triumphantly passed, will be for ever done away. There we shall possess the things we now long for, therefore we shall not need the support of Hope. Thus the second step will finally vanish. But when Faith and Hope shall have had their perfect consummation, Charity will still remain. The third step of the Ladder penetrates the highest heavens, and can never be destroyed. And when the darkness of death is past, and we are admitted into the Grand Lodge above, the region of eternal Light, the bright beams of Charity will be fully infused into our souls; and we shall make our glorious company with the angels and archangels and all the host of heaven. One mind and one voice will animate this heavenly society; and that mind and that voice will celebrate the praises of masonic charity. All will unite in the most perfect harmony to adore the Most High. Mutually rejoicing in each other's happiness, as there will be no wants to relieve, no distress to commiserate, all in that blessed Lodge will be filled with the pure essence of spiritual Freemasonry.

This, then, is the system of Charity which is taught in a Freemasons' Lodge. Is it necessary to enquire whether you feel proud of a science from which such purity flows —from which such blessings are conveyed? Do you feel happy in the prospect of sharing with the Holy Angels in the bliss which celestial charity confers on the just? Deprived of Charity, pleasure with all its allurements—learning with all its privileges—wealth with all its splendour of enjoyment—authority with all its painted pomp —are but a solemn mockery. Though we may possess the gift of prophecy; though we may understand all mysteries and all knowledge; though by Faith we could remove mountains; though we bestow all our goods to feed the poor, and give our bodies to be burned; yet if our hearts be not impressed with this supernal charity, all these possessions, brilliant and imposing though they may appear, will not help us one step on our road to heaven.

If, in the mansions of bliss, there is a graduated scale of rewards, adapted to the different degrees of approval, vouchsafed to individuals at the day of judgment—which is extremely probable, as there are many heavens mentioned in scripture—each will be illuminated with a portion of that Light which streams from the throne of God, in the highest heaven; as the Most Holy place in the Temple was enlightened by the sacred Shekinah. And though the degree of Light and illumination will be, doubtless, proportioned to the class on which it is bestowed, yet whether they be made rulers over ten cities, or over five or over two,[2] whether theirs be the glory of the sun, the moon, or the stars, the very lowest grade of happiness[3] will be favoured with the lucid presence of God, as well as that which may approach the nearest to his celestial throne, though not perhaps to the same extent; and the brotherhood, even of that comparative state of happiness, will receive a vast accession of knowledge and spirituality, and will enjoy, as in a supreme Grand Lodge, a portion of that ineffable Light and Charity, which has constituted, while on earth, the glorious object of their Faith and Hope. The true Freemason, if he have performed his work faithfully, and practised with freedom, fervency, and zeal, the incumbent duties of his profession, shall shine as the brightness of the firmament; and if he have turned many to righteousness, as the stars for ever and ever.[4]

Let us, then, cultivate, not only in tyled Lodges, but in our general commerce with the world, this most excellent quality. Let us, from a genuine principle of refined charity, practise mutual forbearance; and reciprocate a constant interchange of kindness and affection. If Freemasonry be a beneficial institution, let its fruits appear, in the virtuous discharge of the social duties of life; for the Third Degree points to a day of responsibility, when the transient concerns of time shall have passed away—when the world and all its allurements shall have vanished like a morning dream—and purity of heart, induced by the presence of universal Charity, will alone enable us to endure the presence of the glorious Shekinah of God. As Masons, let us use the present world, without abusing our fraternal privileges; for if all our time be expended in the acquirement of worldly knowledge, or in the gaiety of worldly pleasure, and we neglect to enlighten our minds with this celestial virtue, we shall be fatally convinced at that awful period when the everblessed Lodge above shall be opened never to be closed; when the last arrow of the mighty conqueror Death shall have been expended, and his bow broken by the iron hand of time, that St. Paul uttered the words of eternal truth when he said: "though I speak with the tongues of men and of angels, and have not charity, I am become as sounding brass or a tinkling cymbal."

[2] Luke xix. 17. [3] 1 Cor. xv. 41. [4] Dan. xii. 3.

LECTURE III.

THE PERFECTION TO WHICH OPERATIVE OR SCIENTIFIC MASONRY WAS CARRIED IN THE EARLIEST TIMES.

Those tents thou saw'st so pleasant, were the tents
Of wickedness, wherein shall dwell his race
Who slew his brother; studious they appear
Of arts that polish life, inventors rare,
Unmindful of their Maker, though his Spirit
Taught them, but they his gifts acknowledg'd none.
Milton.

THE study of Freemasonry in its several branches, and under every designation by which it has been recognized in all ages from the creation, cannot fail to enhance the moral dignity of man, from the influence which it has ever exercised over human institutions, whether civil or religious. The political relations, which the nomadic tribes of antiquity sustained towards each other, were cemented by the awful sanction of its local name, as the sacred vehicle of religious mystery; and the rites of initiation conveyed privileges which constituted a bond of union amongst individuals of every clime and every language; while under another form, as a medium for the development of scientific knowledge, its influence was no less felt, by its command over the arts which dignified and adorned nations, and contributed to the necessities and elegances of social and domestic life.

The cloud capt towers, the gorgeous palaces,
The solemn temples,

the works of the sculptor, the statuary, the painter, and the engraver, which still live, not only in the desolate and uninhabited places of the earth, forsaken by the hordes which once crowded their streets and swarmed in their pastoral districts—but in the more accessible form of collections, which furnish the museums and depositories of every nation: these contribute to establish the permanency and triumph of Freemasonry; and here the fame of our ancient brethren will live for ever.

It is, however, a favourite theory of modern times, that the earliest inhabitants of the world were imperfectly acquainted with the arts and sciences; and some eminent philosophers have not hesitated to assert, that they were a race of ignorant savages, destitute alike of moral and scientific improvement. Lord Woodhouselee, in his Universal History, says, that "so entire a change must have been operated by the deluge on the face of nature, as totally to extinguish all traces of antediluvian knowledge, and to renew the world to a state of infancy; and we are well assured that the manners, customs, arts, sciences, and political arrangements of the antediluvian ages could have little or no influence on those which succeeded them."

To redeem the character of our ancient brethren from such a reflection is the object of the present Lecture; in which I shall attempt to prove that literature and science, amongst those who practised the Spurious Freemasonry, had attained some state of perfection before the existence of any accredited records which have reached our times; not only in the antediluvian, but also in the earlier periods of the postdiluvian world; and I proceed to adduce a series of evidence which, it is presumed, will establish this remarkable fact.

It is clear that certain sciences were practised before the flood, by the apostate race of Cain. The sacred writings afford a satisfactory illustration of their ingenuity and diligence in the arts of civil life; and the ancient histories of every nation furnish sufficient evidence to confirm the theory; as witness the record of Sanchoniatho, and the Puranas of the East. On the murder of Abel, Cain, with his family, being expelled from Adam's altars, built a city and called it Dedicate or Consecrate, after the name of his eldest son; and his descendants, following this example, improved themselves, not only in geometry and architecture, as branches of Operative Masonry, but made discoveries of other curious arts. Thus Jabal, the eldest son of Lamech, first invented the use of tents, or moveable dwellings, adapted to the use of herdsmen; and taught the art of managing cattle, which heretofore had dispersed themselves wild throughout the open country. Jubal, his third son, was the inventor of music and musical instruments; and Tubal Cain, his youngest son, found out the art of forging and working metals.

The descendants of Seth, the third son of Adam, were very differently employed. They practised what we denominate Speculative Masonry; and lived, according to an Eastern tradition, in the sacred mountain, with great sanctity and purity of manners. They employed themselves principally in the worship and praise of God; and they had sufficient leisure for this delightful exercise, for they lived on the spontaneous fruits of the earth, and neither sowed, reaped, nor gathered harvest. They were ignorant of the baleful passions of envy, hatred, malice or deceit. They daily ascended to the summit of the mountain to worship God, and to visit the body of Adam, as the means of procuring the divine blessing. They seem to have employed their leisure hours in cultivating their minds, and in speculations on the wonderful works of creation. They were chiefly skilful in Astronomy; for they attained no perfection in mechanical arts; as far, at least, as we are able to judge from the Mosaic records; where little is said about them, except in commendation of their peaceful and domestic virtues of social life. They soon discovered that the study of the laws and motions of the heavenly bodies expanded the mind, and led it from the contemplation of the most magnificent objects of nature up to the Almighty Architect. The sun, the moon, and the planets were regarded by them as august objects displaying the unbounded power and goodness of God, in constructing this vast machine for the service of man. This science formed a part of their system of Freemasonry; and some idea of the avidity with which they cultivated it may be formed, from a belief indulged by the Jewish Rabbins that Adam received the rudiments of Astronomy by divine inspiration; and, also, from the fact that his immediate posterity, according to the testimony of Josephus, attained such an accurate knowledge of the periodical motions of the heavenly bodies as to be acquainted wi the Grand period of 600 years, when the sun and moon resume the same comparative situations which they occupied at its commencement.

Shuckford says: "Noah must be well apprized of the usefulness of this study, having lived 600 years before the flood; and he was, without doubt, well acquainted with all the arts of life that had been invented in the first world, and this of observing the stars had been one of them; so that he could not only apprize his children of the necessity of, but also put them into some method of, prosecuting these studies." After the flood, therefore, the line of Ham were by no means ignorant of astronomy; on the contrary, the Phenicians and Egyptians attained a very early knowledge of the planetary revolutions, and even arranged the clusters of stars into the constellations by which they are now distinguished. Thus their principal deity, Cronus or Ham, who invented, as it is supposed, the Spurious Freemasonry, was consecrated into the planet Saturn.[1] Mercury was the presumed residence of Thoth.[2] Isis was called the dog star. Osiris or Nimrod appeared in the constellation of Orion; and Typhon, in Ursa Major.[3] And most of these asterisms were significant emblems of the process of initiation.

It was not curiosity alone that prompted men to apply themselves to astronomical speculations. It proceeded, in some measure, from necessity. For, if the seasons which are distinguished by the movements of the heavenly bodies, are not observed, it would be impossible to succeed in the practice of agriculture. If the duration of the month and year were not accurately determined, a prescribed order could not be established in civil affairs; nor could the days allotted to the exercise of religion be fixed. Thus, as neither agriculture, polity, nor religion could dispense with the want of astronomy, it is evident that mankind were obliged to apply themselves to the sciences from the beginning of the world.

The Indians were a primitive people, and they paid great attention to astronomy, the rudiments of which were probably communicated to them by the Patriarch Noah. A passage in the Chronicon Paschale makes them famous for this science, even before the general disper-

[1] Sanch. in Euseb. præp. evan. l. i. c. 10.
[2] Eratos. Catas. c. 23.
[3] De Isid. and Osir.

sion of mankind. The author says, "at the time when the Tower of Babel was built, a person who was an Indian, of the race of Arphaxad, made his appearance. His name was Andoubarios, and he was famous for wisdom, and a knowledge of astronomy."

Hence the Spurious Freemasonry of both these nations bore an universal reference to this divine science. When the early Egyptians surveyed the heavens with the eye of philosophy, they were struck with the order and regularity of the wonderful orbs of light which illuminated the expanse; and admiring the beautiful system thus pourtrayed in the sky, ascribed the miracle to the two chief luminaries, the Sun and the Moon, which they considered to be eternal, and hence the Deity, because nothing but the Deity could have existed from everlasting. This belief induced them to paint in permanent colours, or carve in relief, upon the walls and ceilings of their most ancient temples and places of initiation, planetary systems, zodiacs, and celestial planispheres; which have been described by Denon, Belzoni, and others, as still remaining at Tintyra, Esneh, the ancient Letopolis, the Temple of Isis at Philoe, Apollinopolis magna or Edfu, &c.

To describe the astronomical systems which prevailed in every nation, would be a task far exceeding my means of information; but a brief exposition of the astronomy of Pythagoras, who carried the spurious Freemasonry to its greatest perfection, may be acceptable, as it displays some of tne refinements of science peculiar to those early times, and was, indeed, a combination of the chief excellencies of each system; for he had travelled through the world to study the wisdom and learning of every people, and had been initiated, as we shall more particularly see in a subsequent Lecture, into the mysteries of all nations. Iamblichus informs us,[4] that he communicated in his Lodges a clear knowledge of all the motions of the stars and spheres, which he modelled on the just proportions of harmony and numbers.[5] He instructed them that the centre of all things is Fire and Light; and this Fire he placed in heaven and called it *Μεσουρανεο.*

[4] Vit. Pyth. c. 6.

[5] Censor. de die natal. c. 13. Pliny. l. 9, c. 21.

because he said, the most excellent body ought to have the most excellent place, viz., the centre.[6] The Egyptian hierophants, from whom he learned much of his astronomy and geometry, taught their disciples that there were eight spheres, the highest of which was the fixed stars, or the region of incorruptible ether, from which all souls emanated, and where spiritual essences dwell.[7] But Pythagoras ventured to differ from his instructors, and made the spheres ten in number, because ten being the most perfect number, or the Tetractys, aptly represented Heaven. By the central fire, Simplicius appears to think he meant the Sun, about which the earth and planets had their periodical revolutions. This interpretation is doubted by others, because his successors made the sun move round the earth. Empedocles, one of his most learned followers, informs us, that "the sun is a great heap of fire, bigger than the moon. The world is circumscribed by the circulation of the sun, and that is the boundary of it." And if the harmonical theory of Pythagoras, with which we have been favoured by Censorinus, be correct, the earth must have been placed by our philosophers in the centre. This writer says: "Pythagoras asserted that the whole world is made according to musical proportion, and that the seven planets, betwixt heaven and earth, have an harmonious motion, and intervals correspondent to musical *diastemes*, and render various sounds, according to their several heights, so consonant, that they make the most sweet melody, but to us inaudible, by reason of the greatness of the noise, which the narrow passages of our ear is not capable to receive." He then goes on to explain that the moon is distant from the earth *one tone;* from the moon to Mercury, a *semitone;* the same from Mercury to Venus; from thence to the sun, a *tone and a half;* from the sun to Mars, *one tone;* and the three remote spaces, viz., to Jupiter, Saturn, and summum cœlum, each a *semitone.* Thus from the earth to the sun, being three tones and a half, he denominated *diapente,* or a musical fifth; from the moon to the sun, and from thence to the supreme heaven, each two tones and a half, which he termed *diatessaron,* or a fourth; and the whole distance from the earth to the supreme heaven being six

[6] Plut. Simplic. [7] Picard. Egypt. Myth. p. 211.

tones, he called the *diapason* concord, because so many tones make an octave or *hypate*.

Much more might be added to prove that the Spurious Freemasonry of ancient times contained a refined knowledge of this noble science, but it is hoped that I have said enough to substantiate the fact.

Astronomy, however, was not the only science which marked the ingenuity and research of our ancient brethren. They excelled in Geometry, Architecture, and the fine arts; and the memorials of a refined taste still exist in the ruins which enrich the countries of the East. According to Josephus,[8] Geometry was known to the antediluvians. "Providence," says he, "found it necessary, for the promotion of virtue, and for cultivating the study and improvement of astronomy and geometry, to give a long date to the life of man; for, agreeably to the computation of the great year, no less a space of time than 600 years was required for making accurate experiments in those sciences." As geometry is a science on which many others depend, this conjecture of the Jewish historian is undoubtedly correct. Cain could scarcely practice architecture with any degree of success without the aid of geometry; nor could he apply himself to apportion and divide the land of Nod amongst his children, had he not possessed some knowledge of this fundamental science.

After the flood, we have positive evidence of the use to which geometry was applied. Indeed, Diodorus, Proclus, and others, attribute the *invention* of it to the Egyptians, under the direction of Mizraim and Thoth. It is certain that they were well versed in the science, which they applied to the construction of edifices, which have, in all ages, gratified and astonished the world. They found it particularly serviceable in ascertaining the situation of landmarks that formed the boundaries of their respective estates, which were usually obliterated and destroyed by the annual inundations of the river Nile; for on this science also the agriculturist placed some reliance for the success of his labours. Herodotus records the practice of geometry in the reign of Sesostris. "This prince," says the historian, "made a regular

[8] Ant. Jud. l. i. c. 4.

distribution of the lands of Egypt. He assigned to every Egyptian a square piece of ground; and his revenues were drawn from the rent which every individual paid him. Whoever was a sufferer by the inundation of the Nile, was permitted to make the king acquainted with his loss. Certain officers were appointed to enquire into the particulars of the injury, that no man might pay beyond his ability."

The principles of geometry were beautifully displayed very soon after the general deluge, in the construction of the Tower of Babel, which is represented as the frustum of a cone, with seven gradations. It was composed of bricks, dried in the sun, each being nineteen and a half feet in length, fifteen feet broad, and seven and a half feet in thickness. The foundation is said to have been half a mile in diameter; the building rising in stages, with an ascending passage on the outside to the top, which, when the work was stopped, was six hundred feet from the ground.

Operative Masonry had thus established its claims to notice at this early period. And its progress was gradual and sure, for a spirit of emulation existed amongst the fraternity, which led the way to great undertakings. The pyramids were constructed with such geometrical exactness, that they served to measure time. A writer in the Classical Journal says, that "whoever built the great pyramid *knew how to take a meridian, which is more than the moderns knew* 250 *years ago.* According to the report of some authors, the northern side of this pyramid is illuminated by the rays of the sun at mid-day from the vernal to the autumnal equinox; but cast a shadow from the autumnal equinox to the vernal. Thus at mid-day at each equinox, the sun will be seen precisely at the apex of the pyramid, by those who place themselves at the centre of the north base."

In the earliest times, Operative Masonry appears to have gone hand in hand with the Spurious branch; and hence, the Cabiri, who are the reputed inventors of the latter, were sometimes called Telchines, because they excelled in the knowledge of architecture and other useful arts, and were particularly skilful in metallurgy, whence they were the reputed children of Tubal Cain or Vulcan; and the latter appears to have been a generic term for every workman in metals who attained a superior degree of excellence. Æschylus introduces Prometheus, who was certainly a Cabirean priest, or in masonic phraseology, the Master of a Lodge of Spurious Freemasons, describing to the Chorus the arts for which mankind were indebted to his prolific genius. "I found them," says he, "dwelling in dismal caverns, which the sun's rays were unable to pierce, mansions more fit for the dead than for the living, ignorant of the seasons, and unskilful in the cultivation of the earth. I instructed them to build houses with timber and stone; I taught them the course of the stars, the recurrence of the seasons, and the science of agriculture; I taught them numbers, and that surpassing science—the knowledge of symbols and hieroglyphical characters, to serve for speech; I instructed them how to tame the ox and steed, and bow their stubborn necks to the yoke; I gave them ships to bear their commerce to the distant shores of the earth, imparted the secret virtues of herbs and plants, and taught them divination, signs and symbols, omens and augury; and, chief of all, explained the art of digging gold and silver, brass and iron, from the prolific earth—and of fabricating instruments for ornament and use."

To the Cabirean Lodges mankind were indebted for much of the useful knowledge they possessed. From their connection with the Spurious Freemasonry, the Cabiri were accounted magicians, who could equally sway the counsels, or wield the thunder of the gods; and hence these remarkable men were subsequently deified, (because tradition had magnified the exploits which they had performed, and the power which they had really exercised,) and the initiated into their mysteries were deemed secure from all temporal dangers and adversities. From them proceeded all the wonders of the Cyclopean Masonry; and the most remarkable structures that adorned the ancient world may be ascribed to their predominant genius. There is, indeed, scarcely a country in existence, how insignificant soever it may appear in the history of the times when it flourished, but retains traces of the skill and science of our ancient brethren.

A striking evidence of the perfection to which the Egyptians carried their knowledge of Operative Masonry must not be omitted: I refer to the immense temples tombs, and catacombs, which display an intimate acquaintance with this science, and also with the arts of printing and engraving. This lavish display of taste and decoration proceeded, in some measure, from the religious awe which temples and receptacles for the dead always inspired in the ancient world; an awe proceeding from the Spurious Freemasonry. The scenes of horror which were displayed during the initiations, were peculiarly calculated to impress the mind with veneration and terror.

The divine vengeance on sacrilege, or the profanation of sacred edifices, was inculcated by scenic exhibitions, pourtraying the infliction of horrible torments on the unhappy perpetrators of this crime. Hence we are informed that the idolaters had such a high veneration for their temples that they frequently approached them on bended knees; and in times of public calamity, the women prostrated themselves in the porticos, sweeping the pavement with the hair of their heads.[9] And Quintilian[10] says, *sacratos morte lapides etiam ossa et cineres, et ossa religiose quiescentia fracta sparsisset urna.* It would require volumes to describe all the palaces, tombs, obelisks, statues, paintings, &c., the remains of which still exist, and which owe their origin to the genius and industry of ancient Operative Masons.

The splendour, taste, and science displayed in the construction of the temple at Jerusalem, with the curious and cunning workmanship of the cherubim and other embellishments which decorated that superb building, the magnificent cities of Thebes, Balbec, and Palmyra, and many other cities in the East, stupendous monuments of which still exist to strike the artists of the present day with wonder and delight, are so many evidences of the triumph of Operative Masonry in the ancient world, and serve to show that how proud soever the philosophy of the present times may be of its lofty elevation, the specimens executed in the most enlightened periods of antiquity, by the artists of Egypt, Greece, and Rome, mutilated though they be, are still considered as studies of the most sublime nature; and a gallery has been collected in the British Museum, at an incredible expense, for that express purpose. Thus it becomes

[9] Arrian. apud Montf. Ant. vol. 2. p. 37. [10] Declaim. 10.

questionable, whether the best efforts of Chantry or Canova can exceed the Jupiter of Phidias, or the Venus of Praxiteles.

From the facts displayed in this Lecture, we may form some idea of the early origin of the liberal sciences, and the perfection to which they were carried in the most remote period of time, amongst those who had strayed widely from the true Light, and practised the substituted anomaly. Before I conclude, however, it may be useful to make a few general references and remarks, not included in the foregoing arrangement. So early as the time of Abraham, Egypt was a great nation. Its Spurious Freemasonry was in full operation, and it possessed a settled government, with civil and religious institutions. Two generations lower, viz., in the time of Jacob, we find distant people flocking hither for initiation and instruction—conveniences for general intercourse having been established by this politic people, in the form of caravans, regularly passing and repassing to and from Palestine and other countries, for the purchase of spices and various articles of merchandise[11]—while the order, state, and ceremony, observed in the court of Pharaoh when Joseph was a captive, indicate that considerable progress had been made in the refinements which accompany civilization. Indeed, Macrobius says that no people in the world were equal to the Egyptians in learning and politeness, and while he makes Egypt, in one place, "the mother of all the arts," he says in another, "the Egyptians *omnium philosophiæ disciplinarum parentes.*"

The book of Job is the oldest written document in the world, and was either the production of that patriarch, or compiled from materials left by him. Now, according to Hales, Job was cotemporary with Nahor, the grandfather of Abraham; while others place him much lower, and make him the same with Jobab, king of Edom, and the son of Zera, of Bozra, the grandson of Esau. In either case he lived before the time of Moses. In this book we find the most indisputable evidences of the high degree of refinement which mankind had then attained. Philosophy was taught in their Lodges, and embodied in the theory and practice of the liberal sciences, grammar,

[11] Gen. xxxvii. 25.

rhetoric, logic, arithmetic, geometry with architecture, civil, military, and naval, music and astronomy. The people were busied in the arts of agriculture, mineralogy, and navigation; and Dr. Hyde asserts that the Chaldee Jews mention the loadstone in their private writings; and that the Arabians understood its uses. The vine and the olive were cultivated for the solace and gratification of the highest grades of society; music in theory and practice was taught; ear-rings and jewels of gold were manufactured and enriched with precious stones; the onyx, the chaste sapphire, the transparent crystal, the topaz, ruby, coral, and pearl are all mentioned as being in requisition for female adornment; and even polished mirrors were constructed for the convenience of decorating their persons with the accessories of dress. The art of glass-blowing was not unknown; and they were acquainted with the smelting and refining of metals. These public and domestic conveniences belonged only to a state far advanced towards moral and intellectual enlightenment.

At the deliverance from Egypt, the Israelites, with Aaron at their head, exhibited a wonderful facility in the art of working metals; for, during the short period that Moses was in the mount, they constructed a mould in which they cast a golden calf, and finished their work with the graver, by decorating it with a variety of ornaments, both polished and annealed. There is no positive evidence to prove this assertion, except the expressive words of Moses, "he fashioned it with a graving tool;"[12] but the presumption is strongly in favour of the fact, because the cherubim and other enrichments of the tabernacle were finished in both these styles; and it is further rendered probable by the very high degree of chemical knowledge which the legislator displayed in destroying the idol; for he reduced it to powder by the agency of fire. These arts were undoubtedly learned in Egypt.

In an enumeration of the ancient learning of the Egyptian hierophants—for it will be remembered that

[12] Ex. xxxii. 4. Jerome translates the passage, *formavit opere fusorio, et fecit ex eis vitulum conflatilem*—he fashioned it by the art of the founder, and made of them a cast calf. Scapula says *υϱαφιδι*, and *υϱαφις*—is an engraver's tool.

all knowledge was imbedded in the Spurious Freemasonry, and the people were miserably ignorant and brutish —Philo names arithmetic, geometry, music, and hieroglyphical philosophy; but others, more correctly, divide it into four parts: mathematical, natural, divine, and moral. The great value which they placed on geography, appears from the description which Clemens Alexandrinus gives of the sacred scribe; who was required to be well skilled in hieroglyphics, cosmography, geography, the motions of the planets, the chorography of Egypt, and a description of the Nile. Whitehurst goes so far as to assert that the first race of men after the flood, much anterior to the Phenician and Egyptian nations, were familiarly acquainted with the laws of gravitation, fluidity, and centrifugal force. The science exhibited by the Sidonians is celebrated both in sacred and profane history. Homer terms them πολυδαιδαλοι, skilled in many arts.

Is it, then, asked, why we find the nations of the east, and Egypt in particular, at the present time, in such a degraded state of mental ignorance and imbecility? I answer,—the natural fertility of that country, by the periodical inundations of its sacred river, yielding abundance without labour, produced indolence; and the people, being at length enervated by sloth and luxury, the taste for cultivating the arts gradually declined, till at length it ended in their total extinction: and we look in vain for a work of genius in times comparatively modern, which will display the science so abundantly lavished on the temples, statues, and catacombs of antiquity. And hence appears the necessity of constant labour and incessant industry in the perfection of human reason and science.

To these causes of a decay of refinement amongst a civilized people, may be added their easy conquest by Barbarians, and the consequent destruction of works of art, and valuable monuments containing the accumulated wisdom of ages. Such were the desolation of Egypt under Cambyses; the destruction of the Alexandrian library by the Saracens; the conquest of Italy and the sack of Rome, first by the Goths, and afterwards by the Huns and Vandals; each tending to extinguish knowledge, and introduce a period of ignorance and mental imbecility. Even the native Americans, savage though they have been for a succession of ages, were, in times too remote for either record or tradition, a wise, civilized, and scientific people. An evidence of this exists in the fact that more than half a century ago two ancient wells were discovered in North America, *walled round with brick.* It is clear, therefore, from this incident, that, as bricks were unknown to the first inhabitants of that country, of whom we possess any authentic knowledge, they must have been used by a people antecedent to them, amongst whom arts and civilization had been cultivated with considerable success. And this primitive people, whoever they might be, were acquainted with the principles of geometry; for the wells were walled in a perfect circle.

There would, however, be a wide difference amongst various nations in the grades of scientific improvement; and I agree with the author of the Origines Biblicæ, that in maritime countries, where the further progress and dispersion of mankind have been stopped by the ocean —in islands—in cities where men have been congregated together for the purposes of commerce—civilization has generally continued to advance with considerable rapidity; whilst in countries where nomadic habits have been induced, the people have descended in the scale of civilization in an equal ratio to the quality of the country, and its means of affording subsistence, operating conjointly with its extent, and the consequent absence of the necessity for its inhabitants to adopt any means of support beyond those which have spontaneously presented themselves, and which have thence become congenial to them. Generally speaking, however, the barometer of civilization would fluctuate as it was operated upon by prosperity or adversity; for while exertion would be stimulated by necessity, plenty would lessen the motives for exertion; and science would accordingly be debased, and in many instances lost, as it is at present in most of the Eastern nations, on whose superiority I have, in this Lecture, had the pleasure to enlarge.

Thus it appears, that the world has had its bright as well as its dark ages; that the human intellect, in times of national peace and prosperity, has displayed its capability of improvement to an almost unlimited extent; and it is a matter of gratifying reflection, that our own times are marked by striking advances in the sciences and arts, although they are yet far from perfection. Novelties are announced almost daily. What the future may produce we are unable to conjecture; but while we have before our eyes the beneficial purposes to which gas and steam have been applied, we must learn to be cautious how we condemn any proposition—strange and startling though it may appear;—for the ingenious efforts of scientific men may perfect designs which may exceed our most sanguine anticipations. This rapid diffusion of knowledge is morally as well as scientifically advantageous to society. He who is ardently attached to the stirring pursuits of science can never be an idle, and scarcely a vicious man. His mental energies are absorbed in the contemplation of a rich series of causes and effects, which cannot fail to produce a feeling of genuine and unremitted benevolence. Carnal indulgences will find it difficult to counterbalance, in such a mind, the attractions of science with its marvellous secrets, its host of new ideas, and the complication of vast designs which it is capable of bringing to perfection.

LECTURE IV.

HISTORICAL ACCOUNT OF THE ORIGIN, PROGRESS, AND DESIGN OF THE SPURIOUS FREEMASONRY.

Underneath the soil, a hundred sacred paths,
Scoop'd through the living rock in winding maze,
Lead to as many caverns dark and deep,
Mid which the hoary sages act their rites
Mysterious—rites of such strange potency,
As done in open day would dim the sun
Though throned in noontide brightness.

Mason.

In every modification of true religion, mysterious doctrines have been proposed by the Divine Author for the exercise of faith, and as a condition of existence. At the Fall, it was propounded as a motive for consolation, under the pressure of that misery and humiliation with which disobedience to the Divine command had plunged the first created pair, that the seed of the woman should bruise the serpent's head. This covenant was included in the Freemasonry of Adam, and illustrated by its symbol, a serpent, and a series of expressive signs and tokens which are still preserved amongst us. The type of this consoling promise, viz., animal sacrifices, was the primary mystery or sacrament which demanded implicit belief; and it was the moving principle which prompted the antediluvian patriarchs to worship God in purity, under the lively hope of profiting by the merits of the promised seed, who should thus atone for Adam's sin, and open to them the gates of heaven.

After the Flood and the renewed apostacy of the idolatrous race of Ham, another mystery or sacrament was enjoined on the patriarchs which was equally incomprehensible, and demanded the tacit acquiescence of the pious worshipper: this was circumcision. In the Mosaic dispensation, the mystery of atonement by blood was more fully developed; and the type was made perfect by the institution of daily and annual sacrifices—the sin and trespass offerings—and more particularly by the scape goat; the offering of Abraham on Mount Moriah having intervened, that the promise and its type might be kept alive in the memory and comprehension of those who adhered to the true worship, and with it to the practice of pure Freemasonry.

Now, it would be known to the Cuthite occupiers of the plain of Shinar, that the true religion was imperfect without the presence of symbol and mystery. In the formation of a new system, therefore, the idea was carried out to an extent never contemplated in the pure times of simple and natural devotion. Instead of adopting the mystery (*Μυστηριον*, *Sacramentum*, an inward grace illustrated by symbols,) as a matter for the exercise of faith, which is the substance of things hoped for, the evidence of things not seen, they embraced the more literal meaning of the word, *(res abscondita,)* and instituted secret rites and ceremonies (*απορρητα*) to conceal certain facts and doctrines from the people, and with a view of perpetuating, amidst darkness and seclusion, the knowledge of important circumstances, which they considered might be usefully transmitted to posterity. Still there was a remarkable rite in the orgies of Mithras, from which it would seem that they retained, amidst all their errors, some indistinct idea of the original purport of the mystery. And this was a kind of sacrament which the hierophant administered to the candidate at his initiation. We have the information from Tertullian,[1] who was well versed in all the mysteries of Paganism; but he erroneously ascribes the origin of the ceremony to Christianity. "A Diabolo scilicet, cujus sunt partes intervertendi veritatem. Qui ipsas quoque res sacramentorum divinorum idolorum mysteriis æmulatur. Tingit et ipse quosdam, utique credentes, et fideles suos: expositionem delictorum de lavacro promittit et si adhuc memini, Mithra signat illic in frontibus milites suos, celebrat et panis oblationem, et imaginem resurrectionis inducit, et sub gladio redimit coronam."

[1] De præscript. c. 40.

The first retrogade step in the departure from truth was taken on the plain of Shinar, by the Cuthite descendants of Ham; although Epiphanius seems to think that the individual guilt of it lies with Serug, the son of Rue in the posterity of Shem, who possessed some authority amongst them.[2] First, the Invisible Deity was worshipped; but soon a perverted ingenuity substituted an emblem, and it was not long before credulity and superstition esteemed the symbol to be divine, and had honours offered at its altar. The primitive object of adoration used to represent the deity was a rough stone, whether a cube or a pyramid. Maximus Tyrius says, that the Arabians worshipped a square stone, and the Paphians a white pyramid.[3] Herodian reports that the Phenicians paid their devotions to a conical pillar. Sometimes these emblems were applied indiscriminately to the same deity. Thus Pausanias affirms, that Jupiter *Μειλιχιος* at Argos and Sicyon was represented in one place by a pyramid, and in the other by a rough stone. And the upright stones consecrated by our Druidical forefathers are still extant in many parts of Britain; but their shapes are so various that they appear to have been determined by accident.

All the migratory tribes, however, who peopled distant countries, did not at once depart from the simplicity of the patriarchal worship. The Greeks were first led astray by the poets Orpheus, Homer, and Hesiod, who applied names and attributed actions to certain individuals whom they elevated to the rank of deities; for, before their time, the mythological worship of this people was directed to an invisible God. The Noachidæ, by the influence of primitive Freemasonry, succeeded for a time in stemming the torrent of idolatrous innovation, and were hence subsequently distinguished by the name of sages, "wise men, philosophers, masters in Israel, &c., and were ever venerated as sacred persons. They consisted of men of the brightest parts and genius, who exerted their utmost abilities in discovering and investigating the various mysteries of nature, from whence to draw improvements and inventions of the most useful consequences; men whose talents were not only employ-

[2] Hæres. l. i. c. 6.

[3] Max. Tyr. Dissert. 38.

ed in speculation, or in private acts of beneficence, but who were also public blessings to the age and country in which they lived, possessed with moderate desires, who knew how to conquer their passions, practisers and teachers of the purest morality, and ever exerting themselves to promote the harmony and felicity of society. They were, therefore, consulted from all parts, and venerated with that sincere homage which is never paid but to real merit; and the greatest and wisest potentates on earth esteemed it an addition to their imperial dignities to be enrolled among such bright ornaments of human nature."[4]

Hence the religion of Freemasonry had not wholly degenerated in the time of Abraham. Melchizedek, king of Salem, is mentioned as a righteous man, as are also Abimelech the Philistine, and his people, Potipherah, the father-in-law of Joseph, Job, Balaam, and Jethro. Speaking of the latter, Calvin said that he was, doubtless, a worshipper of the true God; but adds, "Mihi videtur vitiatum fuisse aliqua exparte illius sacerdotium." All these men were hierophants of the mysteries, and, therefore, Procopius says: "Nec tamen interim abstinebant ab idolatria." Bishop Horsley affirms, that, "in Egypt, idolatry was in its infancy, if it had at all gotten ground, in the days of Joseph, for, when he was brought to Pharaoh to interpret his dream, the holy Patriarch and the Egyptian king speak of God in much the same language, and with the same acknowledgment of his overruling providence."[5] This assertion must be received with the above allowance. The base alloy was already visible in their superstitious rites and ceremonies; for the mysteries were certainly practised in Egypt long before this period. Indeed, idolatry must have made considerable progress in all the nations of the East before the Exodus, or the directions to avoid it in the Mosaic law would not have been so abundant, nor the denunciations against it so appalling. And Job alludes to the superstitions of Egypt when he declares: "if I beheld the sun when it shined, or the moon walking in brightness, and my heart hath been secretly enticed, or my mouth hath kissed my hand (to an idol) I should have denied the God that is above."[6]

[4] Calcott, p. 15. [5] Horsley, Vol. IV. p. 46. [6] Job xxxi. 26.

The Sun, by its name of Luc or Lux,[7] appears to have been the first object of idolatrous worship; but *fire* was its acknowledged emblem; and hence that element soon came in for its share of the devotion in Persia and Peru; while, in the Delta, the symbol was a scarabæus or beetle, which hence was ranked amongst the Egyptian deities. In Gaul and Britain, it was an unhewn stone placed erect. The person represented was soon obliged in all these cases to succumb to the substitute, and thus objects of worship were multiplied, till a present deity was seen in every work of nature.

In like manner the worship of dead men degenerated into the adoration of their representatives. Every apotheosis was the consequence of some real or imaginary benefit rendered to mankind; and that animal which possessed, or was emblematical of similar qualities, was considered sacred to the deified person. Sometimes the significant allusion of their names to those of certain animals, gave the impulse to the same adoption. Thus Isis was worshipped under the figure of a swallow, because Sis was the name of that bird; and each deity was hieroglyphically designated by the picture of his peculiar symbol.

The doctrine of transmigration, or the introduction of the souls of dead men into the bodies of animals, was a fruitful, though more subsequent cause of the superstitious, and even devotional attachment of many nations to the most loathsome animals. If men could be persuaded that the soul of a dead hero had passed into the body of a brute, it would be an easy task to transfer the worship from an invisible god to his visible representative. Thus it was inculcated that the soul of Osiris had passed into a bull, and that of Diana into a cat; these animals were therefore esteemed sacred, and divine honours paid to them as the visible essence of the deity they represented.

[7] Hence Gr. *λυκαβας, a year, or a revolution of Luc, λυκειος, an epithet of Apollo. λυκαβητος, a name of Mount Parnassus*, equivalent to Luca.—Bet. *the Temple of the Sun. λυκοφως, the morning light. λυκνος, a lantern. λευκος, white or shining. λυκος, a wolf*, from its being sacred to Luc or Apollo.—Lat. Lux, *light*. Lucus, *a grove*, from ts being usually planted round the high places of Luc. Lucerna, *a lantern*. Luceo, *to shine*.—Eng. Luck, from the usual metaphor of prosperity being represented by light, and adversity by darkness.—Fab. Mys. Cab. Vol. I. p. 29.

Hieroglyphical writing lent a high sanction to this species of idolatry, and ultimately transferred the rites of divine worship to the father of evil. The hieroglyphic for God was a star, and the symbol to represent a star was a serpent. Hence from the worship of God under that peculiar symbol, proceeded the worship of this reptile; and, hence Satan had temples erected to his honour, and was adored under his own immediate and familiar emblems; being also, like the celestial gods of the heathen world, honoured with divers significant appellations. Forsbroke, in his Encyclopedia of Antiquities, cites a passage from a sermon preached in the year 1633, to this effect: "Some do rightly style him *Poluonomus*, one full of names, as Argus was of eyes. *Persequitus me hostis, cui nomina mille, mille nocendi artes*, as Hierome saith, an enemie pursueth me, which hath a thousand names, a thousand subtil devices to annoy or hurt us. And indeed in the scriptures, both of the Old and New Testaments, we finde a great varietie of names ascribed unto him; as when he is called a serpent, a lion, a dragon, a fox, a cockatrice, the leviathan, the evil one, the tempter, the envious man, the accuser of the brethren, Satan, the devil, &c."

Thus, by the influence of Spurious Freemasonry, the human race, in successive ages, sank from one extravagance to another, till they worshipped as mediators, not only the stars and planets, but also their various symbols and representatives, animals and reptiles, trees and vegetables, stocks and stones, and even the most loathsome insect was not without its devotees. The serpent became one of the greatest and perhaps the most ancient deities; and the besotted people fell down by thousands in devout adoration of a filthy beetle or an insignificant fly. To such an extent of degradation had even the wise and learned Greeks degenerated, that it is said they worshipped one statue of Jupiter covered with horse-dung, and another, called Jupiter Apomyos, in the shape of a fly!

In a word, as Tertullian expresses it, they had "new gods, old gods, barbarous gods, and Greek gods; Roman gods and strange gods; gods whom you have taken captive, and gods whom you have adopted; your own country gods, and common gods; he gods and she gods; married gods and unmarried gods; gods artificers or lazy gods; city gods or peregrine gods; rustic gods or urbane gods;

clownish gods and civil gods; sailing gods and fighting gods."

And yet, amidst all this abomination, it is remarkable how truly they propagated the externals of the Order, and with what fidelity they adhered to the ceremonies and symbolical machinery of the system which inculcated virtue by precept, but failed to enforce it by example. Thus, I quote from Brother Laurie's History of Freemasonry in Scotland:—"Those who were initiated into the Mysteries, were bound by the most awful engagements to conceal the instructions they received, and the ceremonies that were performed. None were admitted as candidates till they arrived at a certain age, and particular persons were appointed to examine and prepare them for the rites of initiation. Those whose conduct was found irregular, or who had been guilty of atrocious crimes, were rejected as unworthy; while the successful candidates were instructed, by significant symbols, in the principles of religion, were exhorted to quell every turbulent appetite and passion, and to merit, by the improvement of their minds and the purity of their hearts, those ineffable benefits which they were still to receive. Significant words were communicated to the members; grand officers presided over their assemblies; their emblems were exactly similar to those of Freemasonry, and the candidate advanced from one degree to another, till he received all the lessons of wisdom and virtue which the priests could impart. But besides these circumstances of resemblance, there are two facts transmitted to us by ancient authors, which have an astonishing similarity to the ceremonies of the third degree of Freemasonry."

In the succession of schools instituted by the philosophers of Greece, every new system laboured to defeat its predecessor; and the great variety of speculations, which have reached our times, only tend to shew the vast superiority of revelation over the vague conclusions of unassisted reason; and all unite to fix the conviction more firmly on our minds, that there exists in the world one only source of truth, whose credibility no argument has been able to shake; and that the Scriptures of the Old and New Testament, like their Divine Author, are the same yesterday, to-day, and for ever.

The distortion by which these great truths were mutilated and disguised, arose out of the fancy which the heathen possessed for allegory and mystification; and, in many instances, separate traditions were blended, which renders the search after truth still more confused and uncertain. Indeed, the primitive traditions "would have been abundantly more clear," says Bryant, "if the Greeks had not abused the terms traditionally delivered, and transposed them to words in their own language. Nothing has produced greater confusion in ancient history, than the propensity which the Greeks had of reducing every unknown term to some word with which they were better acquainted. They could not rest till they had formed every thing by their own idiom, and made every nation speak the language of Greece." After all, there might have been some design in this, for Strabo confesses that "it is impossible to persuade females and the uneducated multitude to embrace religion by reason and philosophy; and, therefore, *we are obliged to resort to superstition*, which cannot be accomplished without the intermixture of fable. The thunderbolt, shields, tridents, serpents, spears, attributed to the gods, like all the system of polytheism, *are but fictions;* but the legislature made use of these things, to keep the silly multitude in awe through the influence of superstition."[8]

The true explication of the complicated system of hieroglyphics which had been imbedded in the Mysteries was believed to be attainable by initiation only. The acquisition of this knowledge was reputed to convey a high degree of satisfaction and delight; and the initiated were accustomed to boast, that on them the LIGHT shone abundantly and exclusively;[9] that they only were entitled to exclaim: "I have escaped an evil—I have acquired a benefit;" that all learning and knowledge, and every other acquirement were theirs alone; that the Mysteries were the only things of any value in this life; and that in the next, the initiated were certain of admission into the happy gardens of Elysium. In a word, to say nothing of the fact, that no person was capable of holding any office of trust without a previous knowledge of these orgies, initiation was reputed to convey absolute per-

[8] Strabo. Geogr. l. i. p. 13. [9] Aristoph. Ran. Act 1.

fection; and it was implicitly believed that the poor forlorn wretches who were not entitled to a participation of its privileges, were sure to lead a life of extreme misery and privation, and at last be condemned to eternal torment in the dark shades of Tartarus. Servius on I Georg. speaking of the mystical van of Bacchus, says, *et sic homines ejus mysteriis purgabantur sicut vannes frumenta purgantur.*

Warburton gathers, from a remark of Origen against Celsus, that nothing absurd was *taught* in the Mysteries; thus drawing a clear line of distinction between doctrine and practice. It is quite certain that the latter was extremely defective; for these institutions contained much vice and abomination. Like the true Freemasonry, indeed, they encouraged the cultivation of science, which was hence practised with great success in those countries where initiation was most in request; and the high degree of perfection which the fine arts attained in the heathen world was owing, in a great measure, to the patronage and example of the chief officers of the mysteries. And such an example of fraternal union appears to have subsisted amongst the initiated of every clime, that the Mysteries of vanquished nations were ever respected, and in all public treaties were specially exempted from desecration.[10]

It was the unanimous opinion of antiquity that the mysteries were pure at their original institution; and that it was owing to a series of imperceptible causes that they were subsequently deteriorated. Thus Livy says: "Many institutions, contributing to the improvement of both the body and mind, were imported from Greece." And Cicero testifies the same thing. "Though Athens produced many excellent expedients to improve the human mind, nothing was better than the mysteries, which are truly called *initia*, or rudiments of life; for they not only teach mankind to live happily in this world, but to hope for more supreme happiness hereafter." Plato had before expressed a similar opinion; and to add greater weight to the testimony, he put it into the mouth of Socrates, who had been accused of despising these institutions.

[10] Thus when the Eleusinians submitted to Athens, it was agreed that, on the surrender of their property, they should be still protected in the celebration of their mysteries. (Paus. Attic. 38.)

"Initiation," says he, "symbolically signified, that whoever was not admitted into the lesser, and made perfect by the greater mysteries, should be punished by wallowing in the mire and dirt of Hades; but he that had been purified and perfected, should, on the contrary, dwell with the gods." And Isocrates commends them as fortifying the mind against the fear of death, and inspiring hopes of a happy immortality.

When such was the veneration for these Rites, it may be easily conceived that initiation would be in great request. And accordingly we find that all, who had any regard for their personal reputation or future happiness, were anxious to acquire a competent knowledge of the Mysteries through that legitimate medium. This was a Freemasonry which penetrated through all ranks of mankind except the very lowest; because the requisites for initiation were, that a man should be a *free born* denizen of the country, of mature age, sound judgment, and strict morality.[11] Hence, neither slaves nor foreigners could be admitted;[12] because the doctrines therein revealed were considered of too much value to be entrusted to the keeping of those who had no interest in the general welfare of the community. St. Austin, quoting Varro, says that such a communication might have been prejudicial to the state; for slaves were not unfrequently plotters of mischief, and fomenters of sedition; and a suspicion whispered against the truth of the popular religion would have constituted a fearful engine in the hands of an artful and enterprising conspirator, by which the people might have been moved at pleasure. The vulgar were therefore kept in awe by the supposition of some hidden mystery, which it would be fatal to penetrate.[13]

The effects which were thus produced, even in the most refined states, and periods, have excited the indignation of all posterity. The uninitiated and slaves were

[11] "Since the benefits of initiation were so vastly great, no wonder if the hierophants were very cautious what persons they admitted to it; therefore such as were convicted of witchcraft, or any other heinous crime, or had committed murder, though against their wills, were debarred from these mysteries; and, though in later ages, all persons, barbarians excepted, were admitted to them, yet in the primitive times, the Athenians excluded all strangers, that is, all that were not members of their own commonwealth." (Potter, Arch. vol. 1. p. 419.)

[12] Diod. Sic. 5.

[13] Liban. Decl. 19.

considered no better than outcasts; and the laws, even of Lycurgus, maintained the policy of brutifying their minds to the lowest point. "Never was human nature degraded," says Mitford, "by system, to such a degree as in the miserable Helots. Every imaginable method was taken to set them at the widest distance from their haughty masters. Even vice was commanded to them. They were compelled to drunkenness, for the purpose of exhibiting to the young Lacedemonians the ridiculous and contemptible condition to which men are reduced by it. They were forbidden every thing manly; and they were commanded every thing humiliating, of which man is capable while beasts are not."[14]

By requiring virtue in every candidate, it was intended to prevent the commission of *public* crime; for it is well known that, unlike the Freemasonry of which they vainly imagined themselves to be possessed, the indulgence of private vices was at least connived at in these institutions, if not openly encouraged.

The Lesser Mysteries were accessible to all ranks and descriptions of people—even women and children were not rejected. "Influunt turbæ," says Apuleius, "sacris divinis initiatæ, viri fæminæque, omnis ætatis, et omnis dignitatis." But these inferior celebrations consisted merely of a few simple rites, which constituted the ceremony of admission to the practice of their religious duties, like Jewish circumcision, or Christian baptism; and all the information communicated at that solemnity was limited to a few mythological facts respecting the principal deities, which might tend to confirm the aspirant in his belief of the virtues which would arise from a steady conformity to the current system of polytheism.

> Discite justitiam moniti, ed non temnere Divos.
>
> ÆN. vi. 620.

The lesser festival, says Archbishop Potter, was used as a preparation to the greater; for no persons were initiated in the greater, unless they had been purified at the lesser; the manner of which purification was this: Having kept themselves chaste and unpolluted nine days, they came and offered sacrifices and prayers, wearing

[14] Mitford. Greece. i. 317.

crowns and garlands of flowers, which were called *Ismera* or *Imera;* they had also, under their feet, Jupiter's skin, which was the skin of a victim offered to that god. The person that assisted them herein was called *Udranus*, from *udor*, i. e. water; which was used at most purifications; themselves were named *Mustæ*, i. e. persons initiated. About a year after, having sacrificed a sow to Ceres, they were admitted to the superior Degrees.[15]

But the Greater Mysteries, which contained the doctrines so clearly revealed in the Mosaic history, and which appertain to the designs of Providence in the salvation of man[16]—veiled, indeed, and often misunderstood—were of too serious a nature to be thus freely exposed. They were communicated only to a select few, and even to them under the most awful sanctions. This will account for the silence of the early historians on most of these subjects. Cuvier concludes, most unphilosophically, that all remembrance of the Deluge was lost because it is not mentioned by Sanchoniatho, neither "are any traces of it to be found in Egypt in ancient records." The fact is, that this knowledge was preserved in the Mysteries by the Anaglyph, or sacred character of the priests; and to whomsoever it might be revealed, its publication was prohibited under heavy penalties. As in the genuine Freemasonry, secrecy was recommended and enforced by every possible expedient. The Egyptians set up a statue of Harpocrates, with his right hand on his heart, and his left pendant by his side, and full of eyes and ears, but without a tongue—to intimate that whatever may be seen and heard in the mysterious celebrations, ought never to be spoken. The Greeks, in like manner, erected a statue of brass at Athens without a tongue, to enjoin secrecy; and the Romans had a goddess of Silence, who was represented with her forefinger on her lips.

These practical lessons made such an impression on the people, that from a simple suspicion that Eschylus had introduced into one of his plays some reference to the mysterious doctrines, the poet preserved his life only by taking sanctuary at the altar of Bacchus, until he had an opportunity of appealing to the Areopagus.[17] Pausa-

[15] Potter Arch. i. 420. [16] Clem. Alex. Strom. 5.
[17] Ibid. Strom. 2. Aristot. l. 3. c. 1.

nias, in his History of Greece, assigns to the mysteries such a venerable sanctity that he is obliged to pass over them in silence.[18] And, in another place, he excuses himself from making a revelation of their secrets by a very ingenious device. "I intended," he says, "to have entered on a particular description of the Eleusinian temple at Athens, and all its services; but my design was prevented by a prohibition *communicated to me in a dream.*[19] And he accuses Homer[20] of boldness for the insertion of certain particulars in his poem *respecting the souls in Hades,* or, in other words, respecting the initiations. Horace was thus pointed in his opinion respecting those who betrayed the secrets of the Spurious Freemasonry:—

> Est et fideli tuta silentio
> Marces: vetabo qui Cereris sacrum
> Vulgarit arcanæ, sub iisdem
> Sit trabibus, fragilemve mecum
> Solvat Phaselum.
>
> OD. iii. 2. 25.

Indeed, the priests of all nations were so chary in the revelation of their sacred Mysteries, that it constituted their chief boast that no one was able "to lift up their veil."

To make the impression still more affecting, the Greater Mysteries were celebrated at dead of night, in the deep recesses of caverns, amidst darkness and seclusion, attended with horrible representations of the sufferings which departed souls endured who had died without regeneration, or, which is the same thing, who had incurred the displeasure of those in whose custody these institutions were placed.

> And many a godlike form there met his eye,
> And many an emblem dark of mystery.
>
> SOUTHEY. *Kehama.* xvi. 2.

And the open sanction of the civil magistrate[21] was added, if it be true that the Senate assembled after each celebration, to enquire whether it had been conducted according to the prescribed formula, without irregularity or profanation.

When the mind had been subdued by these scenes to

[18] Messen. iv. 33. [19] Paus. l. i. 14. [20] Messen. p. 17.
[21] Andoc. de Mys. vol. I. p. 159.

the requisite point of implicit submission and unreserved faith and obedience, the ineffable doctrines, on which the whole fabric of true religion rests, were gradually unfolded as profound secrets, the very whisper of any one of which could only be atoned for with life. "Si quis arcanæ mysteria Cereris sacra vulgasset, lege morti addicebatur." These were the Unity and Trinity of the Godhead, including the startling fact, that the popular deities of their mythology were only dead men, who had been canonized by their ancestors for benefits rendered to mankind; the creation and institution of a Sabbath; the fall of man by means of a serpent-tempter, and his restoration through the voluntary obedience of a Mediator, who should bruise the serpent's head; the universal deluge; and a future state, with its necessary concomitant, the immortality of the soul.

These are doctrines which were essential to the true Freemasonry in all ages of the world; and still remain to invigorate our Order with the vivifying principle of religion, without which Freemasonry would be a skeleton of dry bones, and unworthy the attention of a rational being. That they formed part of the imitative systems of antiquity, there is no lack of proof. On all the above points the evidence is full and clear; not consisting in detached and solitary allusions, and dark hints thinly dispersed throughout the writings of antiquity, but broadly declared in language which cannot admit of cavil or doubt.

And there is nothing in the admission of this fact which is inconsistent with the attributes of the Deity. If the Governor of the Universe thought proper to permit such an universal defection from truth, it was intended not only to conduce to some further purposes of his providence, but as a means of contributing to the perfection of those secret purposes which were designed for the ultimate benefit of all his creatures. King, in the "Origin of Evil," maintains the principle, that if God had been inclined to have removed this evil, it would have been at the sacrifice of a certain portion of good. On a full inquiry into this intricate subject, we shall find that, as St. Paul assures us,[22] he did permit idolatry and its attendant

[22] Acts. xiv. 16.

mysteries to exist amongst mankind, for the purpose of conveying throughout the whole world the sublime truths connected with his gracious purposes respecting our salvation, although human perversity studiously endeavoured to throw them into shade.

LECTURE V.

ON THE ORIGIN OF HIEROGLYPHICS.

But on the south, a long majestic race
Of Egypt's priests the gilded niches grace,
Who measured earth, described the starry spheres,
And trac'd the long records of lunar years.
Between the statues obelisks were plac'd
And the learn'd walls with hieroglyphics grac'd.

Pope.

I HAVE asserted, and in a future Lecture shall endeavour to prove, that a system of symbolical instruction was profusely used in the Spurious Freemasonry of ancient times—but this is not enough for my purpose. I must first make it appear that the elementary principles of the system originated amongst the sons of Light; trace its existence in the infancy of time, and show that it pervaded the more ancient institutions of truth, and was sanctioned by the approbation of the Deity.

The knowledge of symbols is of great importance in the illustration of Freemasonry, because they were used in all its branches, whether Speculative, Operative, or Spurious. A dissertation, therefore, on their nature and properties will be of peculiar utility, because the chief excellence of our sublime science consists in its emblems, which embody every thing that is commendable and praiseworthy in the system. I assume that alphabetical characters, in their primitive state, were but a series of substantive emblems, or simple representations of language, which itself, in the first ages of the world, was so figurative as to constitute a speaking picture.

Shuckford, in his Connection of Sacred and Profane History, has expressed an opinion that "the first language had but one part of speech; and consisted chiefly of a few names for the creatures and things mankind had to do with." The arguments used in support of this proposition do not appear conclusive. The art of thinking, which is the arrangement of our ideas from the perceptions of natural objects, cannot exist without some degree of reason; and the various and abstruse combinations of reason will scarcely be produced without the use of words expressing *qualities*, action, or passion, as well as connectives to draw consequences, or blend ideas which are relative, uniform, and rational. Adam was possessed of this faculty, for he named the animals from the observation of individual properties possessed by each. Thus his perception furnished him with ideas; his ideas produced reasoning, and reasoning was completed by the use of language. He observed that each beast had some symbolical property, and the word which expressed it was adopted as the name of the animal. If it be objected that, before the Fall, animals were equally peaceable, and that it was during this season of quiet and tractability that Adam gave them names, the conclusion will be the same, so far as respects the argument in question; for it is sufficient to know that the names he gave them were expressive of those actual qualities by which they were afterwards distinguished, for the knowledge of their future characteristic properties might have been dictated by inspiration.

And this is confirmed by the method which Eve afterwards observed in giving names to her children. When Cain was born, she said: "I have acquired *possession* of a man of my own species: I will therefore call him Cain;" which word signifies acquisition or possession. Her children she bore in *sorrow and pain*, in consequence of the curse, and therefore she named her second son Abel, which signifies affliction.[1] After the murder of Abel and the migration of Cain, God *appointed* her another son, whom she named Seth, because that word signifies to appoint. These are evidently deductions drawn from premises, which is reasoning in its simplest or most elementary state, and constituted the germ of picture writing,

[1] Dr. Lamb (Hierogl. p. 57) interprets these names differently. Cain, he says, means *man of my womb; Abel, son of a living creature;* Seth, *of fair complexion.*

which was the earliest form that written characters assumed. But this reasoning could scarcely have been used without words expressing something more than the abstract names of animals.

But God conversed with Adam in the garden of Eden, and communicated to him his relative situation, both with regard to himself as his superior, and to the animal which he had placed in subjection under him. He gav him rules and directions for the government of his con duct, and threatened the infliction of a terrible penalty in case of disobedience. But could all this have been effected with the assistance of that limited degree of knowledge which Adam is said to have enjoyed in paradise, aided by the confined faculty of speech which the use of only *one sort of words* could afford? Could the denunciation of the penalty which produced such dreadful effects as to need the revelation of a Saviour to soothe the troubled minds of our first parents; could the sentence of banishment, and the curse of thorns and thistles have been pronounced without some other aid? Surely not. And the divine beneficence would not have left his favoured creature darkened by ignorance, without the power of self-improvement, except by the slow and gradual progess of human sagacity and invention. We know that man was endowed with reason and speech; we conclude that he was also endowed with words sufficient to use those faculties, for his own immediate gratification and benefit; and these words being figures of the things represented, constituted the first approach to hieroglyphics or alphabetical characters.

Expressive symbols, however, were coeval with the creation of the first man, of which the divine covenant itself is an example; for the trees of life and knowledge were emblematical of life and happiness, or death and misery. The latter symbol was realized by the transgression of Adam when the Shekinah was introduced to figure the divine displeasure. At the deluge the olive leaf was a symbol of peace, and the rainbow of reconciliation. Thus early had the system an existence.

It is true, grammar was not reduced into the form of a distinct science until the experience of many ages, and the invention of many arts and sciences had taught mankind the necessity of placing language under certain laws, in order to render it fixed and permanent; for so long as it continued arbitrary and changeable, there existed no certain method of distinguishing the thing meant by the thing expressed. The common intercourse of mankind would indeed, during the first ages, tend to prevent this effect; but when mankind were dispersed over the whole face of the earth, and the intercourse of different nations was only accidental and casual, many essential alterations would ensue to change the nature and idiom of the original language without the protection of grammar. But when language became restricted within certain prescribed limits, numerous and rapid improvements would take place. Expressions and phrases would become more precise and correct; less circumlocution would be necessary: and the introduction of new words, as occasion might require, would obviate the harshness necessarily attending that recurrence of the same expression which is now called *tautology*. The first languages were less comprehensive and more simple than those of later date, but they do not yield to any in sublimity and force.

It was in this state of language that alphabetical characters were probably first used. They were purely hieroglyphical; and there is great probability that the progress of refinement would improve and simplify these primitive characters, which, as in the known case of China, would be infinite in number and diversity, by the substitution of signs that would be more easy of adaptation to general use. Accordingly, in the alphabets of Abubkr, preserved by Ben Washih we may trace, without any difficulty, the connection between concurrent alphabets, and the transitions from one to another, as the ideas of men developed themselves, and suggested the utility of a comprehensive system of notation which might blend simplicity and usefulness. "The original mode of writing," says Spineto,[2] "was the exact figure of the object which, for the sake of diminishing labour, became first a simple drawing of the outline; and ultimately an arbitrary mark, which produced the three different modes of writing amongst the Egyptiuns, generally designated by the appellations of hieroglyphic, demotic, and hieratic."

[2] Hier. ix. 297.

Another cause hastened and advanced the art of a conventional system of written signs or characters, as a means of recording events, or transmitting knowledge to posterity; viz. the imagery in which primitive language was clothed. Rhetoric is a science which sprang naturally out of language; for the rudest savages will express, with simple energy, love and hatred, accusation, persuasion, and defence. Hence this science existed in the very first ages; unrestricted, indeed, by rule or method, and governed only by the passions and affections of those who used it. Primitive argumentation was rude and unembellished; and directed solely to the purpose in view. A striking instance of this is exhibited in Cain's defence against the divine accusation. At first he sternly denies any knowledge of the fate of his brother; but, to qualify this bold falsehood, he resorts to subterfuge: "Am I my brother's keeper? When his sentence is pronounced, he endeavours, by a subdued language, to awaken the pity of his judge, in mitigation of punishment: "And Cain said unto the Lord, my punishment is greater than I can bear. Behold thou hast driven me out this day from the face of the earth, and from thy face shall I be hid; and I shall be a fugitive and a vagabond in the earth; and it shall come to pass that every one that findeth me shall slay me.[3] Another specimen of this sort of rhetoric occurs in the address of Lamech to his wives; and these are sufficient to authorise the conclusion, that the language of Adam and the first world was sufficiently copious not merely for the purposes of a civil and social state, but it possessed enough of character to convey to posterity the great truths of creation and providence.

Before language assumed the form of copiousness it has since attained, it would perhaps be difficult to express a flow of ideas without circumlocution, or the use of symbolical imagery; and thus, what are now esteemed the graces and ornaments of style, were originally adopted from necessity. And this very necessity would suggest a form of written expression to perpetuate facts. Thus, in what is called the Nabathean alphabet, which is reputed

[3] This speech would form a striking Picture, if printed in hieroglyphical characters.

to be antediluvian, this method was used. If, for instance, they wished to record the fact of a man having died a violent death, they used these characters.

And nothing could more strongly express the seven kinds of violent death, than these figures, viz.: death by lightning, the guillotine, by a serpent, a hatchet, poison, a dagger, or the cord.

In the early simplicity of an unformed language, qualities were described tropically, or by the use of visible objects which appeared to possess similar attributes. Thus, to express the quality of firmness of mind, and personal strength and courage, recourse was had to some stately or majestic production of nature; and the *oak* and the *lion*, being observed to display the quality of firmness in its highest perfection, were used to convey the idea. Hence a warrior was termed a lion or an oak; while on the other hand a weak and irresolute man was designated by a reed; insincerity by a serpent, and fidelity by a dog. These figures, if scrawled with a staff upon sand, would have been picture-writing. But the probabilities are, that historical events, at the least, would be depicted in symbols on tablets, for preservation by the heads of tribes, or as the hieroglyphics or sacred writings of their respective families; including all the great events and predictions which it would concern posterity to know. This was a part of the true, and the origin of the Spurious Freemasonry of ancient times; and hence the heathen probably derived the traditions of truth which their systems undoubtedly contained.

The above practice, being necessarily prevalent in general use, it may be readily conceived that when mankind first began to feel the necessity of some method of written communication, it would be at once transferred to the tablet. Accordingly, we find that the origin of hieroglyphics was this very picture-writing; which would be exceedingly simple, and consist merely of a representation of any concise fact they wished to record, by scrawling some visible object connected with it. Experience would soon proclaim the total inadequacy of this plan. Gradual improvements arose to meet the necessities of ripening knowledge, and *hiero-*

glyphics were invented, to designate invisible objects or qualities; and, in process of time, these were combined and formed into a regular system. But whether the use of alphabetical characters sprang out of hieroglyphics, is a question on which the evidence is very imperfect and unsatisfactory. The truth is, that in the most early times letters and hieroglyphics were probably the same;[4] and they were the ripened fruits of a system of picture-writing, by exchanging the hieroglyphic for a phonetic character. "When once this important discovery was made, these characters would shortly be reduced to the same, or nearly the same, form as we now find them. The number of consonants does not depend upon the genius of each particular language, but upon certain organs of the animal man; and, as these are uniform throughout the whole race, the same alphabet would be applicable to every language. This discovery would soon be known to the neighbouring nations; and in no very long time it would be generally adopted. Each separate people would not repeat the process by which the first inventor had arrived at so happy a result; but would, if I may be allowed the expression, translate their own pictures into the two and twenty sounds already provided for them. And hence it is that we find almost every nation claiming to itself the discovery of letters. Each one, no doubt, may put in a claim for

[4] "The letters of the ancient Egyptians, like those of the Hebrews, and of several other nations, may have been distinguished by names, which primarily expressed leading ideas, and, at the same time, were appropriated also to a variety of objects, in which those leading ideas presented themselves. In this case, the term could be represented by the figure of either of the objects to which it was applied. Let us, for example, suppose that the letter B was called *Bai*, and that such a term primarily imported *being* or *existing*. We are told, that *Bai* was the Egyptian denomination for a branch of the palm tree, and that this tree was anciently regarded as an emblem of being, existence, or immortality. Again, Horapollo says, *Bai* signified a hawk, the soul, and the wind; therefore, the Egyptians used the hawk as a symbol for the soul. The Greeks called the palm branch *Baion* or *Bais:* and *Beta* or *Baita*, the letter B, preserves the sound of the Hebrew *Beth*, or the Egyptian *Bai*, but the idea of the name in Greek, may be collected from *Bei-bai-oo*, to confirm, establish, or place in a permanent state of existence. The Latins called this letter Be, nearly the simple name of the Bai, or symbolical palm branch. And Be in the Celtic, conveys the same leading idea of *existence*. Irish Be, is the term for life; Cornish, signifies Be, am, art, is, existent." (Dav. Celt. Res. p. 339.)

this honour, as far as it consists in having reduced pictures to a phonetic language, after that the first discoveries had given them the key."[5]

The question is, by whom were letters actually invented? It may be surmised, from the assertions of ancient authors, that such characters were in use before the flood. Pliny affirms that the Pelasgi, the founder of whom was a man in Japhet's line in the eldest times, first brought letters into Latinum; and that they were in Italy before the Lydian colony under Tyrrhenus came thither and expelled them. And the Lydian colony was but four generations after the time of Menes. The most ancient Greek letters were called Pelasgic; and the Pelasgi were termed divine, because, says Eustàtius, they, amongst all the Greeks, were the only preservers of letters, after the flood.

Sanchoniatho, however, attributes the invention of letters to Thoth, the grandson of Ham. But Thoth received the elements of this knowledge from Noah; for the above author expressly asserts that Thoth imitated the art of picture-writing practised by Ouranus or Noah; and delineated the sacred characters that formed the elements of this kind of writing. It was owing to the exertions and learning of this prince, that the Egyptians soared so far beyond the rest of the world in the arts and sciences, and the refinements and even elegancies of social life. While many of the tribes which had migrated, remained in a state of semi-barbarism, Egypt became a populous, well-governed, powerful, and happy people. And with them the use of letters and hieroglyphical characters of most extensive meaning and application, was carried to a perfection unknown to the rest of the world.

If these testimonies be admitted, it will appear that letters, or phonetic characters, were used by Noah, *after* the flood; and we may very reasonably conjecture that he was not ignorant of them *before* that event, because he was 600 years of age when he entered the ark; and there is no existing evidence to prove that he invented them afterwards.

If we take another line of argument, the result will

[5] Lamb. Hier. p. 2.

be the same. Pliny says that letters were *always* found among the Assyrians; and that the ancient Hebrew and the Assyrian letters were the same. The reason why we meet with no supposed author of the Assyrian letters is, that they were certainly not invented by that people. Mankind had lived many hundred years before the flood, and it is scarcely to be believed that they lived without the use of alphabetical characters. It is highly probable, then, that Noah was skilled in them, and taught them to his children. The knowledge of this art he might receive from Methusaleh, the son of Enoch, to whom his father had communicated much of the information which he had collected by study and experience. And in Jonathan's Targum on Genesis, we find Enoch termed the Great Scribe. Eupolemus says that Enoch was instructed *in all things* by angels, letters, of course, included. Bar Hebreus affirms that Enoch was the first who invented books, and different sorts of writing. All these authorities combine to verify that fragment of Alexander Polyhistor, preserved by Scaliger, where mention is made of the keeping of certain records written *before the flood.*

Hales conjectures, "from the whole of ancient history, both sacred and profane, that the art of alphabetical writing not only could, but actually did, precede the establishment of hieroglyphics; and that the invention of alphabetical language was not superinduced by a mixture of other nations; nor could it be so superinduced. First, The book of the genealogy of the antediluvian patriarchs from Adam to Noah, is evidently represented as a written record. Gen. v. 1. And, indeed, how could it possibly record their names, and their generations, residues of life, and total ages, without written words? How could oral tradition hand down, through two and twenty centuries, to the deluge, unimpaired, thirty large and unconnected numbers, rising from a hundred to near a thousand years? Secondly, some Jewish and Oriental traditions ascribe the invention of writing to Seth, the son of Adam; others to Enoch, the seventh from Adam; whether well-founded or not, it proves the prevailing opinion that letters were of antediluvian date."[6]

[6] Hales. Anal. Chron. Vol. I. p. 370.

In the mass of facts here collected, it may be supposed, that, under some circumstances, the ideas attached to letters and hieroglyphics have been confounded, and the one may have frequently been mistaken for the other. The use of hieroglyphics amongst idolaters, appears, from the above reasoning, to have been almost coeval with that apostacy which seduced men from the knowledge of God and the practice of true religion. The hierophant was very fond of delivering his instructions in an ambiguous manner; for it was believed that learning would be deteriorated, and science insulted, if they were displayed so plainly as to be intelligible to the vulgar and uninitiated.[7] Sanchoniatho informs us that Thoth drew the portraitures of the gods in mystical characters, and inscribed columns with hieroglyphics;[8] an evident proof that symbolical instruction was used in his days; and he flourished only three generations after the flood.

The truth being thus artfully concealed from the people, error gradually usurped its place; polytheism was insensibly introduced, and each emblem was worshipped as a god. This perversion was secretly encouraged by the priests, until the error became engrafted into the whole system of worship practised by almost every nation under the sun. Thus Apuleius, when describing the wonders which he beheld during his initiation into the Spurious Freemasonry, says that the hierophant took certain mysterious writings out of the sanctuary, which contained the Signs, Words, and Tokens, expressed by marks, symbols, and figures of animals, so intricately combined, that it was impossible to understand them without a deliberate and accurate explanation.[9]

In Egypt, as we have seen, the use of symbols may be almost identified with the colonization of that country; for we are told that the pyramids, at their original erection, were covered with hieroglyphical characters, which have been defaced by time and exposure to the weather. Every historical and religious truth taught to the aspirants in the Spurious Freemasonry were wrapped in

[7] Procl. in Tim. Platon. l. 1. Cicero de divin. l. 1. Plin. Nat. Hist. l. 2. c. 12.

[8] Euseb. de præp. evan. l. 1. c. 9.

[9] Apul. Metam. l. 2.

hieroglyphics; and isolated facts in morality and physics were frequently blended, or designated by a compound symbol; and the invention of phonetic characters was the result. Thus the science was not only difficult of attainment, but uncertain when accomplished. It is historically clear that to Egypt every people resorted for information on the essential parts of symbolical knowledge; without which, even the initiations themselves would have failed to convey any additional privileges; and this knowledge was therefore thrown by the priests into the most abstruse and difficult form, and every successive Degree had its peculiar system of appropriate emblems.

The hieroglyphics of Egypt, which will be more particularly considered in a subsequent Lecture, were thus of a varying and uncertain character; and different ages furnished new symbols, probably when the more ancient ones became known. Thus, Dr. Young says: "several of the manuscripts on papyrus, which have been carefully published in Hamilton's Description of Egypt, exhibited very frequently the same text in different forms, deviating more or less from the perfect resemblance of the objects intended to be delineated, till they became, in many cases, mere lines and curves, and dashes and flourishes; but still answering, character for character, to the hieroglyphical or hieratic writing of the same chapters, found in other manuscripts, and of which the identity was sufficiently indicated; besides the coincidence, by the similarity of the larger tablets, or pictural representations, at the head of each chapter or column, which are almost universally found on the margins of manuscripts of a mythological nature. And the enchorial inscription of the Pillar of Rosetta resembled very accurately, in its general appearance, the most unpicturesque of these manuscripts. It did not, however, by any means agree, character for character, with the 'sacred letters' of the first inscription, though in many instances, by means of some intermediate steps derived from the manuscripts on papyrus, the characters could be traced into each other with sufficient accuracy to supersede every idea of any essential diversity in the principles of representation employed. The want of a more perfect correspondence could only be explained, by considering the sacred characters as the remains of a more ancient and solemn mode of expression, which had been superseded, in common life, by other words and phrases; and, in several cases, it seemed probable, that the forms of the characters had been so far degraded and confused, that the addition of a greater number of distinguished epithets have become necessary, in order that the sense might be rendered intelligible."

LECTURE VI.

EXEMPLIFICATION OF THE SYMBOLS USED IN THOSE SPURIOUS INSTITUTIONS WHICH ATTAINED THE MOST PERMANENT CELEBRITY IN THE ANCIENT WORLD.

After these appeared
A crew who, under names of old renown,
Osiris, Isis, Orus, and their train,
With monstrous shapes and sorceries abused
Fanatic Egypt and her priests, to seek
Their wandering gods, disguised in brutish forms
Rather than human.

Milton.

In ancient times, when leaders and commanders were chosen by lot, Dionysius of Syracuse drew the letter M, which a friend, in the anxiety of his mind, interpreted unfavourably, and exclaimed: "You will acquit yourself *foolishly*, O Dionysius, and your oration will be laughed at; for your initial means *Μωρολογεῖς*." Dionysius was of a different opinion; for he felt confident of his own powers, and replied: "You are mistaken, friend, my lot is *Μοναρχησω*; I shall be a monarch." And he was right; for his speech produced such a strong impression on the audience, that he was chosen general of the Syracusian army on the spot. Here we have a striking evidence of the very equivocal nature of signs and symbols at that early period. Hieroglyphics of every kind were of doubtful interpretation, even to the initiated, except they had been admitted to the very highest degrees. And here—what was the secret? It was nothing less than a development of the plan of human salvation by the future advent of a Man-God, or Mediator. Thus was Christianity, under the direction of Providence, the aim and end of these remarkable institutions. But this great truth, and its details, in the shape of tradition and prophecy, were buried so deeply in hieroglyphics as to be unintelligible to common comprehensions; and the popular versions were so much at variance with each other, that little credit could be attached to any of them. They resembled the superstitious figments of our own times, which induce, in the minds of weak and uninstructed persons, a belief in the efficacy of charms for agues, toothache, fits, and sciatica; amulets to prevent mischance and danger; philters for love, and omens which foretell the accidents of life. Such a circle of awful mystery was drawn around the hieroglyphical knowledge of ancient times, by the hierophant of the Spurious Freemasonry, that the people bowed before the symbols inscribed on tombs, obelisks, and temples, and worshipped them with great devotion, as though they were instinct with the divine essence, and possessed perception and power to bless or ban; to distribute benefits or inflict calamities.

We have seen, in the preceding Lecture, that the origin of hieroglyphics was picture-writing. This was very simple, and consisted merely of the representation of any concise fact it was thought desirable to record, by scrawling some visible object connected with it. Experience soon proclaimed the inadequacy of this plan. Gradual improvements arose to meet the necessities of ripening knowledge; and hieroglyphics were invented to designate invisible objects and qualities; and in process of time these were combined and formed into a regular system. Thus they considered the hawk as an emblem of the supreme Deity because of its piercing sight and swiftness; the asp, the cat, and the beetle were also honoured as images of the Divine power; the first as not being subject to old age, and moving without the assistance of limbs; the cat, because they imagined she conceived by her ear, and brought forth her young by her mouth, representing the generation of speech; and the beetle, because they supposed there was no female in the whole species. The crocodile also they took to be another image of the Deity, because, of all animals, it has no tongue, which organ God has no occasion for.[1]

[1] Univ. Hist. vol. I. p. 232.

The method adopted by the Chinese is thus explained by Li Yang Ping; and has been communicated by that eminent scholar and antiquary, Sir William Jones. "Th ancient characters used in this country were the outline of visible objects, earthly and celestial. But as thing merely intellectual could not be expressed by thos figures, the grammarians of China contrived to represen the various operations of the mind by metaphors drawı from the productions of nature; thus the idea of rough ness and rotundity, of motion and rest, were conveyed tc the eye by signs representing a mountain, the sky, a river, and the earth; the figure of the sun, moon, and stars, differently combined, stood for smoothness and splendour, for any thing artfully wrought or woven with delicate workmanship; extension, growth, increase, and many other qualities, were painted in characters taken from the clouds, from the firmament, and from the vegetable part of the creation; the different ways of moving, agility and slowness, idleness and diligence, were expressed by various insects, birds, fish, and quadrupeds. In this manner passions and sentiments were traced by the pencil; and ideas not subject to any sense, were exhibited to the sight, until by degrees new combinations were invented, new expressions added; the characters deviated imperceptibly from their primitive shape; and the Chinese language became not only clear and forcible, but rich and elegant in the highest degree."

It is asserted by Bin Washih, that the first dynasty of the earliest Egyptian kings "invented, each according to his own genius and understanding, a particular alphabet, in order that none should know them but the *sons of Wisdom*. Few, therefore, are found who understand them in our time. They took the figures of different instruments, trees, plants, quadrupeds, birds or their parts, and of planets and fixed stars. In this manner these hieroglyphical alphabets became innumerable. They were not arranged at all in the order of our letters; but they had proper characters agreed upon by the inventors of these alphabets, and which differed in their figure and order; viz.: they expressed water by an indented line. They understood the secrets of nature, and endeavoured to express everything by an appropriate sign, so that they might express it by its appearance."[2]

The Egyptian writing, at the period of its greatest perfection, was of three sorts; the Epistolic, the Hieroglyphic, and the Symbolic; while, in addition to these, the priests had another species of picture-writing, which was termed Hierogrammatic. This latter they entrusted to none but those of their own order. Modern writers have subdivided the above into Pure hieroglyphics, or pictures; Linear hieroglyphics, or emblems; Phonetic hieroglyphics, or the representatives of sounds; and Demotic, or Epistolographic or Enchorial writing for the business of common life. And they invented another system of magical communication which imbedded Cabalistic secrets in comprehensive phrases, that were not only mysterious, but absolutely formidable to the ignorant. Thus soothsayers were called, *magic alarm posts;* philters and dangerous compounds, *treasure chambers;* the knowledge of spirits, *astrological tables;* mysterious things, *conjuring spirits;* pyramids, *secrets of the stars*, &c. But the symbolic writing was most comprehensive, and, for greater secrecy, became subdivided into three parts, which were denominated the Curiologic, the Tropical, and the Allegorical, each admitting of a different method of interpretation, the secret of which was communicated only to a select few. Thus, for instance, in the Curiologic style, the moon was pictured by a crescent, tropically by a cat, and allegorically by the figure of Isis, or a veiled female.

Bin Washih, above cited, gives an account of the following series of hieroglyphics as existing in a temple in Upper Egypt; which is valuable because it contains a vivid picture of the legend of initiation into the mysteries. "This building was a temple of Adonis, whom the sun and moon serve. It represents *a coffin* adorned with curious figures and admirable ornaments. *A sprig of vine*

[2] The above author has enumerated a vast variety of alphabets, and with great industry has collected the hieroglyphical characters of most of them, including antediluvian alphabets, those of the kings and philosophers, one for each of the twelve signs, and the seven planets, &c., to the number of eighty, which embody an abundance of symbols used in the mysteries, as well as many which have been incorporated into genuine Freemasonry.

growing, with its leaves spread over it. The divinity was standing upon the coffin, with a staff in his hand, out of the end of which a tree shot forth and overshadowed it. Behind the coffin was seen a pit full of blazing fire, and four angels catching serpents, scorpions, and other noxious reptiles, throwing them into it. On his head a crown of glory; on his right the sun, and on his left the moon, and in his hand a ring with the twelve signs of the Zodiac. Before the coffin an olive tree sprouted forth, under the branches of which different kinds of animals were collected. On the left, and a little further back, a high mountain was seen, with seven golden towers supporting the sky. A hand stretched forth from this sky, poured out light, and pointed with its fingers to the olive tree. Here was also the figure of a man whose head was in the sky, and whose feet were on the earth. His hands and feet were bound. Before the deity stood seven censers, two pots, a vase filled with perfumes, spices, and a bottle with a long neck (retort), containing storax. The hieroglyphic representing day, was under his right foot, and the hieroglyphic representing night under his left. Before the divinity was laid, on a high desk, the book of universal nature, whereon a representation and names of the planets, the constellations, the stations, and every thing that is found in the highest heavens, were painted. There was also an urn filled half with earth and half with sand, (viz., the hieroglyphics of earth and sand being represented therein). A suspended, ever-burning lamp, dates, and olives, in a vase of emerald. A table of black basalt with seven lines, the four elements, the figure of a man carrying away a dead body, and a dog upon a lion These, O brother," says the author, "are the mysterious keys of the treasures and secrets of ancient and modern knowledge. The wise may guess the whole from a part."

The spirit of modern discovery has furnished the world with a more correct knowledge of Egyptian hieroglyphics; and the investigations of Denon, Champollion, Belzoni, Salt, Dr. Young, and others, have stamped the impress of truth on an abstruse and difficult subject, which has puzzled all antiquity. From this source we learn that the unity of the deity was symbolized by a rude sort of mallet or hammer; and a plurality of gods by three of the same to represent the triad. Phre, by a point within a circle; Cneph, by a serpent or a cross within a circle; a female by a semicircle and an oval. Hyperion, by an anchor; country, a ladder with four staves; land, a saltire cross within a circle; divinity, a sistrum; a tear was literally represented, according to Young, by a drop from an eye; but Salt is of opinion, that this emblem represented the goddess Athor in the form of a cow. The symbol of life was a cross and circle, commonly called the crux ansata; sometimes it was a lamp, and sometimes it was represented by water, because that element is essential to animal and vegetable existence. This was sensibly felt in Egypt, where vegetation depended entirely on the inundation of their sacred river. The emblem of eternity was a serpent; of immortality, two semicircles and the crux ansata. Equity was designated by a plume of feathers; silence by a peach tree; and the mouth by a palm tree. Three heads conjoined, symbolized counsel; three arms, action; three legs, expedition; and three hearts, courage. A rite or ceremony was designated by the All-seeing Eye, and an indented line; and joy, by an equilateral triangle. Spring, summer, autumn, and winter, were symbolized by a dog, a lion, a serpent, and a wolf. The moon, by a cat with two kittens, one black and the other white, denoting its phases; and equity, by a crown of ostrich plumes, or of the bird Phœnicopteros.

Champollion thus describes the hieroglyphics on a bas relief which forms the architrave of the door of entrance to the tomb of Pharaoh Ramses:—In the centre is the sun with the head of a ram; an emblem of the monarch of the day retiring in the west to cheer the southern hemisphere with his radiant beams; and is adored by the king kneeling. On the east is the goddess Nephthys, and in the west Isis. Near to the sun is a scarabæus, a symbol of regeneration. The king kneels on the celestial mountain, which supports also the feet of the two goddesses. The general interpretation of these hieroglyphics means that the monarch, during his life, like the sun in his course from east to west, enlightened and regenerated his country, and was the source of all the blessings, civil and religious, which a happy people enjoyed.

The hieroglyphical researches of Champollion, Salt, and others, have furnished a phonetic alphabet, in which each letter is represented by a variety of symbols or characters. But even this arrangement, how correct soever it may be in principle, presents some natural difficulties. The Egyptian alphabet did not contain more than twenty characters; but the above writers have produced upwards of a hundred phonetic signs. Some confusion will, therefore, necessarily arise in the interpretation of a monumental inscription, when several hieroglyphics are appropriated to the same letter. I subjoin a few of these phonetic signs in illustration of my subject.

A—A human figure kneeling; a goose; a twisted rope.

A N—A winged eye.

A Y—A hawk; a volute.

B—A man's leg; a sheep.

D—Two horizontal lines; a scarabæus; the left hand.

E—A feather; a knife blade.

G or K—A level or quadrant.

J—A man's arm.

L—A lion seated.

M—A bier; an owl; a crown.

N—A line wavy; the crux ansata.

O—A volute; a fan.

P or. Ph—A square.

R—A weaver's shuttle; a point within a circle; an undulating serpent.

S—A star; an egg; a naked figure.

T—A human hand.

Th—A semicircle.

Z—A cross rising from a heart.

Of all the hieroglyphical systems which pervaded the heathen world, or were introduced into the Spurious Freemasonry, none could compete, in accuracy of intention, or comprehensiveness of meaning, with the symbols of Pythagoras; and they form the connecting link between the spurious and the true Freemasonry. In former publications I have had occasion to introduce brief sketches of this great philosopher and Freemason, and his system of hieroglyphics. Indeed, in every work professedly on Freemasonry, the subject is indispensable, as it forms a part of our own private lectures; and many of the emblems possess a reference in common with those of our Order. It has been even asserted by an ancient writer on Masonry, that Pythagoras "journeydde ffor kunnynge yn Egypte, and in Syria, and yn everyche londe, whereas the Venetians hadde plaunted Maçonrye, and wynnynge entraunce yn al lodges of maçonnes, he lerned muche, and retournedde and woned yn Grecia Magna, wacksynge and becomynge a myghtye wysacre, and gratelyche renowned, and her he framed a grate lodge at Groton (Crotona) and maked manye maçonnes, some whereoffe dyde journye yn Fraunce, and maked manye maçonnes; wherefromme, yn processe of tyme, the arte passede yn Englonde." Under such circumstances, a clear and somewhat copious dissertation on his system of symbolical instruction may be both useful and entertaining. And to make the subject intelligible, I shall give a brief sketch of his life and initiations.

The country of Pythagoras does not seem to be well settled. Some say he was a Simian, some a Tyrrhenian, and others a Tyrian; but it is clear that his birth and future eminence were foretold by the oracle at Delphos. In his youth, his person was so beautiful as to have obtained for him the surname of the Samian Comet, or the fair haired Samian. He had many masters, whose names are famous in science and philosophy. Pherecydes, Anaximander, and Thales, were amongst the number; and all were astonished at the quickness of his understanding and the excellency of his judgment. He travelled through Phenicia, and was initiated into the mysteries of Tyre and Byblus, and from thence he proceeded to Egypt, where, after an extraordinary display of fortitude and perseverance, he was received into the sacred institutions of that country.[3] Here he was favoured with full instruction

[3] His probation is thus described by the authors of the Universal History. "Designing to travel into Egypt, he desired Polycrates, the tyrant of Samos, to recommend him by letter to Amasis, king of Egypt, who was his particular friend, that he might have the freer admission to the secret learning of the priests. He obtained also of Amasis letters to the priests, ordering them to communicate their knowledge to him. He went first to those of Heliopolis, who referred him to the college at Memphis, as their senior; and from Memphis he was sent, under the same pretext, to Thebes. After much tergiversation, not daring to disobey the king's command by any farther dilatory excuses, they endeavoured to deter Pythagoras from his purpose, by the infinite labour and trouble he was to expect; enjoining him, in his noviciate, things that

by the priests at Heliopolis, Memphis, and Thebes, in all the secrets of their mysterious learning—Geometry. Astronomy, Philosophy, and particularly in the knowledge of hieroglyphical symbols, which were so extensively applied, that the wisdom and experience, civil, religious, or political, of this remarkable people, could only be acquired by a perfect understanding of their principles and application, and the art of deciphering the characters, under every combination adopted by the Egyptian hierophants to conceal their mysteries from profane inspection.

After visiting Babylon, where he was instructed in Music, Arithmetic, and other mathematical sciences, he had the advantage of communication with many learned Jews, from whom he derived a knowledge of that divine science which we call Speculative Masonry. And archbishop Usher affirms that he transferred many of their doctrines into his own system of philosophy.[4] He increased his knowledge by conversing with the Persian Magi, and the Brahmins of India; and in the fifty-sixth year of his age, he began to communicate his knowledge to his own countrymen. For this purpose he visited successively Samos, Delos, Delphi, Crete, Sparta, Olympia, Phlius; and having filled all Greece with the fame of his institutions, he passed over to Italy; settled at Crotona, and died there, after disseminating his philosophy with such effect, that Italy was named in his honour, Magna Grecia.

At Crotona he established his first lodge of philosophers;[5] modelling his ceremonies and doctrines on a plan improved from the rites of Orpheus, of Egypt, of Samothrace, India, Chaldea, Tyre, Judea, and the mysteries of Eleusis. Laertius says that six hundred persons underwent a severe probation of five years, silence, during which period they were instructed in the exoteric doc-

are very hard, and contrary to the religion of the Greeks. And when he had undergone all this trial with invincible courage, he obliged them at length, against their wills, to admit him to a participation of their sacred mysteries and profound learning."

[4] Annal. p. 151.

[5] Valerius Maximus relates that when Pythagoras founded his school, he was asked what was the name of his system? To this question he replied: I am not *sophos*, wise, but *philo-sophos*, a lover of wisdom; and my disciples shall be called Philosophers.

trines of his system; hearing his lectures from behind a screen, without enjoying the privilege of being admitted to his presence. This was termed the nocturnal *acroasis*. After having worthily passed their probation, they were admitted to participate in the esoteric secrets, and became a part of his family; but if the patience or constancy of any one failed during this long trial, he was rejected with scorn, and a tomb was erected for him; because he was accounted morally dead; and if any of the Pythagorean brotherhood met this unfortunate outcast in their walks, they either passed him without notice, or used the more mortifying ceremony of saluting him by a false name.

An universal bond of brotherhood was inculcated by this great philosopher upon his esoteric followers, and Cicero informs us that this maxim was constantly in his mouth—"the design of friendship is to make two or more—one. Men ought to be united." From such a system of training, the disciples of Pythagoras became so celebrated for their fraternal affection towards each other, that when any remarkable instance of friendship was displayed, it became a common proverb—they are members of the Pythagorean Society.

The principal and most efficacious of their doctrines, says Iamblichus,[6] they kept secret amongst themselves, with perfect *echemythia* towards the uninitiated. They did not commit them to writing, but transmitted them to their successors by oral communication as the most abstruse mysteries of the gods. By this means nothing of moment became publicly known. Their peculiar secrets were only known within the walls of their lodges, which were always kept closely tyled; and, if by any accident, profane persons were found amongst them, they signified their meaning one to another by signs and symbols.

From the picture drawn by Porphyry, Laertius, Cicero, and others, there appears to have been something very dignified and almost superhuman in the person and appearance of this celebrated Freemason. He wore a white robe or gown, as an emblem of purity; and was of a comely and divine presence. Porphyry informs us

[6] Cap. 17.

that by abstemiousness and moderation in diet, he preserved his body in a state of perfect regularity, and kept his passions in subjection. He was addicted to neither joy nor grief; and his mind was constantly calm and serene. He was never seen in a condition of anger or ebriety, and, in his public disputations, refrained alik from ridicule, scoffs, and personal allusions. In a word his disciples conceived him to be one of the celestial deities, who had descended from heaven for the reformation of mankind.

The hieroglyphics or symbols of Pythagoras, which constitute the object of our present enquiry, contained his esoteric doctrines, and were of two classes; the one a visible emblem, as an animal, or some geometrical figure; the other, a short and pithy sentence or apothegm, which possessed the quality of combining many ideas or sparks of truth, as Iamblichus expresses it, for those that are able to enkindle them, and constituted a lecture in itself; for one great feature in the system of Pythagoras was to comprehend many things in few words.[7] And these apothegms were so highly esteemed, that some have compared them to "the divine oracles of Apollo."

The first class of hieroglyphics may be thus briefly explained. The equilateral triangle was the deity; for Pythagoras taught that whatsoever had a middle was a triform; and the triform figure constituted perfection. It was, indeed, esteemed the most sacred of emblems, and when an obligation of more than usual importance was administered, it was universally given in a triangle, and when so taken none were ever known to violate it. So highly did the ancients esteem the figure, that it be came among them an object of worship, and the great principle of animated existence, and they gave it the name of God, affirming that it represented the animal, mineral, and vegetable creation. The sacred Delta is usually placed in all squares and circles; and as it is supposed to extend its ramifications through all matter and space, it is considered the *summum bonum* of existence. A ship, a chariot, and fire, represented by the monad or number one, were symbolical of love, concord, piety, and

[7] Stob. Ser. 35.

friendship. They also referred to an hermaphrodite, because the monad partakes of the nature of odd and even;[8] for being added to odd it makes even, and being added to even makes odd.[9] A key was a symbol of the tetrad, and the tetrad was God, because he is the key—keeper of nature. It was also an emblem of the soul, which consists of four parts,—mind, science, opinion, and sense. The duad represented Light, and the pentad, darkness. The hexad or triple triangle was an emblem of health; but Pierius thinks the word υγιεια should be inscribed within the exterior angles. The decad or number ten was used to typify heaven, the universe, age, fate, and power; and a series of reasons were assigned for each similitude. The symbol was ten commas or jods placed in the order of the first four digits; for ten was produced from four, the Tetractys or Sacred Name.

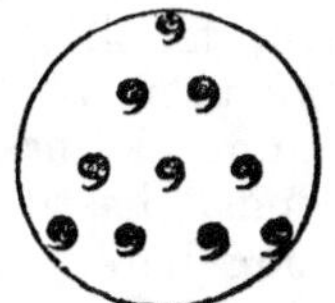

On this symbol Pierius thus comments: Decadis autem vis est quaternarius numerus; secundum enim compositionem a monade ad quaternarium punctis in unum contractis ac supputatis, decas fit. Decies autem decem, centum; decies centum, mille; millia decies, summa perfectissima.

Schalichius said that Pythagoras made the monad and the duad the origin of all things. "One, the father, two, the mother, one and two, in the divine essence, producing four, the Tetractys, the idea of all things, which are consummated in the number ten." This Pythagoras styles "eternal nature's fountain;—no other than the knowledge of things in the divine mind, intellectually operating. From this fountain of eternal nature floweth down the Pythagoric numbers, one and two, which form eternity, in the fountain of the immense ocean, was, shall

[8] Macrob. in Som. Scip. l. 1. c. 6. [9] Theon. Smyrn. Mathem. c. 5.

be, and always is, plenteously streaming. Thus one was by the ancients termed Jupiter, two, Juno, wife and sister to Jupiter. In Ida, Jupiter and Juno sat as one and two in the streaming idea of the Tetractys; whenc flow the principles of all things, Form and Matter."[10]

An anchor represented magnanimity and fortitude "These," said Pythagoras, "no tempest can shake Virtue alone is firm; every thing else is unstable." Fortitude was also symbolized by a rock amidst the waves of the sea. A bridle was symbolical of wisdom; because, as a horse cannot be governed without a bridle, so also are riches without wisdom unmanageable and pernicious. The poppy was an emblem of a city; and its multitude of seeds represented the abundant population. The iris signified eloquence; the hyacinth, wisdom; the myrtle, grace; and the hyssop, the expiation of sin. The fig represented humanity, and sometimes sycophancy; the pomegranate, populousness; the ivy, antiquity; the thistle, disease; the toadstool, folly or stupidity; ears of corn, fertility; the branch of palm was a token of joy, and used as an emblem to express the conviction that trouble had been exchanged for prosperity; the willow, bonds, chastity and barrenness; and the rose, modesty. Long hair was a symbol of mourning, and short hair of joy. Honey was used to intimate to the initiated, that the individual presenting it was free from malice or any other evil passion. A ring betokened ignorance, because ignorance enslaves the mind, as the finger is bound and fettered with this little circle of gold. A crown symbolized the laws; and, therefore, the phrase, "pluck not a crown," meant, offend not the laws which are the crown of a nation. The rainbow was an emblem of the sun's splendour; the balance of avarice; anger was represented by fire, and contention by a sword. A torch, from its united qualities of brightness and purity, was an emblem of philosophy.

The use of animal hieroglyphics amongst the followers of Pythagoras, was very extensive in its application and symbolical meaning. According to this system, the ox was an emblem of patient industry; the elephant, of fidelity, justice, and piety; the bull, of ferocity; the horse

[10] Stanl. Hist. Phil. vol. 3. P. 1. p. 140.

of fame and swiftness; the dog, of fidelity, friendship, memory and gratitude; the lamb, of innocence; the ram, of boldness, profanity, and slander; the ass, of laziness and indocility; the camel, of strength and abstinence· the mule, of sterility; the hare, of timidity and fecundi ty; the mole, of opacity of intellect; the hawk, of victory the kite, of navigation; the dove, of chastity; the stork, of filial piety; the parrot, of eloquence; the cock, of pugnacity, and, as a "monitor of the hours," he was a symbol of time; the goose, of vigilance; the heron of a tempest; the quail, of impurity; the thrush, of deafness; the kingfisher seated on its nest, of tranquillity; the red-breast, of solitude; a swallow, of sloth and idleness, because it appears to labour only a small part of the year.

Again, Spring was hieroglyphically painted by a basket of flowers; Summer, by a sheaf of corn; Autumn, by a cornucopia of fruits; and Winter, by a convivial party seated round a well furnished table before a blazing fire.

Geometrical figures are ever found amongst the symbols of Pythagoras, and he philosophised very frequently, in his private schools or lodges, on the elementary principles of that science—a point, a line, a superficies, and a solid; for they comprehended his favourite number, the tetrad; and he believed the quadrangular figure to symbolize the divine essence. Stanley presents us with a brief sketch of his lecture on these leading principles. "A point is correspondent to the monad: the monad is indivisible—so is the point. The monad is the principle of numbers, as the point is of lines. A line is correspondent with the duad; both are considered by transition. A line is length without breadth, extending betwixt two points. A superficies corresponds to the triad; besides length, whereby it was a duad, it receives a third distance, breadth. Again, setting down three points, two opposite, and the third at the juncture of the lines made by the two, we represent a superficies. The solid figure, and the body, as a pyramid, answers the tetrad; if we lay down, as before, three points, and set over them another point, behold the pyramidical form of a solid body, which hath three dimensions—length, breadth, and thickness."

The elements were symbolized by geometrical figures,

of which Pythagoras entertained the opinion that they were five in number. Earth was figured by a cube; fire by a pyramid; air by an octaedron; water by an icosaedron; and the sphere by a dodecaedron, which was hence used as a symbol of the universe. "If," said Pythagoras, "upon an octangular tube we erect a pyramid by four equi-crural triangles, it makes a dodecaedron, wherein the cube is, as it were, mother, and the pyramid, father." Again, a cube was an emblem of the Supreme Deity, as was also the equilateral triangle; while the scalene triangle figured the nature of demons, because its sides and angles were all unequal. When two scaleni of equal dimensions are united by the smallest of the lines which include the right angle, they form an obtuse angled triangle of the isosceles kind, when, by the larger of these two lines, an acute angled triangle would appear. But, in the latter case, their angles are to each other, in the arithmetical proportion of one, two, and three. They form an equilateral triangle, which may be justly considered as the most perfect of all trilateral forms, for the following reasons:—First, because it is equal in all its relations;—secondly, because it is capable of being reduced into the scalene and isosceles forms;—thirdly, because it is infinitely divisible, or may be infinitely multiplied into similar triangles equal to each other, without alteration of its form or relations;—and fourthly, because in every such division it observes the geometrical progression of the tetrad; and therefore it may be considered as a symbolical representation of that species of proportion.

The problems which he had the credit of inventing were these:

1. There are only three equilateral and equiangular polygons, which occupy the space about a point, viz., the equilateral triangle, the square, and the hexagon.

2. The internal angles of a triangle are equal to two right angles.

3. In any right angled triangle, the square which is described, upon the side subtending the right angle, is equal to the squares described upon the sides which contain the right angle.

Pythagoras used to deliver a most admirable lecture on the emblem of an angle of ninety degrees or a square, placed on a perpendicular line, usually denominated the letter Y. This figure symbolized the three stages of human life, and had a further reference to the three steps or degrees used in the Spurious Freemasonry. The first stage is early youth, a state of preparation for the active business of life, and open to the impressions both of good and evil, according to the prevalence and effect of admonition and example. The youth is thus supposed to pass along the inferior limb of the figure, till he arrives at the angle where two lines diverge to the right and to the left, which was supposed to take place when he attained his maturity and discretion. The former represents the narrow path of virtue, which, if he be so fortunate as to choose, his life will be honourable, and his death glorious and full of hope. But should he, unhappily, turn on the way of pleasure and carnal indulgence towards the left, which appears broader, and consequently more joyous and tempting, his course will be full of trouble and sorrow; sloth and luxury will enervate his body, debase his mind, and poison his enjoyments, and he will close his life in ignominy, and his memory will be covered with reproach. Some think that he carried the comparison beyond the grave, and referred it to the two states of reward and punishment which distinguish a future life.[11]

The symbolical precepts of Pythagoras are too numerous to be fully explained within the confined limits of a single Lecture. I shall, however, select a few of the most significant, to illustrate the use that was made of this kind of imagery in the Pythagorean lodges. He taught that the virtues which had the most beneficial tendency to adorn and dignify the nature of man were two-fold, viz., *to speak truth, and render benefits to our fellow creatures*, these being essential points of theoretical and practical virtue, and make mankind resemble the celestial deities; for God himself is in his body Light, and in in his soul truth.

By the precept, *worship the gods with your feet uncovered*,

[11] It is probable Pythagoras might have taken the idea of this symbol from the ancient Grecian fable of the two ways in hell—that to the right leading to all pleasure and happiness, and the other to endless misery. It was introduced by Virgil into his great poem. (Æn. vi. 540.)

he represented hypocrisy; for he said that the soul, thus symbolized by the feet, ought to be naked during the time employed in sacrifice.

He recommended his followers to *decline highways and walk in foot-paths;* thus enforcing upon them the necessity of avoiding the pleasures and allurements of the world, and devoting themselves to the more strict and private pursuits of piety and philosophy.

Turn away a sharp sword; or, in plainer language, use prudence; and, in your intercourse with mankind, shew that your initiation has conferred its proportionate degree of purity, by the due government of your passions, by keeping a tongue of good report, and by avoiding anger, wrath, and evil speaking.

Take off your right shoe first, but put your left foot first into the bath. Good actions were symbolized by *the right*, and evil ones by *the left.* It is, therefore, by the exercise of judgment and right reason, and a due application of the lessons taught in the Lodge, that the former will be cherished, and the latter rejected.

Discourse not of the Pythagorean philosophy without Light, was another maxim, by which he recommended prudence; and it was hence symbolized, as in our Lodges, by a blazing star. Without light, this philosophy could not be acquired; but, by its prudent study, the industrious candidate gradually emerged out of darkness, and became enlightened with the true wisdom, which was inculcated in the esoteric, or higher degrees of the Spurious Freemasonry.

When in travel, turn not back, for, if you do, the furies will accompany you. This symbol was more beautifully expressed by the Saviour of mankind. "No man having put his hand to the plough, and looking back, is fit for the kingdom of heaven."[12] The Pythagorean symbol had a similar reference. The study of philosophy, once commenced, should never be relinquished, lest it produce an unavailing repentance, which was considered equivalent to Erinnys or the fury.

Look not in a glass by candle-light. Pursue Lux and not Lumen; the reality and not the shadow or reflection.

[12] Luke ix. 62. The same idea is terrifically painted in the parable of the unclean spirit. Luke xi. 26.

Philosophy[13] is a steady, substantial reality, and not a flickering blaze, which expires when the light from which it emanates, and to which it owes its existence, is withdrawn.

Do not give the right hand of fellowship to every one, indiscriminately. If you enter into a league of friendship with uninitiated persons, it is possible you may be betrayed; for, none are worthy of esteem and confidence, but such as have been tried and proved by long discipline, and found faithful. To such the grip may be safely given, without fear or scruple.

Eat not the heart. A very pithy and important symbol. It recommends to the fraternity to be obliging, communicative to each other, and void of envy. The interpretation of this emblem is given in the masonic distich:

> And all the contentions 'mongst Masons should be,
> Who better can work, and who better agree.

Break not bread. Avoid slander and defamation; for they may separate friends and change them into enemies. *Sleep not at noon.* Do not close your eyes to the Light, when it invites your attention; or to instruction, when it is most clear and refulgent. Against the crime of suicide, Pythagoras gave his disciples this admonition: *Do not quit your station without orders.* And finally, as a persuasive against changing meekness into anger, he directed them, *never to roast that which is boiled.*

From this copious specimen of the Pythagorean symbols, their nature and characteristic properties may be fairly estimated. The dictates of sound wisdom are observable throughout the mass, although it is, in some instances, debased by redundant metaphors and absurd trifling. The sterling wheat is mixed with chaff. As a whole, however, his system was noble, stately, and dignified, and approached nearer to the foundation of true Light, than any other that existed in the heathen world, notwithstanding the defective opinions which Pythagoras entertained respecting God, and the true principles of divine worship. Had he lived half a dozen

[13] It will be understood that, in these illustrations, the word *philosophy*, as used by Pythagoras, invariably refers to the doctrines of the spurious Freemasonry taught in his lodges.

centuries later, he would have maintained a distinguished rank amongst the holy Fathers of Christianity.

It will be apparent from the reasoning and examples contained in this Lecture, that the use and application of hieroglyphics was in all nations the same, viz.: to conceal important truths, and to illustrate valuable doctrines; nor is there any nation, either ancient or modern, but who veiled their abstruse knowledge in the "cloudy garment of hieroglyphics."[14] In Britain, the system was carried out to an extent which equalled in ingenuity, if it fell short in copiousness of application, either of the instances which I have endeavoured to explain, differing, indeed, from the Egyptian arrangement, in that the symbols were not ostentatiously displayed on public monuments, but remained during the entire existence of the druidical religion, in the custody of the three orders of the priesthood, and transmitted solely by oral communication.

These hieroglyphics were used not only for the purpose of embodying thought and ideas, but an efficient scheme of augury was accomplished by their assistance. And the science of vaticination assumed, ultimately, so much importance in Britain, that it was deemed to be the chief advantage derivable from initiation; whence it was termed *rhyn*, or the secret. The method is known, and appears to have been as follows: trees of various kinds were acknowledged symbols of qualities. The tall and straight poplar denoted uprightness or integrity; the aspen, from the quivering motion of its foliage, symbolized instability or inconstancy; the oak, firmness; the birch, liberality, readiness, or complacency in doing a kind action. Thus, if a young woman accepted the addresses of her lover, she presented him with a branch of the birch tree; but if he were rejected, a twig of

[14] "The coronation of the king of Pegu (if we may credit Vincent le Blanc, as he relates it in his Travels,) is wholy hieroglyphical; for he is invested or inaugurated with a Diadem of Lead, to signifie that all things should be performed in weight and measure, and an axe is put into his hand, to denote that he should administer justice; he takes his oath upon a small vessel of emerald, in which some of the ashes of the first kings of Pegu lie enshrined, to put into him a remembrance of human frailty; he is attired or adorned with a Turkish robe, lined or furred with the skins of white hares, to intimate his subsequent innocence." Philpot's Heraldry, p. 25—26.

hazle was the substitute. From a combination of these symbolical trees, marked by some mystical process, divination was practised and responses pronounced.[15]

From being symbols of qualities, these trees or sprigs at length became the representatives, first of things in general, then of sounds, and lastly of alphabetical characters; and this was the result:

A—The fir tree.
B—The birch.
C—The hazle.
D—The oak.
E—The aspen.
F—The alder.
G—The ivy.
I—The yew.
L—The quicken tree.
M—The vine.
N—The ash.
O—The furze.
R—The elder.
S—The willow
U—The heath.

Subsequently the alphabet was formed of shoots of the apple tree cut in various forms, which was substituted as the more simple and certain process. But whether this was derived from the alphabet of the Dioscorides, and introduced by the Phenician merchants, I shall not attempt to decide, as it forms no part of my enquiry; but leave it to the judgment of my readers by introducing both.

A B C D E F G H I J C H L M N O P R S T U V W Z

The reader will have no difficulty in tracing the rudiments of our Roman letters, in the above tally alphabet of the Druids. In all nations, alphabetical characters were not only used as symbols but were considered to possess supernatural virtues. Thus Colphotorios, the

[15] Thus Taliesin boasted of his knowledge in this art.

I am acquainted with every *sprig*,
In the cave of the Arch diviner. (W. Arch. i. 34.)

Again, in a Poem entitled: "The First Greeting of Taliesin."

The points of the counterfeited trees,
What is it they whisper so forcibly?
Or what various breathings
Are in their trunks?
These are read by the Sages
Who are versed in science. (Ibid. i. 33.)

philosopher, who was "deeply learned in the knowledge of spirits and cabalistic spells, in talismans, astrological aspects, and in magic and the black art, invented an alphabet to conceal his secrets. Philosophers and learned men have used this alphabet in their books and writings n preference to others, on account of its different extraordinary qualities. The alphabet of the sign Aquarius, under the influence of Saturn, was used by the Chaldeans and Sabeans in their incantation books, and also in their inscriptions relative to the science of spirits. And one of the first Pharaohs of Egypt constructed wonderful talismans and magical alarm posts, in an alphabet of his own invention."[16] In like manner the druidical alphabet was esteemed to be magical. Ledwich says the same thing of the Irish alphabet, which was hence called *Bethluisnion na ogma*, or the alphabet of cabalistical letters; and it is well known that the Runic characters were used by Odin for magical charms and imprecations.

The general symbols of the Druids were, however, more diffuse and extensively diversified; and, like the hieroglyphics of other nations, were used as a mantle to conceal the acroatic or ineffable doctrines and secrets of their Spurious Freemasonry. Thus the serpent or dragon was a received hieroglyphic of the deity; and an egg of the creation or deluge; whence the ovum anguinum became the distinguishing mark of a druid, as the representative of him, who created the world out of chaos, and renewed it again after its destruction by the waters of the Deluge. The same spiritual officer was also known by his wand or rod, and his rings and glains; all emblematical of some peculiar properties which were supposed to be vested in him by virtue of his sacred character. The rod signified peace; the ring, eternity and power; and the glain, or boat of glass, was a symbol of preservation. These were sacred amulets, and believed, from their symbolical properties, to possess a secret power of averting danger. The goddess Ceridwen was symbolized or represented by a ship, a hen, a mare, a cow, a grain of wheat, and other emblems; by a scientific combination of which, various points in her character

16 Hammer. p. 7. 12. In this book are a host of testimonies to the same effect.

and history were exemplified. The cauldron of the goddess was emblematical of the arts and sciences; a bull represented the sun, and a beaver the patriarch Hu or Noah; for which this reason has been assigned. "The patriarch had built himself a vessel or house, in which he had lived in the midst of the waters; and which had deposited that venerable personage and his family safe upon dry ground. So the beaver is not only an amphibious animal, but also a distinguished architect. He is said to build a house of two stories; one of which is in the water and the other above the water; and out of the latter he has an egress to dry ground."[17]

The bee was an emblem of industry; the primrose, of dignity and power; the vervain of vaticination; the selago of divine grace. The oak was an hieroglyphic of the supreme god; and also symbolized an expanded mind, as the reed figured deceit, and the aspen leaf instability. The misletoe was an emblem of fecundity; the rainbow of protection; and for this purpose it was feigned to surround the candidate during his initiation. The white trefoil was a symbol of union, not only from the circumstance of its including the mystical triad; but also because the Druids saw, or pretended to see, in every leaf, a faint representation of the lunette or six days moon, which was an object of their veneration from its resemblance to a boat or ark. It was the powerful pledge or symbol which demanded and conveyed mutual aid in the moment of peril; a never-failing token of everlasting brotherhood, esteem, goodwill, and assistance, even unto death. The chain was symbolical of the penance imposed on every candidate for initiation by his confinement in the pastos. The phrase, "he submitted to the chain," implied that he had endured the rigours of preparation and initiation with patience and fortitude. The spica, or ear of corn, was an emblem of plenty and prosperity; and a wheat straw was an invaluable symbol, and the conservator of many potent virtues.

Thus I close my view of the hieroglyphics and symbols which were peculiar to the Spurious Freemasonry; and it will be observed that the hierophant made a marked distinction between them. Thus hieroglyphics, as the

[17] Dav. Dru. p. 267.

word implies, were used to represent divine or supernatural things, while symbols were confined to those which were sensible and natural; and hence, in the spirit of their maxim, that sacred things should be confined to sacred persons, hieroglyphical knowledge was in the custody of the priests alone; while others of the initiated were amused with symbolical illustrations. This distinc tion was too refined for general use, and, therefore, th priests were ultimately obliged to invent a new kind of hieroglyphic to preserve their peculiar secrets from being known.

Now though we deny that our system of Freemasonry was derived from the mysteries of heathen nations—for the offspring of pollution can never be made pure—yet I see no reason to reject the theory that, at its restoration by the Essenes and their successors, nay, probably at the building of king Solomon's temple, an arrangement, corresponding, in some of its component parts, with the symbolical system of Egypt, might, (for it is impossible to speak decisively on so intricate a point,) be incorporated into the original science; and be retained as a convenient mode of embodying and transmitting solemn truths, not only to secure their preservation, but also to produce a striking and permanent effect upon the mind. The extent to which they corresponded will be seen in a subsequent Lecture.

LECTURE VII.

THE TRUE FREEMASONRY IN ALL AGES SHEWN TO HAVE BEEN "VEILED IN ALLEGORY AND ILLUSTRATED BY SYMBOLS."

Lo, where our silent emblems breathe
Their sacred influence o'er the soul,
In mystic order rang'd: while round the whole
A starry zone the sister virtues wreathe.
Ye, who by compass, square, and line,
Those hidden truths can well divine,
To all besides unknown.

Waller Rodwell Wright.

Speculative Freemasonry, as preserved and practised by the small portion of mankind who had not deviated from the true worship of the Creator, ran, like an irregular vein of gold amidst a heavy stratum of impure metal, throughout all the mysterious institutions of the ancient world; and its symbols and hieroglyphical interpretations, though of pure origin, became to a certain extent polluted by their introduction into the system of Spurious Freemasonry for the purpose of conferring a real value on its complicated ceremonies.

It will, therefore, be highly interesting to inquire in what manner, and to what extent the Jewish and Christian symbols may be assimilated with those of Freemasonry. But whatever might be the utility and worth of symbolical instruction in the caverns of initiation, we find it enunciated with still greater clearness and perspicuity under the patriarchal, Mosaic, and Christian dispensations; and even invested with the sanction of the Deity.

The ancient mythologies of all nations, display, in striking colours, the fondness of an unsophisticated people for allegory; and the history of the heathen deities affords ample evidence of the existence of such a taste. In the infancy of the world poetry reigned triumphantly over the human heart, and expanded itself, not merely in thought, but in allegorical language and design. If the ideas of an uncultivated race were confined within narrow limits, they were rendered expressive by being embodied in poetical language, and embellished with figures of rhetoric, whence originated the art of picture-writing; which, as we have seen, was probably used before the Flood. But of all others, the Hebrew language was peculiarly susceptible of allegorical imagery. Take an instance from the prophecy of Isaiah. "My hand hath found, as a nest, the riches of the people; and as one gathereth eggs that are left, have I gathered all the earth; and there was none that moved the wing, or opened the mouth, or peeped. Shall the axe boast itself against him that heweth therewith? Or shall the saw magnify itself against him that shaketh it? As if the rod should shake itself against them that lift it up, or as if the staff should lift up itself as if it were no wood. Therefore shall the Lord send among his fat ones leanness; and under his glory he shall kindle a burning like the burning of a fire. And the Light of Israel shall be for a fire, and his Holy One for a flame; and it shall burn and devour his thorns and his briars in one day; and shall consume the glory of his forest, and of his fruitful field, both soul and body; and they shall be as when a standard-bearer fainteth."[1]

This passage has been selected at random: it is full of types or hieroglyphics. And throughout the whole of the Jewish writings, they, in like manner, abound. Nothing, indeed, could be more general than the use of symbolical machinery amongst that people, if we may believe the testimony of learned men. It was engrafted into their system of worship, formed a constituent part of the mysteries of their religion, and was carried into operation in all their public and private avocations. No certain canon has been laid down for their interpretation; but there is a general reference to a more perfect system of religion, of which all their rites and ceremonies were

[1] Isai. x. 14. 18.

types and shadows. The leading truths cannot be mistaken, but the details admit of various and contradictory explanations. Thus the tree of Life, Jacob's Vision, the manna, the brazen serpent, the scape goat, the Sun of righteousness, &c. are symbols of a nature too plain and unequivocal to be mistaken. But the inferior emblems have been matter of endless conjecture.

Some of these hieroglyphical symbols have been considered of local operation by one commentator; while another, adopting a more general view, has differed widely in his exposition. Some are content with the simple and obvious meaning; others reason upon them analogically; while a third party resort to allegory and mystery for the true sense; and from these causes are often led astray by doubtful interpretations; but all agree that an emblematical signification is to be looked for in the ceremonies of the Jewish religion, and the circumstances attending the establishment of the Jewish polity. Thus by one writer the ten plagues of Egypt are explained in reference to the ten torments and pains of hell. "1. As the water was turned into blood; so all things shall be turned to the destruction of the ungodly. 2. Their frogs, signify horror of conscience. 3. Their lice, a restless and unquiet mind. 4. The flies denote that they shall be destitute of all help. 5. By the murrain of beasts, the perpetual punishment of their bodies was typified. 6. By boils, anguish of mind. 7. By hail, continual terror. 8. By locusts, the want of every good thing. 9. By the darkness, their loss of the favour of God. 10. And everlasting death, by the death of their first-born."[2] While Augustine refers these ten plagues to the transgression of the ten precepts of the moral law; and others to the same number of mercies which were vouchsafed to the people during their sojournings in the wilderness.

The dying Jacob, when blessing his children, used a series of a significant emblems to express the character and fortunes of their respective descendants; which were treasured up in their memory, and used as the insignia of the tribes after the great deliverance from Egyptian bondage. In the ancient book of Job, hieroglyphical

[2] Willet. Hexapla. p. 128.

modes of expression frequently occur. The swiftness of time is symbolized by a weaver's shuttle; and the hypocrite's hope by a spider's web. The knowledge of the Deity is described as being "high as the heavens, deeper than hell, longer than the earth, and broader than the sea." Man is symbolized by a flower of the field; prosperity by a lighted candle; and adversity by a candle extinguished.

The pledge of fidelity and token of renunciation amongst the Jews, was, taking off a shoe; and joining of hands was a symbol of friendship and fidelity. Going barefoot was an emblem of sorrow and purity of heart; as were also sackcloth and ashes.[3] David uses the emblem of a tree planted by the water side, to denote a just and upright man; and chaff for the worthless. To represent the divine justice he takes the similitude of a bow. The land of Israel is designated by the emblem of a vineyard; and the people by a vine. The expiation of sin was symbolized by hyssop; righteousness by a palm tree; which was also a peculiar type of Judea; and hence on some Roman coins, women are depicted seated under the palm tree, overwhelmed with grief; and circumscribed JUDÆA CAPTA. Mercy or piety were symbolically expressed by the cedar or citron tree; indecision by the failing of water brooks; irresolution by the perishing of summer fruits; instability by the evanescence of a morning cloud, and the withering away of seed that taketh no root; despair by the silence of the harp; righteousness and faithfulness by a girdle; strength by a lock of hair; and industry by the ant. The emblem to express the brevity of life was a hand-breadth.[4]

When the prophets communicated the will of God, it was frequently accomplished by the use of symbols or images of material things. As the rending of Samuel's mantle was a type to denote Saul's loss of the kingdom; the destruction of the altar at Bethel and the withering

[3] Achilles strewed ashes on his head when overwhelmed with sorrow on hearing of the death of Patroclus. Il. xviii. 23.

[4] On this emblem Pierius says:—"In divinis literis, ut multorum theologorum est interpretatio παλαιστῃ, vitæ brevis est quasi hieroglyphicum. Nam Psalmo, &c. Traductione, quam Ruffinus citat, scriptum est—Ecce veteres posuisti dies meos.

of Jeroboam's hand were symbols of the reformation by Josiah. Zedekiah, though a false prophet, used the common imagery when he made him horns of iron, as an emblem of the destruction of the Syrians. Isaiah pronounced the annihilation of Sennacherib's army by the symbol of a hook in his nose and a bridle in his lips; and the lenghthened life of Hezekiah by the retrogradation of the sun's shadow on the dial. The same prophet typified the captivity of Egypt and Ethiopia by walking naked and barefoot. Jeremiah symbolized the destruction of the people by a linen girdle; and their misery by bottles filled with wine; the power of God by a potter; and the destruction of the Jews by breaking a potter's vessel. By bonds and yokes he figured their captivity under Nebuchadnezzar; and by the type of good and bad figs, the return of the Jews with Zerubbabel, after the seventy years should be accomplished, and the land had enjoyed her sabbaths.

Ezekiel shewed the fearful judgments which awaited his countrymen, by the type of hair; and their slavery by a chain, by two eagles and a vine, and by a boiling pot. The fearful chambers of imagery which the Lord revealed to him in a vision, were the caverns of initiation into the Spurious Freemasonry. The hope of Israel's restoration was symbolized by a resurrection of dry bones. By the emblem of a gourd, the disaffection of Judah was reproved; the success of Zerubbabel was shown by a golden candlestick; and the two anointed ones by as many olive trees; while the violated covenant, and the quarrel between the two brothers, Judah and Israel, is forcibly displayed by that significant emblem, the two staves, Beauty and Bands.[5]

Such is a brief outline, copiously illustrated by facts, of the hieroglyphical system of the Jews at the period of their greatest glory. It was not enough that the doctrine should be enunciated simply by the use of metaphorical language in their conversation and writings; but it was plainly and obviously exhibited by the frequent use of material symbols, like those employed in Freemasonry. In some cases emblematical imagery was ex-

[5] It will be needless to observe that all the above illustrations are taken from the Holy Scriptures.

tended to apologue or fable. Of this nature is the message of Jehoash to Amaziah:—"The thistle that was in Lebanon, sent to the cedar that was in Lebanon, saying, give thy daughter to my son to wife; and there passed by a wild beast that was in Lebanon, and trode down the thistle."[6] Hence we perceive that the frequent mention in scripture of men who "understand dark sayings, riddles, and parables," referred to the interpretation of hieroglyphical symbols. And it appears probable that the "difficult questions" of Sheba, and those which Dius says passed between Solomon and Hiram, were of the same description. A remarkable specimen how prevalent this kind of knowledge was amongst the Jews, is found in the writings of their great historian, Josephus; and I quote a passage in which this learned writer explains the secret meaning of many emblematical decorations which Moses had introduced into the tabernacle. "To any man," he says, "who deliberately and candidly examines the matter, it will plainly appear that the structure of the tabernacle, the sacerdotal garments, and the various vessels and instruments appertaining to the service of the altar, bear a strict analogy to the structure of the universe. The three divisions of the tabernacle may be compared to the earth, the sea, and the heavens; the two first of which divisions were open to the priests in general, whilst every person was forbidden to enter into the last, it being peculiarly appropriated to the residence of the Almighty. The twelve months of the year are signified by the same number of loaves of shew bread, which were placed on the table. The seven lamps over the branches of the golden candlestick, refer to the seven planets; and the seventy pieces of which the candlestick is composed to the twelve signs of the Zodiac. The four colours which are wrought into the curtains, as well the curtains themselves, are intended to represent the four elements. The earth, from which the flax is produced, was typified by the fine linen. The sea is represented by the purple colour, which derives its origin from the blood of the fish murex. The violet colour is an emblem of the air, as

[6] 2 Kings. xiv. 9. There are several instances of this in the Old Testament. See Judges. xi. Ezek. xxiv. xxvii. &c,

the crimson is of the fire. With respect to the garment of the High Priest, the linen of which it is composed, represents the whole earth, and its violet colour the heavens. The pomegranates refer to the lightning, and the noise of the bells to the thunder. The ephod, with its four several colours, has a reference to the nature of the universe; and the intermixture of gold to the rays of the sun. The essen, or rationale, which is placed in the middle of the garment, denotes the situation of the earth, in the centre of the universe. The girdle which passes round the body of the priests, is a symbol of the sea environing the earth. The sun and moon may be supposed to be expressed by the two sardonyx stones; and either the twelve months, or the signs of the zodiac by the twelve other stones. The violet colour of the tiara resembles heaven; and it would have manifested a great want of reverence to the Deity to have inscribed his Sacred Name on any other colour. The splendour and majesty of the Supreme Being are signified by the triple crown, and the plate of gold."[7]

The same method of inculcating moral and theological truths was used by the Saviour of mankind. This great pattern of all that was good and virtuous, confessed that while he spake to his disciples plainly, and interpreted to them freely the meaning of all the symbols in which his discourses were enfolded, he addressed the people in parables, that "seeing, they might not see, and hearing, they might not understand."[8] He designated himself by various similitudes, to exhibit the different points in his character, or to illustrate the doctrines which he came to teach. If he represented himself under the symbol of a vine, and his disciples as the branches, it was to pourtray his character as the Father of mankind; and to shew the intimate connection which subsists between him and his favourite people. And this emblem was in perfect keeping with the ancient system; for Judea was usually symbolized by a vineyard. A door or a way pointed out the doctrine of salvation through faith in his name; and was further emblematical of the sprinkling which the Jews of old were commanded to perform on the side-

[7] Jos. Ant. Jud. b. 3. c. 7.

[8] Mark.iv. 11, 12.

posts and upper door-posts of their houses, that they might be saved, when the destroying angel passed through the land of Egypt to exterminate the first-born. A shepherd denotes the manhood of Christ; light and truth his Godhead. His doctrine was compared to leaven put into a lump of dough; and to figure the unlimited dominion which his religion should ultimately assume, he likened his disciples to a city set on a hill. The kingdom of heaven was a sublime object kept perpetually in view by a succession of striking and significant metaphors; all uniting their aid to confirm the great truth of Christian revelation, a future state of rewards and punishments.

By the emblem of a single eye, he referred to the light of truth; and by a wedding garment, to personal holiness. He compared his church to a grain of mustard seed, because of the smallness and obscurity of its origin, and its gradual enlargement to cover the whole earth; and to a net, which contained both good and worthless fishes, as the church receives members of every kind—but as the fisherman separates them, and casts the bad away, so will the Great Fisherman, at the day of judgment, separate the worthy from the wicked members of his church, and cast the latter into the lake that burneth with fire and brimstone. He also adopted various emblems to point out the repentant sinner, and the joyful acclamations with which his contrition is received by the hosts of heaven; such as, the lost sheep, the piece of silver, and the prodigal; while impenitent sinners were symbolized by tares, the barren fig tree, and the demoniac. Hypocritical pride and malice, he designated by the emblem of a beam and a mote. If he spake of living waters, he referred to the Holy Spirit of God, which had been frequently represented under that symbol by the Jewish prophets; and if he mentioned a strait gate, the symbol plainly meant a pure and holy life. He described his church under the figure of a pearl; the world as a cultivated field; the angels as reapers; and the final consummation of all things as a harvest. Thus was symbolical instruction used and applied by Jesus Christ. He knew the constitutional indifference of mankind too well to confide in the common method of conveying knowledge; and adopted the system of association, which is more efficacious in making permanent impressions than any other which philosophy could invent.

I have said that the Jewish religion is a type of Christianity. Let us, then, examine how the early Christian writers allegorized and explained the symbols which they found in the tabernacle or temple worship. The passover was an important ceremony which the Israelites were enjoined to observe with ritual punctuality throughout their generations; and indeed it was a type of the sacrifice of Christ, the true paschal lamb. Every ceremony attending this ordinance has therefore been taken symbolically, and applied to the Christian dispensation. Thus the time of killing the passover, viz., in the fourteenth day, or full of the moon, when nights were light, and darkness superseded, has been considered an emblem of Christ coming as a Light to lighten the Gentiles, and the glory of the people of Israel. And it is remarkable that the Messiah was actually slain at the feast of the passover. On the tenth day of the month the Jews were directed to take a lamb, and keep it four days before it was killed. In like manner Christ entered Jerusalem on the tenth day of the same month, and was sacrificed on the fourteenth.

The paschal lamb was an emblem of Christ. It was without spot or blemish—Christ was without sin. It was a male—Christ was strong and powerful; and a male was further a symbol of perfection; which equally applies to Christ, for he was free from sin. The lamb was to be a year old, and consequently at its full strength—Christ was sacrificed in the vigour of manhood. A lamb is patient—so was Christ. Innocent—Christ was the same. The blood of the lamb was shed—as was also that of Christ. By this ceremony the Jews were protected from the destroying angel—by Christ's death we are delivered from the power of Satan. The blood of the lamb, in order to be efficacious, was to be sprinkled on the door-posts—the blood of Christ must be sprinkled on our hearts by faith. The lamb was to be eaten whole—Christ is a full and perfect sacrifice for the sins of the world. There are many and various interpretations of such types; but this specimen will be amply sufficient to display the general nature of their application and reference.

The construction, furniture, and ornaments of the tabernacle have been a fertile source of allegorical exposition. I have already adduced the opinion of Josephus on the subject; and I shall subjoin that of many eminent Christian writers. By its three divisions were symbolized the three Orders of the Church—Bishops, Priests, and Deacons; and in a more extended sense it has been considered as referring to the whole community of the faithful. As the High Priest only could enter into the Holy of Holies, so this division was emblematical of Christ our High Priest, who is now in the holiest place of heaven as our mediator. The holy place was accessible to the priests; and is thus an emblem of the ministers of the Church. While the third division, or Court, being open to the people, was a type of the whole company of the faithful wheresoever dispersed under the wide canopy of heaven. The large outer Court prefiguring the mission to the Gentiles; while the doors of the sanctuary were composed of fir and olive to signify peace on earth; and the two leaves of that which led to the Oracle symbolized the two theological virtues, Faith and Hope.

In the table for the Shewbread, the shittim wood of which it was composed, was emblematical of the Holy Scriptures; the four feet symbolized the four senses in which they conceived those holy writings ought to be understood; viz. historically, allegorically, tropologically, and anagogically, the four rings referred to the four evangelists. By the divers vessels used in the tabernacle worship, we have been called on to understand the diversity of gifts, communicated by the Holy Spirit; the twelve loaves symbolized the twelve tribes, including the whole Israel of God; the altar of incense, prayer, and thanksgiving; and the crown, eternal life. The golden candlestick was an emblem of Christ; the metal, denoting the purity of divine grace; the seven branches containing lamps, the seven spirits of God; and the knops and flowers, the graces and ornaments of a pious Christian's life. The ten curtains of the tabernacle referred to the Decalogue; the hair covering impervious to the weather, was emblematical of the priests and ministers who defend the church from heresy; the red skins denoted those who suffered martyrdom for their faith; while the whole four coverings which defended the tabernacle, pointed to the protection which Christ has promised to his church—that the gates of hell shall not prevail against it. The boards or pillars were symbols of the faithful; the bars, of the pastors of the church; and the foundation, Jesus Christ the Messiah of God.

The inner veil represented the heavens, which Christ hath opened to us by his blood. And, not to follow up this part of the subject till it becomes tedious, the ark of the Covenant was a symbol of the divine presence; the cherubim with which the doors and veils were profusely adorned, were emblematical of ministering spirits who execute the will and pleasure of the Deity; the palm trees denoted patience; and the golden cherubim of the Mercy Seat, referred to the quadruple figure which was revealed to Ezekiel and St. John by visions, composed of a man, an ox, a lion, and an eagle, facing respectively the south, west, east, and north, and signified the union of fire, light, and air, which were the usual similitudes under which the divine essence had been manifested to man.

The Apocalypse abounds with types and symbols; but as this Lecture has already been extended to an unusual length, and having other matters of great importance to bring forward, I shall merely notice a few. By a crystal river was symbolized the pure doctrines of Christianity; trees of life, signified holy men; and frogs, impurity. By dogs, and sorcerers, and whoremongers, and murderers, were typified brutal, obscene, and unbelieving men, persecutors, and atheists; by the waters of life, eternal happiness.

From a careful perusal of the writings of the early Christian Fathers, we find a variety of characteristic signs used by the first professors of our faith. Did they wish to express adoration, their eyes and hands were lifted up to heaven.[9] Contrition was symbolized by

[9] It is worthy of remark that the Greek word for a man, *ανθρωπος*, appears to have been derived from *αναθρων*,, *sursum aspiciens*, looking upward. In Ovid's account of the creation, reference is made to this distinction of man from the beasts.

Pronaque cum spectent animalia cætera terram

bending the knees; gratitude by prostration; humility by uncovering the head, or by kneeling down and spreading forth the hands; piety by stretching out the right arm with the hand open: supplication by placing both hand on the heart; liberality by throwing back the right hand innocence by washing the hands; fear by casting th eyes to the ground; and blessing by the imposition of hands. The sign of Faith was an upright posture of the body; Hope, lifting up the hands; and Charity rising from the knees. They adopted likewise the Pythagorean pentalpha, as the sign of salutation; the five wounds of Christ being imagined to correspond with the five angular points of the figure. This was the portraiture. Again, the body of Christ, when extended on the Cross, was considered a symbol of the Jewish Temple; his head, the Holy of Holies; his breast, the altar; his feet, the eastern portal; and his stretched out hands, the north and south doors of the edifice. "In like manner the same figure, called by Bishop Kennet, the *pentangle of Solomon*, which was used as the banner of Antiochus Soter, was employed all over Asia in ancient times as a charm against witchcraft. It was anciently in use among the Jews, as a symbol betokening safety; and to this day the English shepherd cuts it on the grass, or in the green sward, little thinking of its ancient composition and signification; the entire figure representing the Greek characters υγεαι health."[10]

These tokens are curious, and the Free and Accepted Mason will derive much gratification from finding that the same observances which he has been taught to esteem, as being the conservators of great symbolical

Os homini sublime dedit; cælumque tueri
Jussit et erectos ad sidera tollere vultus.

And our own Young has deduced from man's upright form a lesson of devotion.

Nature no such hard task enjoins; she gave
A make to man directive of his thought;
A make set upright, pointing to the stars;
As who should say—read thy chief lesson there.

[10] Cruciana p. 285.

truths and important moral references, were employed by the early teachers of our most holy faith to embody and express, with significancy and truth, the internal feelings and emotions of the heart.

It is wonderful to reflect on the facility with which the hieroglyphics of heathenism passed into Christianity Mr. Hope[11] has furnished a lucid view of the subject, which may not be inappropriately quoted at the conclusion of this Lecture, although I must admit that, in some particulars, the comparison is strained. "Among the first Christians, the emblems of heathen deities or worship, rendered allusive to the parables of our Saviour, or the points of his doctrine, from being odious and profane, became suddenly objects of respect and veneration. Thus the vine, the genii sporting among its tendrils, and the various processes of converting its fruit into the most universal of beverages, all belonging, among the heathens, to the rites of Bacchus, were by the first Christians rendered symbolical of the labours in the vineyard of the faith; or, perhaps, the cup of wine which our Saviour, at the last supper, presented to his disciples as the type of his own blood, and were thence introduced in the edifices and tombs of Christians, as we see in numberless early Christian monuments, which not only deceived the Pagans, who knew not the subterfuge, but the later Christians also, who had again forgotten it, and who have mistaken most of these works for heathen relics. As the vine of Bacchus furnished the emblem for the wine, so did the ear of corn of Ceres furnish that for the bread, which, on the eve of his crucifixion, our Saviour divided among his disciples.

The palm branch, which, among heathens, denoted worldly victories, was made among Christians to mark the triumphs of the cross, and was wrested from the hands of heathen gods to be placed in those of a saint or martyr. Venus' dove became the Holy Ghost; Diana's stag, the Christian soul thirsting for the living waters; Juno's peacock, under the name of the phœnix, that soul after the resurrection. One evangelist was gifted with Jupiter's eagle; another with Cybele's lion; and winged genii and cupids became angels and cherubs.

[11] Archit. p. 180.

Even the sphinx, the griffin, and the chimera of mythology, were by the Christians adopted as having the same power of warding off evil spirits and fascination which was supposed to belong to the head of the Gorgon. The holy image of the cross itself was disguised in the semblance of an insignificant ornament. At Lavinia, in the posterior pediment of that small edifice called the Temple of Chiturnus, we see that cross composed of acanthus leaves, so blended among the surrounding scrolls of vine and poppy as to have escaped the eye of later and less sharp-sighted Christians. Afterwards, a more distinctly formed cross, covered with gems, was used as the emblem of the Christian faith; and it was not till the sixth century that the body of Christ was exhibited on it; nor was it till the council was held at Constantinople, in 692, that the superseding of allegory by actual representation was positively enjoined.

To the insignia borrowed from polytheism, the Christians still added others, useful in allaying the wrath which more undisguised representations would have raised. The lamb was made to designate the meek and faithful Christian; twelve such, in regular procession, represented the Apostles; and a thirteenth, more exalted than the rest, and adorned by a nimbus, was our Saviour. As the Greek word for a fish, *Ιχθυος* contained the initials of *Ιεσους Χριστος θεος Υιος ο Σοτηρ*, even the inhabitants of the deep were made to represent Christ; and the rough outline of the fish, formed of two curves, meeting in a point at their extremities, was made to enclose, under the name *vesica piscis*, the figure of our Saviour in his glorified state, or of the Madona, or of the patron saint; and displayed in the pediments, or over the porches of churches, or in the seats of bishops, as objects destined to call forth the recollection of these holy personages."

In the above illustrations, the well-instructed Mason will find many things which he has already learned in the several Degrees of his Order; for the great union of Speculative and Operative Masonry at the building of the Temple introduced a series of Jewish symbols, which will for ever remain to dignify and adorn the science. The architectural emblems of the First Degree may be rather considered of Sidonian extraction, as they emanate almost entirely from Operative Masonry; but though they appear to the uninitiated as mere instruments of manual labour, yet, as they embody a mass of moral reference, we consider them to be jewels of inestimable value. And are they not so? How did Solomon inculcate industry? Go to the ant, said he. If, in like manner, we desire to teach morality and justice, what better reference can we have than to the Master's jewel? If equality, that attribute of the Deity,

> Who sees with equal eye as God of all,
> A hero perish or a sparrow fall;

we point to that of the Senior Warden; of integrity, to that of the Junior Warden; and each reads the Mason a lecture, which is highly calculated to make him a wiser and a better man. What can be more beautiful or more significant than the Immovable Jewels? Even the simple working tools of an Entered Apprentice embody the wisdom and utility which alone would enhance the practice of virtue, and enrich the mind with precepts of inestimable value.

Do we pass on to the Second and Third Degrees; the symbolical interpretation of each Floor Cloth increases in interest as we gradually advance through the field of corn by the river side,[12] past the enriched pillars of the temple to the awful Sanctum Sanctorum, where ethereal Light, the essence and perfection of Freemasonry, enthroned between the Cherubim of the Mercy Seat, shall reign for ever and ever.

[12] Hutchinson has ventured a curious opinion respecting the above symbol, which I do not think has been adopted by any other writer. Being one of the attributes of Ceres, he is rather inclined to refer it to the spurious than the true Free Masonry. "The application which is made of the word Sibboleth amongst Masons is a testimony of their retaining their original vow uninfringed, and their first faith with the Brotherhood uncorrupted. And to render their words and phrases more abstruse and obscure, they selected such as by acceptation in the Scriptures, or otherwise, might puzzle the ignorant by a double implication. Thus Sibboleth, should we have adopted the Eleusinian mysteries, would answer, as an avowal of our profession; the same implying *ears of corn.* But it has its etymology or derivation from the following compounds in the Greek language, as it is adopted by Masons, viz.: **σιβο** *colo;* and **λιθον** *lapis:* so **Σιβολιθον** Sibbolithon, *colo Lapidem,* implies that they retain and keep inviolate their obligations as the *Juramentum per Jovem Lapidem,* the most obligatory oath held amongst the heathen."—Hutch. Spirit of Masonry. Ed. 1775 p. 181.

LECTURE VIII.

ENQUIRY WHETHER THE UNION OF SPECULATIVE AND OPERATIVE MASONRY WAS ACCOMPLISHED AT THE BUILDING OF KING SOLOMON'S TEMPLE.

A kingly pile sublime.
For this exhausted mines
Supplied the golden store;
For this the central caverns gave their gems;
For this the woodman's axe
Open'd the cedar forest to the sun;
The silkworm of the East
Spun her sepulchral egg. *Southey.*

THE chain of social relations is constituted on such a just and equitable principle of mutual dependency and mutual aid, that if a single link be broken, a sense of disorganization is felt from the highest down to the most inferior class in the community. Precisely thus it is in the system of Freemasonry which we profess. Taken collectively as a speculative and operative science, it is the pride of human institutions. Separate these component parts, and it becomes meagre, useless, and void of meaning. No person who has been initiated into Freemasonry can have paid the slightest attention to its principles without discovering that it is composed of two parts—morality and science. And these are interwoven with such delicacy and art, that every scientific illustration conveys some moral truth, or points, with unerring certainty, to the Great Architect of the Universe, as the divine source of all knowledge, and the sole object of human adoration. When the rich treasures of masonic lore are unfolded, the heart is improved by its moral disquisitions, and the affections tempered into soberness and brotherly love. And if historic records of the science be investigated, we shall find, in the example of our ancient brethren, many instances of lofty virtue and scientific excellence which are worthy of imitation. The union of Speculative and Operative Masonry, by which our sublime science was modelled into its present form, is an event which we hail with pleasure, and reflect on with admiration. It took place at the building of King Solomon's Temple, which hence constitutes one of the most important occurrences in the history of Freemasonry, and contributes its aid towards hallowing the floor of a Mason's Lodge. The subject is, therefore, of sufficient interest to demand the cool and impartial consideration of every brother who wishes to understand the great principles of the science into which he has been initiated.

In this Lecture, therefore, I will endeavour to disentangle the subject from some of its difficulties, and to explain the particular circumstances which produced the union of these two branches of our science, in an intelligible and, I trust, satisfactory manner. For this purpose I shall take a brief view of Operative Masonry as it passed through the descendants of those primitive people who had renounced the pure worship of the Creator, and practised the Spurious Freemasonry, which was of human invention.

It may not, perhaps, be necessary to recall to your recollection the fact, that pure or Speculative Masonry was conveyed, along with the true religion, by the posterity—or, at least, by a portion of the posterity—of Shem and Japheth; while the arts and sciences attached to Operative Masonry were cultivated with triumphant success by the rest of the world. Before the time when temples were furnished with roofs, architecture had effected a considerable degree of refinement, which was displayed in the altars, pavements, and appendages to places of religious worship. Recent researches in Egypt have produced a series of interesting facts which prove the antiquity of architecture amongst its early inhabitants. From Wilkinson's Materia Hieroglyphica, we learn, that before the building of King Solomon's Temple, the Temple of Ammon was erected, and embellished by a succession of Egyptian Princes. Its original founder is unknown, but Thotmos III. 1367, A. A. C. added sculptures, colonnades, and obelisks. Amon-me-ameneto built a propylon and an avenue of sphinxes; and Ramses III. added a side temple, and enriched its walls with many sculptures. This was the monarch whose daughter was married to King Solomon. The great temple at Ypsambul, with its gigantic statues and rich ornaments, was erected by Amon-me-Ramses, 160 years before the Temple at Jerusalem. Egyptian architecture, in its palmy state, was so sublime, that modern writers are struck with astonishment and awe at contemplating its vast remains. Denon says: "With the Egyptians the idea of the immortality of God is presented in the eternity of his temples. I have not words to express my feelings as I stood beneath the portico of Tentyra, and thought upon that nation of men who were capable of conceiving, executing, decorating, and enriching this edifice with every thing that could speak to the eye and to the soul.' Champollion exclaims: "Imagination sinks abashed at the foot of the 140 columns of the hypostyle hall of Carnac or Ammon." To give some idea of the vastness of this latter temple, it may only be necessary to state, that each of these 140 columns was of the same diameter, and not much inferior in altitude, to the London monument on Fish Street Hill. What an immense idea must we form of the genius, as well as of the population and resources, of a country which was capable of erecting such stupendous buildings?

In the catalogue of expert architects of antiquity, the Tyrians will occupy a high and conspicuous place. Their ancestors had been masters of Egypt for more than two centuries; and when driven forth 700 years before the period to which I now desire to call your attention, viz., the era of King Solomon, carried with them the learning and talent for which that nation was so justly celebrated. And the posterity of these architects, living in constant communication with Egypt, were further improved by studying the great examples which the temples and monuments of that people exhibited, and which were unequalled in any other part of the globe.

——————————Art thrives most
Where Commerce has enriched the busy coast.
He catches all improvements in his flight,
Spreads foreign wonders in his country's sight;
Imports what others have invented well,
And stirs his own to match them or excel. *Cowper.*

Their fame was so celebrated, that every thing which displayed superior taste or elegance, not only in the erection of splendid buildings, but in ornamented glass, working of metals, fine linen, or rich colours, was, by universal consent, distinguished by the epithet of Sidonian.[1] Two hundred years before the building of the Temple, the city of Tyre was erected "by a body of Sidonian masons from Gabala, under their Grand Master, and proper princes or directors, who finished the lofty buildings of the city, with its strong walls and aqueducts, in a manner which greatly conduced to the honour and renown of those who planned and conducted this grand design."[2]

Here, then, we have a specimen of the skill displayed by the early Tyrian architects. Their city, though perhaps in its infancy, of no considerable magnitude, contained in its magnificent columns, porticos, and palaces,[3] the germ of scientific knowledge. But it was a body without a soul. It wanted the invigorating impulse which can only be supplied by a full revelation of the Omnipresent Deity. This vivifying principle was inherent in Speculative Masonry. And when Operative Architecture was animated by this pure spirit, it produced a building which was the admiration and wonder of the ancient world; and for richness and glory has not been exceeded, even in the bright era of science which succeeded the invention of printing, when all the knowledge and experience of former times became accessible to every enquirer. "Religion," says a modern writer, "thus being the parent of architecture—and a style, a symbol, device, or emblem, appropriated at first to religion and to nothing else—its object is to produce a devout abstraction in the spectator. The effect is heightened by its antiquity, and a certain mystery veiling it. It follows, then, that all styles of architecture are hieroglyphics upon a large scale, exhibiting to the heedful eye, forms of worship widely differing from each other; and proving, that in almost every religion with which we are acquainted, the form of the temple was the *hierogram* of its god, or of the peculiar opinions of its votaries."[4]

[1] Strabo. l. 16.
[2] Noorth. Const. p. 19.
[3] Menand. ap. Jos. Ant. Jud. l. viii. c. 2.
[4] Bardwell's Temples, p. 55.

Hastening to the time of the monarchy in Israel, we find Hiram, King of Tyre, much celebrated for his architectural knowledge. He spread out the city to the temple of Jupiter, by adding many magnificent buildings, constructed of immense blocks of stone united with cement of the same colour;[5] amongst which were two new temples, one of which was consecrated to Hercules, and the other to Astarte, the queen of heaven. And the temple of Hercules soon became a central point, round which all the Phenician nations assembled to celebrate the rites of worship, as the Jews were commanded to do at Jerusalem, and the pugnacious States of Greece at the temple of Jupiter Olympus.

The Spurious Freemasonry of the Tyrians was called the Mysteries of Thammuz. It was celebrated by Hiram with all the pomp and solemnity which characterized these institutions in any part of the world. And while the Tyrians practised Operative Masonry as a science from which they derived both pleasure and profit, their near neighbours were engaged in the beauteous celebrations of Speculative Masonry, under the superintendence of their Grand Master, David, King of Israel.[6] A league of the strictest amity and brotherly love subsisted between these celebrated men, as the representatives and Grand Masters of the two branches or divisions of Freemasonry. Nearly three thousand years had elapsed since they were rent asunder by the violation of Brotherly love in the first fratricide; and they were soon to be reunited for another period of equal longitude. Passing events hastened the accomplishment of an union so pregnant with beneficial consequences to all posterity. Let us, then, consider the proximate causes by which this great design was accomplished.

When David found his flourishing kingdom in a state

[5] Alex. Mag. l. 2.

[6] "In the first ages of the world, between the Jews and the Phenicians, there happened a great disagreement in maintaining of interests, rites, and ceremonies; but after some debate between them, the Jews taking a fancy to the Phenician worship, the Phenicians answered their kindness by affecting their mysterious doctrines and ceremonies; and so they exchanged the one for the other. The Jews sent their traditions, laws, and mysteries, in lieu of which was returned, a set method of idolatry. This went on from the time of the Judges; yet grew not up to its mature and full perfection till Solomon's time." (Sammes. Brit. p. 73.)

of profound peace, he had leisure to reflect on the impropiety, and, as he humbly thought, the sinfulness of dwelling in a princely palace, while the Ark of God, and the sacred symbols of his majesty, were deposited in a fragile and insecure tabernacle. Animated by divine wisdom,

> Beneath whose clear discerning eye
> The visionary shadows fly,
> Of folly's painted show;
> He saw through every fair disguise,
> That all but virtue's solid joys
> Is vanity and woe.
>
> *Carter.*

And impressed with the pious principle that the most effectual method of securing God's favour was by providing and maintaining a national Temple for his worship, he conceived the magnificent design of erecting a building to the honour of God which should eclipse all the temples then existing in the world. The idea was sublime, but its execution was not permitted. The man after God's own heart devoutly bowed to the decision, and contented himself with procuring plans from the architects of Tyre, and collecting materials for the work, in perfect acquiescence with the divine promise that it should be completed by the wisest and most accomplished of his children. This assurance animated his zeal; and with prodigious labour and expense he heaped together vast treasures of gold and silver, wood and stone; which after his death were still more extensively increased by Solomon his son, and successor to the throne. Soon, however, this wise king became conscious, from an examination of the plans left to him by his father, that the work was on too extensive a scale to be executed by his own unaided resources; and, therefore, he made that famous application to the Grand Master of Operative Masonry which is recorded in the books of Kings and Chronicles.

This application constitutes an era of great importance in the annals of both Speculative and Operative Masonry. The critical moment, which was to determine whether they should remain forever separate, was at hand. Various causes contributed to accelerate their union; and the embassy of Solomon to Hiram, his father's friend, was the immediate agent of its triumphant completion.

The children of Israel, in every age from their miraculous deliverance out of captivity, had been inordinately attached to the subtilties of Egyptian Freemasonry. St. Chrysostom has recorded that they entertained an increasing fondness for the fascinating splendours of this spurious system. And it could scarcely be otherwise. Man is by nature prone to superstition—fond of prodigies and tales of wild adventure. Traditions of the wonders contained in the mysteries of Thammuz, descended from father to son; augmented, as unguarded traditions always are, by exaggerated statements and fabulous narrations, which absorbed the attention of the Israelitish youth, and excited the voluptuous desire to participate in imaginary pleasures that were denied by the practice of their own religion. The means of gratification were at hand. The Tyrians held their Lodges periodically, in which the Spurious Freemasonry was celebrated in all its imposing splendour. The beautiful temples and places of initiation were thrown open to the enlightened Epopts. And we need scarcely wonder that they were highly attractive. In fact, nothing could resist the influence produced by the mysterious rites of these splendid apartments, which the architectural taste and genius of that people had furnished and decorated with every requisite which might give effect to the ceremonies. The people of the Lord were seduced by the pompous rites and magnificent festivals of Tyre, and longed to unite their voices in the fascinating harmony which chanted the praises and recounted the presumed virtues of fictitious deities. This propensity was not unobserved by him who seeth all things, and knoweth the very thoughts and intents of the heart. He saw—he pitied human weakness—and graciously resolved to wean his people from these allurements. For the purpose, therefore, of inducing them to adhere to their own worship in preference to the idolatries which accompanied the imperfect system practised at Tyre, he permitted a gorgeous temple to be erected for their use, which excelled, beyond all comparison, every existing edifice in riches and glory.

It is clear that there was a familiar intercourse between the Israelites and the Tyrians, which was facilitated by the use of a common language; for the Punic tongue, according to Dr. Pritchard, was nearly pure Phenician or

Hebrew.[7] This, indeed, was a necessary preliminary, without which, no benefits of any importance could have been realized. And it may be presumed that the Light was permitted to illuminate this branch of Spurious Freemasonry, with a greater degree of brilliancy than was conveyed to those which were removed to a greater distance from its source. The ancestors of these Tyrians, when they ruled in Egypt, worshipped the true God, and practised the true Freemasonry; neither had they much degenerated in the time of Abraham; as is evidenced in the history of Abimelech. A portion, therefore, of its benignant spirit might still remain to hallow the league between David and Hiram. Is it probable, then, that any of the Israelites were actually initiated into the Tyrian Freemasonry? It is probable; not only from the above reasoning, but from the fact that they were members of the Lodges of Operative Masonry; and the more permanent and endearing connections of husband and wife, parent and child, were common amongst them; and the most expert architect and designer that the world ever beheld, sprang from such an union.

From these united causes Hiram was induced to return an answer to Solomon's communication, which contained the language of amity and esteem. He agreed to extend the fraternal bond of that charity and brotherly love which was common to both the true and Spurious Freemasonry, by furnishing cedars and other timber from the forest of Lebanon for the erection of a temple to the living God; and providing the most expert architects in his dominions for its construction; on the simple condition of receiving certain supplies of provisions in exchange. And he performed his contract with princely munificence and masonic candour.

But even this would have been insufficient to produce any satisfactory result, without the presence of a Master mind to animate and direct the proceedings. And the King of Tyre furnished this Master mind in the person of his chief architect Hiram Abiff, by whom the reunion of Speculative and Operative Masonry was to be consummated. Having been born and educated in Tyre, he had

[7] See Bochart's Geog. Sac. p. 800, and also Conybeare's Theological Lectures. The Tyrian language was indeed a dialect of the Hebrew.

received initiation from the priests of that people; and it is highly probable that he had risen to the rank of an Hierophant or Grand Master of the Spurious Freemasonry. But his mother was an Israelite, and it is scarcely credible that his great and aspiring genius would be contented with any thing less than a perfect knowledge of all the rites and ceremonies attached to the Jewish religion as well as those of his own country; or that he would remain blind to the superior advantages which the true Freemasonry presented. In a word, he was inspired by Jehovah to distinguish between good and evil—right and wrong.

> ——————him within a finer mould
> She wrought, and tempered with a purer flame.
> To him the Sire Omnipotent unfolds
> The world's harmonious volume, there to read
> The transcript of himself. *Akenside.*

And what was the fruit of this knowledge? An earnest desire to perform the will, and to promote the glory of God. He soon acquired the influence of talent with the Grand Masters; and, by a judicious exercise of prudence and zeal, he induced them to unite the essentials of both systems, viz., their morality, brotherly love, and science, and to constitute one Grand Lodge in which these principles should form the bond of union. This Grand Lodge was the main spring that moved and directed the vast machinery which was put in motion to construct that magnificent edifice; and Hiram Abiff was the animus which directed every movement. Both sacred and profane records fully prove that this curious artist justly merited the honourable apellation of Great, whether we consider him in his moral or scientific character. As an architect none could ever compete with him, not even Aholiab and Bezaleel, though inspired from on high. As an embroiderer he stood unrivalled; as a sculptor antiquity can produce no parallel; and as a mechanic he outshone all his predecessors. "He was the most accomplished designer and operator upon earth," says Anderson, "whose abilities were not confined to building only, but extended to all kinds of work, whether in gold, silver, brass, or iron; whether in linen, tapestry, or embroidery; whether considered as an architect, statuary, founder or designer, he equally excelled. From his designs, and under his direction, all the rich and splendid furniture of the temple, and its several appendages, were begun, carried on, and finished.[8]

Every preliminary being at length arranged, Hiram Abiff proceeded to execute his high commission. He formed Lodges of Master Masons, Fellow Crafts, and Entered Apprentices; each class under its Grand Lodge of Excellent or Superexcellent Masters. Numbers of the Israelitish people were admitted into the inferior degrees; while their chiefs and princes were exalted to the highest honours of the Craft. There are extant amongst Masons many remarkable traditions respecting the formation and management of these Lodges, in each degree of the united system, both in the quarries, the forest, and at Jerusalem; with the mode of working, and the amount of wages. A brief detail of the plans which were used on this great occasion may be interesting to some, and acceptable to all.

First, there was one supreme Grand Lodge, in which Wisdom, Strength, and Beauty were personified in the three Grand Masters—S K I—H K T—H A B. No other persons were permitted to share in the knowledge of those vast designs which formed the subjects of consultation with the illustrious Three. They alone were in possession of the true secrets of a Master Mason; and when the foundations of the Temple were laid, they placed these secrets in a sure and safe depository, that if accident or the decrees of heaven should throw over them the shade of temporary oblivion, they might still, at some future period, reappear as guides and beacons to posterity. This was called the Sacred Lodge. It was held in a crypt beneath the spot where the Sanctum Sanctorum, or Holy of Holies, was placed in the bowels of Mount Moriah.[9] Of this Lodge it was that Solomon our supreme Grand Master said: "Wisdom hath builded her house; she hath hewn out her seven pillars."[10] And it was by the exer-

[8] Noorth. Const. p. 33.

[9] Maundrell says that "in a garden lying at the foot of Mount Moriah, he was shewn several large vaults, running at least fifty yards under ground. They were built in two aisles, arched at the top with huge firm stone, and sustained with tall pillars, consisting each of one single stone, two yards in diameter. This might possibly be some work made to enlarge the area of the temple; for Josephus describes something like it."

[10] Prov. ix. 1.

cise of the Wisdom[11] which was inherent in him, and of which he was the personification as the first Great Pillar of the Grand Lodge, that he preserved the secrets of a Master Mason from utter extinction.

With this Grand Lodge originated the union of Speculative and Operative Masonry; an union which produced the temple at Jerusalem, which was so celebrated throughout the ancient world. Speculative Masonry was represented by Wisdom, in the person of king Solomon; and Operative Masonry by Strength in the person of king Hiram; while Hiram Abiff, or Beauty, was the personification of both united. With these elements a system was constructed which still exists in all its purity and elegance; and will contribute blessings to the human race till time shall be no more. It is presumed that Solomon, who married an Egyptian Princess,[12] had been initiated into the Spurious Freemasonry of that people; and had thus acquired a knowledge of the mysterious principles of their architecture; and of the system of symbolical machinery which distinguished all the Eastern institutions. This knowledge would render the above union more easy of accomplishment; and hence Operative Masonry being endued with all the advantages derivable

[11] In speaking of the Wisdom of our Grand Master, a decisive testimony of which is contained in our Sacred Books, (Kings iii. 12.—2 Chron. i. 11, 12.) Josephus notices some curious instances of the superstitions which had been engrafted thereon in subsequent ages. "These extraordinary gifts were not bestowed upon Solomon in vain; for he composed charms and incantations for expelling the diseases of the human body. He left several manuscript forms of conjuration, by means of which people obtained an effectual relief from evil spirits, which never returned; and his directions for removing complaints of this nature are to this time much practised by the people of our nation. I was present when a countryman of mine, named Eleazar, dispossessed divers persons before Vespasian, his sons, and several officers and soldiers. A ring, under the seal of which a certain root was conveyed, was applied to the nostrils, and it being smelt to by the demoniac, the evil spirit was instantly drawn out by the nose. In this operation the man was thrown down by the spirit. Eleazar repeated charms and incantations invented by Solomon, whose name he frequently introduced, and adjured the devil to trouble the party no more. After this, Eleazar placed a vessel of water near a man who was possessed, and adjured the devil, upon quitting the person, to overturn it, which was accordingly done. This was an incontrovertible testimony of the wisdom of Solomon." (Ant. Jud. b. viii. c. 2.)

[12] This union was not forbidden in the Jewish law. (Deut. xxiii. 7.) The Jews were allowed to marry with any nation that practised the rite of circumcision.

from Light, Charity, and Morality, was elevated into a science capable of forming vast designs, and of astonishing mankind by the perfection and rapidity of their execution.

> Virtue alone outbuilds the pyramids;
> Her monuments shall last, when Egypt's fall.
> *Young.*

There was also a subordinate Grand Lodge of Operative Masons, in which Beauty presided in the person of Hiram Abiff, and his Wardens were the noble princes Tito Harodim and Adoniram; who were placed at the head of the levies from Jerusalem. The Masters of the twelve tribes were appointed by King Solomon to superintend the work.

Joabert	presided over	the tribe of	Judah.
Stolkyn	"	"	Benjamin.
Terry	"	"	Simeon.
Morphey	"	"	Ephraim.
Alcuber	"	"	Manasseh.
Dorson	"	"	Zebulun.
Kerim	"	"	Dan.
Berthemar	"	"	Asher.
Tito	"	"	Naphtali.
Terbal	"	"	Reuben.
Benachard	"	"	Issachar.
Tabar	"	"	Gad.

These twelve presidents rendered a daily account of their respective tribes, and received the power of punishment and reward according to desert. They were also the medium for distributing the workmen's wages. The apprentices, fellow crafts, and masters, were partitioned into Lodges, and the utmost regularity was preserved throughout the whole undertaking. In the quarries of Tyre were two Lodges of Superexcellent Masters, as Supervisors of the work; over which Tito Zadok, the High Priest, presided: these were the Harodim. There were also six Lodges of Excellent Masters; eight Grand Architects, and sixteen Architects—men of superior talent, who had been selected for their proficiency in the sciences, and placed as superintendents over the workmen. This was a necessary provision; for thus they were enabled to regulate the proceedings, and to preserve order and arrangement in the several departments which were assigned to them. There were three classes of Masters in thirty-six Lodges, called the Menatzchim; and 700 Lodges of Ghiblim, or Operative Fellow Crafts, under Hiram Abiff, their Grand Master. The number of persons employed in every department amounted to 113,600, besides 70,000 labourers.[13] In the forest of Lebanon the same classes were arranged, although varying in numbers, with the addition of 10,000 Entered Apprentices, in 100 Lodges; over which Adoniram was constituted Grand Master.[14] It will be observed that each of the above degrees had its distinguishing signs, words, and tokens; without which confusion and disorder could scarcely have been prevented. The Apprentices messed by *seven* in a company, and the Fellow Crafts by *five*. The Masters and Wardens of all these Lodges were men of enlightened minds and matured understandings, well skilled in geometry and the rules of proportion. They trained their respective brethren and fellows to the practice of blending moral virtue with the pursuits of science; and inculcated Charity or Brotherly Love as the distinguishing feature of their profession. Nor were the Cardinal and Theological Virtues omitted in their dispositions. What were the results of this moral and scientific training? Why, it produced an inviolate adherence to order, and a spirit of Fraternal union, which gave energy and permanence to the institution; and enabled it to survive the wreck of mighty empires, and even to resist the destroying hand of time.

Hence, 'midst the ruins of three thousand years,
Unhurt, unchang'd, Freemasonry appears.
Her towers and monuments may fade away,
Her truth and social love shall ne'er decay.

Woods.

Thus was constituted the united system of Speculative and Operative Masonry, a system which, in all ages, has

[13] Jos. Ant. Jud. b. viii. c. 2.

[14] There may appear a discrepancy in this estimate of numbers. Some think that the only actual Freemasons who were present at this building were the 3,300 overseers mentioned, 1 Kings v. 160, added to the 300 who were called Ghiblimites, and were in fact masters over the rest. This account, therefore, gives 300 Masters, 15,000 Fellow Crafts, and 2100 Entered Apprentices in 300 Lodges. But I am inclined to think that the statement in the text is more in unison with ancient masonic belief.

refined the feelings, and purified the heart, which has been productive of human happiness, and led the enquiring brother from the works of nature up to nature's God.

When a sufficient quantity of stone and timber had been provided, the brethren were assembled in the extensive plains between Succoth and Zarthan, where the whole materials were arranged, squared, and carved; having been first carefully measured under the architect's own eye, and the shape delineated by dark lines; each Lodge having its particular mark and number, that specimens of imperfect workmanship might be known and submitted to general reprobation. These preliminaries being completed, the workmen were at length conducted to the summit of Mount Moriah; and with materials thus scientifically prepared, the building was completed without the assistance of axe, hammer, or metal tool; that nought might be heard amongst the workmen of Zion but harmony and peace.

> No workman's steel, no pondrous axes rung,
> Like some tall palm the noiseless fabric sprung.
>
> *Heber.*

There appears to have been a peculiar idea of pollution in the use of iron tools about the holy structure of a temple. In the directions given by the Almighty to Moses from Mount Sinai, respecting the construction of the tabernacle, and more particularly about the altar, the use of metal tools is prohibited in the strongest terms.[15] And David, in the prospect of the temple's desecration by unsanctified hands, complains,[16] as the greatest aggravation of insult which the adversary could offer, that the carved work thereof was broken down with axes and hammers.

But while specimens of imperfect labour were marked with censure, superior merit was rewarded by a public testimony of approbation. This formed a passport to favour and employment in other countries when the temple at Jerusalem was finished. Nothing could have a stronger tendency to rouse dormant talent, or to excite virtuous emulation, than the system of reward which was adopted on this occasion. A number of gold medals

[15] Exod. xx. 25. [16] Ps. lxxiv. 6.

were provided, of the size of a Shekel, with the word FREE impressed on both sides. These were presented to deserving men, and worn by them as proud trophies of merit. And they constituted an undeniable certificate of qualification for great undertakings which required the united aid of genius, learning, and experience.

During the preparation, according to the legends of Freemasonry, the workmen's wages were paid daily, weekly, monthly, and quarterly, in their respective Lodges; and when the temple was nearly completed, they were paid in the Middle Chamber. This celebrated apartment was accessible by a winding staircase of stone; the foot of which was guarded by the Junior Warden, and the summit by the Senior Warden of a Fellow Crafts' Lodge. And how were these wages paid? Without fear or scruple, says the legend, because their employers were entitled to their unlimited confidence. And if an unauthorised hand was stretched out to receive the remuneration of a Craftsman, punishment was summary and certain, so strictly were the arrangements of discipline enforced. The coin in which they were paid was a Shekel of silver, which weighed about half an ounce, and was of the value of two shillings and sixpence of our present currency.

It bore an one side a pot of manna, circumscribed SHEKEL OF ISRAEL, and on the reverse, the budded rod of Aaron, and the legend JERUSALEM THE HOLY.[17] The

[17] "Some of these Shekels were in the possession of Maimonides, and the Rabbi Azarias among the Jews, and of Morinas, Montanus, Villipandus, and others among the Christians. The mark on one side is supposed to have been Aaron's miraculous rod budding for the almonds; and on the other, the pot of manna. The letters over this last, not being

amount paid to each individual was equal to the number of his Degree squared. Thus the Apprentices received one Shekel per day. Those who had attained the second or Fellow Craft's Degree were paid 2×2=4 Shekels. The third Degree, 9 Shekels. And advancing in the same graduated scale to the highest, or Superexcellent Degree, which was the ninth, each brother received 9 × 9=81 Shekels, or £10 2*s.* 6*d.* of our money. The aggregate amount of wages paid for this splendid edifice is said to have been nearly equal to £100,000,000 of our present money.

"The whole expense of this building," says Prideaux, "was so prodigious as gives reason to think that the talents, whereby the sum is reckoned, were another sort of talents of far less value than the Mosaic talents; for what is said to be given by David, and contributed by the princes towards the building of the Temple at Jerusalem, if valued by their talents, exceeded the value of £800,000,000 of our money, which was enough wherewith to have built all that temple of solid silver."[18] How were these vast sums raised? Villipandus asserts—although I confess that his authority is not of much value—that David left behind him treasures, to the amount of £911,416,207; and we know that the princes of Israel presented a greater sum than David. In addition to these treasures, Solomon devoted the greater part of his immense riches to the same purpose. Every voyage to Ophir produced 450 talents,[19] which amounts to £3,240,000 sterling of our present money.[20]

plain enough, are variously conjectured to stand for the name of God, of Israel, David or Jerusalem; as for the inscriptions round the two sides, except a small variation of the character and orthography between those extant coins, they plainly answer to those in the modern Hebrew; on the one side, Skekel Israel;—and on the reverse, Jerushalaim Hakadosha." (Univ. Hist. vol. 2. p. 212.)

[18] Prid. Con. vol. 1. p. 6. [19] 1 Chron. xxii. 14.

[20] Agathercides (p. 60.) tells us that "the Alileans and Cassandrians in the southern parts of Arabia had gold in that plenty amongst them, that they would give double the weight of gold for iron, triple its weight for brass, and ten times its weight for silver; and that in digging the earth they found it in gobbits of pure gold, which needed no refining, and that the least of them were as big as olive stones, but others much larger. No other author speaks of any other place in the world where it was ever found in the like plenty." (Prid. Con. vol. 1. p. 10.) The Dean further says, that the sum amassed towards building the temple by David exceeded all the specie now to be found on the face of the earth. (Ibid. vol. 2. p. 406.)

I flatter myself that sufficient evidence has been adduced to substantiate a fact, concerning which many intelligent Masons have confessed themselves to have been much bewildered. I dare not produce any internal proofs drawn from the construction of our machinery in corroboration of the above reasoning; but every brother who has seriously considered the mechanism of the Third Degree, will be enabled to furnish them for the satisfaction of his own mind. I could imagine some slight objections that might be urged; but they are of little importance when put in competition with the weight of evidence in favour of the view which I have here taken of the union of Speculative and Operative Masonry at this precise period. The Wisdom of Solomon—the Strength of Hiram—the Beauty of Hiram Abiff, all combine to render this interpretation at the least feasible; and where records are wanting, truth can only be obtained by collating and comparing historical facts which are certain and undisputed.

At the building of King Solomon's Temple we find Lodges—Signs and Tokens—and all the paraphernalia by which Secret Societies in all ages have been distinguished. Here were also gradations of rank, from the royal Grand Master, down to the lowest Entered Apprentice, and the Ish Sabbal. Lectures in Morals and Science were delivered by the Masters of Lodges, for the mental improvement of the brethren; and a series of regulations were promulgated for the preservation of order and decorum amongst such a vast concourse of workmen, which were enforced with the strictest severity of perfect discipline. These are symptoms of Freemasonry in its most palmy state; and whatever advantages we may possess from the progress of civilization, and the harmonizing effect of scientific arrangement, it is a question whether our Freemasonry is more perfect in its details, than was the system under the government of the Sacred Grand Lodge at Jerusalem. It was a pattern which we may profitably imitate; and doubts may exist whether, in our age of mental enlightenment, fewer instances of a departure from rectitude would be exhibited amongst ourselves, were we congregated to the number of nearly 200,000 men of all ranks and classes in society. So excellent were the arrangements, and so successful the results of the union of Speculative and Operative Masonry.

LECTURE IX.

THE DETAILS OF THIS FAMOUS EDIFICE CONSIDERED, FOR THE PURPOSE OF SHEWING THAT THE ABOVE UNION CONVEYED ESSENTIAL BENEFITS TO MANKIND.

Sound the full harmonious song;
To Masonry divine the strain prolong;
And first the grateful tribute bring
To the great, the sapient king;
Who, inspired by power divine,
Made wisdom, strength, and beauty all combine
To frame, confirm, and deck the vast design.
Masonic Ode.

THE harmony and union which existed amongst the Masons who were employed to build the Temple at Jerusalem, has been eulogised both in sacred and profane history. This agreement arose from the judicious regulations which the wisdom of Solomon suggested for the government of the various Lodges spread over the plains of Zeredatha, and the forest of Lebanon; and subsequently transferred to the holy mountain of Moriah. For "brotherly love and immutable fidelity," says Calcott, "presented themselves to his mind, as the most proper basis for an institution, whose aim and end should be to establish permanent unity among its members; and to render them a society, who, while they enjoyed the most perfect felicity, would be of considerable utility to mankind. And being desirous to transmit it, under the ancient restrictions, as a blessing to future ages, Solomon decreed, that whenever they should assemble in their Lodges, to discourse upon and improve themselves in the arts and sciences, and whatever else should be deemed proper topics to increase their knowledge, they should likewise instruct each other in secrecy and prudence, morality and good fellowship; and for these purposes he established certain peculiar rules and customs to be invariably observed in their conversations, that their minds might be enriched by a perfect acquaintance with, and practice of, every moral, social, and religious duty; lest, while they were so highly honoured by being employed in raising a temple to the Great Jehovah, they should neglect to secure to themselves a happy admittance into the celestial Lodge, of which the temple was only to be a type."

The method of preparing the materials of elegant structures remote from their intended site, so as to unite without any visible interstices, was an art which the Tyrian workmen derived from Egypt. The expert artists of that extraordinary country were famous for unique productions accomplished by this process. The great father of history has recorded the fact. He says: "The most celebrated of the ancient statuaries, Telecles and Theodorus, the sons of Rhoecus, made for the Samians the image of the Pythian Apollo. And it is said that one-half of the image was executed in Samos by Telecles, and the other half at Ephesus by Theodorus; and that both parts, when put together, agreed so well with each other, as to appear precisely as if they had been the work of one person; and that this kind of workmanship was never practised by the Greeks, but was very common among the Egyptians; for that with them it was not usual to judge of the symmetry of a figure by the sight of the whole, as with the Greeks; but that when the stones were quarried and properly cut out, they then proceeded by proportion from the smallest to the greatest; and dividing the whole fabric of the body into one and twenty parts and a quarter, they arranged the whole symmetry accordingly. And hence, when their artists consult with each other about the magnitude of any figure, although separated from each other, they still make the results agree so well, that this peculiarity of their practice excites the greatest astonishment. And that the image in Samos, according to this refinement of the Egyptians, being divided from the summit of the head and as far as the middle, is still perfectly consistent with itself, and in all parts alike."

The same description of masonry was used in the walls

of Byzantium, which were erected about the time when the Tyrians built Carthage, and long before the Temple of Solomon was designed. These walls, says Herodian, were composed of such immense blocks, so curiously squared, and artfully joined, as to appear like one entire stone.

The site of the Temple had been revealed to David by God himself, in answer to his fervent supplications;[1] and it was denominated "the Field of the Wood." On that consecrated spot Abraham proved his intuitive faith, by leading his only and well-beloved son Isaac a destined victim to the altar of his God. Here, on the floor of Araunah the Jebusite, David offered his mediatorial sacrifice, by which the plague was stayed. Here, also, the Almighty shewed to him the plan of that glorious Temple, which was afterwards completed by his illustrious son; and on that sacred spot God declared he would establish his most Holy Name.

Preparations were made for the foundation by forming vaulted passages and filling up vast hollows, to produce a level space of sufficient capacity and firmness to contain and support the intended building. There are many Rabbinical traditions afloat in the Mishna and Gemara, respecting the existence of a subterraneous communication between the Temple and the royal palace, which had been secretly constructed, as a private passage for the use of King Solomon and his successors. This is said to have been an avenue which led to a small vaulted chamber underneath the Sanctum Sanctorum. It was furnished with an altar and its appendages, calculated to promote a devout abstraction, holy thoughts, and pious feelings. In this place, it is presumed, the king spent much time in meditation and prayer, apart from the toils of government and the cares of the world. Here he found leisure to reflect on the attributes of the Deity, and the mercy and loving kindness which had exalted him to the summit of glory, and placed him at the head of all earthly sovereigns.

The existence of this private passage has been questioned. But vaults formed a necessary part of temple architecture in Egypt, at this early period. The

[1] Ps. cxxxii. 1—5.

pyramids and sphynxes were all furnished with arched vaults.[2] They contained, indeed, but one small apartment, accessible only by long, intricate, and contracted passages, except in the subterranean cavities, which were probably known to none but the priests and hierophants. These secret crypts communicated equally with a chamber in the adjoining sphynx, and with each other. They were used for the purpose of initiation into the Spurious Freemasonry. We have reason to believe that all the early public buildings contained subterraneous vaults, intended for the mysterious celebrations, or as receptacles for the preservation of such facts or doctrines as were considered improper to be publicly known.

Besides, vaults are mentioned by Josephus as existing beneath both the temple and the palace,[3] and they were repeated by Herod on the re-construction of these edifices.[4] It is probable, therefore, that there was some ground for the tradition; nor can we altogether reject the evidence which is contained in one of the Apocryphal books of our Scriptures. It is thus recorded as an undoubted fact, that when the desolation of the temple was about to be accomplished by Nebuchadnezzar, the priests furtively conveyed the sacred fire from the altar, and concealed *it in a vault*, where it remained till the re-edification of that sacred structure. And it was then revived by a process which Nehemiah dictated to the priests.[5] Jeremiah the prophet, also, as it is recorded in the same book, hid the tabernacle, the ark, and the altar of incense, in a vault or cave, and closed up the place so securely, that it could not be discovered; but he predicted that these holy utensils should be found when, in God's good time, the restoration of Israel

[2] "Recent discoveries in Ethiopia have brought to light," says a writer on the Egyptian antiquities in the British Museum, "arches regularly constructed with the *keystone.* The same arch is also found in the vaulted roof of a small building or portico in the Egyptian style, which is attached to one of the sides of the largest pyramids at Assour. At Jebel Barkal, Mr. Waddington observed an arched roof in a portico attached to a pyramid." These pyramids are supposed to be of higher antiquity than the building of King Solomon's Temple.

[3] Ant. Jud. b. viii. c. 2.

[4] Ibid. b. xv. c. 14.

[5] 2 Mac. i. 19—22.

should be accomplished.[6] A most extraordinary corroborating fact, if fact it be, is related by Philostorgius, and after him by Nicephorus, that, at the clearing of the foundations,[7] when Julian the apostate set himself to re-build the temple, a stone was taken up that covered the mouth of a deep, four-square cave, cut out of the rock, into which one of the labourers being let down by a rope, found it full of water to the middle of the leg, and in the midst *a pillar reaching a little above the water, whereon lay a roll or book wrapped up in a fine linen cloth.* Being drawn up, the linen was observed to be fresh and undecayed, and the book being unfolded, was found, to the amazement both of Jews and Gentiles, to contain the first words of the Gospel of St. John, written in capital letters. IN THE BEGINNING WAS THE WORD, AND THE WORD WAS WITH GOD, AND THE WORD WAS GOD. And Maundrell says, that "in a garden at the foot of Mount Moriah, on the south side, he was shewn several large vaults, annexed to the mountain, and running at least fifty yards under ground. They were built in two aisles, *arched at top with huge firm stone, and sustained with tall pillars*, consisting each of a single stone, and two yards in diameter."

Shall we, then, doubt, in the face of such credible authorities, that there did exist some secret passages in the foundations of the temple, which were accessible to few, and those only in the very highest rank of priests or prophets? May we not rather conclude that the wisdom of Solomon would induce him to construct a place for secret communings with his God; which would derive additional sanctity by its connection with that awful spot, consecrated by His immediate and perpetual presence? If this reasoning possess any force, we may suppose it to have been within the secret recesses of this holy apartment that his repentance was awakened, and his piety revived, after his melancholy apostacy;

[6] 2 Mac. ii. 5, 6, 7. See also a confirmation of this tradition in the Elucidarium ascribed to St. Austin. (c. 24.) But he says that they will be restored by the two translated ones, Enoch and Elijah. But the Rabbins (vid. Buxtorf, in 2 Mac. ii.) have a fancy that the ark had been previously hidden in Solomon's vault by Josiah; (2 Chron. xxxv. 3.) and that it shall not be found till the advent of their expected Messiah.

[7] Philost. l. 7. c. 14. Niceph. l. 10. p. 76.

and when he composed that remarkable production which commences—"Vanity of vanities, all is vanity;"[8] and concludes—"Fear God and keep his commandments, for this is the whole duty of man. For God shall bring every work into judgment; with every secret thing, whether it be good or whether it be evil."[9]

The harmony of arrangement resulting from the union of Speculative and Operative Masonry, perfected by the deliberations of Wisdom, Strength, and Beauty, in the Sacred Lodge, was not without its beneficial results. For when the labours of the expert Craftsmen in the forest of Lebanon, the quarries of Tyre, and the plains of Zarthan, were tested at Jerusalem, each part fitted with such perfect exactness, that it was difficult to distinguish the joints. It did not require the use of either axe, hammer, or other metal tool, and the building appeared as though it had been formed out of a single block of highly polished marble. Hence the admiration of strangers was so strongly excited by its finished appearance, that they were inclined to consider it rather as a work of the Great Architect of the Universe, than an exertion of human ingenuity and skill. Without such a perfect disquisition as I have described, it would be impossible to conjecture how the Temple, complicated in its construction, and magnificent in its decorations, as it was, should have occupied such a very short period of time from the foundation to the cape stone. For, while this famous edifice was prepared for divine worship in little more than seven years, the Temple of Diana at Ephesus, inferior in point of splendour, is said to have occupied a period of 220 years in building. The cape stone was celebrated with masonic honours; and the Dedication stands forth in the records of antiquity, as a festival perfectly unexampled and alone. "Magnificent must have been the sight, to see the young king, clothed in royalty, officiating as priest before the immense alter, while the thousands of Levites and priests on the east side, habited in surplices, with harps, cymbals, and trumpets in their hands, led the eye to the beautiful Pillars flanking the doors of the temple, now thrown open, and displaying the interior brilliantly lighted up;

[8] Eccles. i. 2. [9] Ibid. xii. 13, 14.

while the burnished gold of the floor, the ceiling, and the walls, with the precious gems with which they were enriched, reflecting the light on all sides, would completely overwhelm the imagination, were it not excited by the view of the embroidered veil, to consider the yet more awful glories of the Most Holy Place And astounding must have been the din of the instruments of the four thousand Levites, led on by the priests with one hundred and twenty trumpets, directing the choruses of the immense congregation, as they chaunted the sublime compositions of the royal Psalmist in the grand intonations of the Hebrew language, like the "roaring of many waters."[10]

Josephus has given the following description of the Temple: "The foundation was sunk to an astonishing depth, and composed of stones of singular magnitude, and so hard a quality, as to resist the worm and the inclemency of the weather; and being closely mortised into the rock with great ingenuity, they formed a basis adequate to the support of the intended structure. The Temple was sixty cubits high,[11] and sixty cubits also in length; and the breadth was twenty cubits. Above this was another stage of equal dimensions. So that the height of the whole structure was one hundred and twenty cubits. The walls were composed entirely of white stone; and the front of the building was towards the east. The porch was twenty cubits in length, ten in breadth, and one hundred and twenty in height. Round the outward walls were erected thirty cells or small houses, communicating with each other, and forming galleries, and at the same time answering the purpose of buttresses, by supporting the walls. These cells were each five cubits square, and twenty cubits high. Over these were two other floors of the same proportion, and the uppermost of the cells were on a level with the lower story of the fabric. They were fastened together by large beams, so disposed as to make them appear of one piece, and as if they gave additional strength to the walls. Under the beams was a variety of carving, gilding, fretwork, and other curious ornaments. The walls and ceilings were lined with cedar,

[10] Bardwell's Temples. p. 87.

[11] The cubit may be estimated at eighteen inches.

and the wainscots were embellished with a profusion of splendid ornaments of the purest gold. The fabric was composed of stones polished to the utmost degree of excellence, and put together with such ingenuity, that the smallest interstice was not to be perceived. The whole, in short, was so wonderfully executed, that it appeared to be the effect of Divine Providence, rather than of human art."[12]

Egypt was the great source of all eastern learning and knowledge. But its science was eclipsed and superseded by this famous structure; and for many years, if not for ever, it declined before the superior brightness of sacred architecture, resulting from the union of Speculative and Operative Masonry. The Egyptian temples were vast, striking, and sublime; but there were wanting in their construction the charms of symmetry, and the graces of chaste decoration, which rendered the Temple of Solomon so famous. Here was magnificence in its most gorgeous form; but it was a magnificence tempered by delicacy of design and accuracy of execution. Unity and proportion were displayed in all its parts, and a correct taste was never violated by the introduction of discordant members or inappropriate ornaments. There was not a solitary blot in the whole building—not a single deformity to abstract the attention from its beauties—all was replete with deep feeling; and the secret sympathies which elevated the soul from the temple to the Deity, operated in each member and in the whole. This singleness of purpose—this inimitable result of genius and taste united with consummate skill—it was that excited the admiration of foreign architects on their visits to this monument of WISDOM, STRENGTH, and BEAUTY, and the triumph of sacred architecture was perfect and complete.

This model of perfection was, indeed, a perfect gem. The scale on which it was planned was peculiarly adapted to its situation. When illuminated by the sun's rays, it shone brilliantly on the heights of Moriah, and seemed, at a distance, like a celestial palace composed of ivory inlaid with veins of precious metal. And the splendour of its appearance will fully justify the rapturous expressions of the Jews concerning its beauty and sublimity. It was

[12] Jos. Ant. Jud. b. viii. 2.

truly a work of art worthy of being beloved—a work which any nation or people would have regarded with pride and veneration.

I now proceed to offer a few remarks on some of the details. And first, on the two famous Pillars which stood at the entrance of the porch. In the absence of that sublime principle of vital religion which preserved a just idea of the nature and attributes of God, and the spirituality of his worship, the nations of the earth entertained an uniform veneration for upright pillars of stone. In the first ages of idolatry, the rites of divine worship were conducted without any idols, or visible representations of the deity. After the erection of Jacob's pillar at Bethel,[13] the neighbouring nations set up rude stones,[14] generally black or of a dark colour,[15] to denote God's invisibility. These were termed Betulia, and served for objects of worship. To them succeeded, at a later period, rude attempts to imitate the human form, carved out of blocks of wood. And when the art of statuary was perfected, the most delicately executed images were erected, not only of wood and stone, but of brass, ivory, and the precious metals. These statues were possessed of a two-fold application; first, they were considered as symbols of God's presence; and secondly, as visible emblems of security and protection. And after the image had been adopted and solemnly consecrated as the tutelary deity of a particular city or country, the inhabitants thought themselves perfectly safe so long as they retained possession of the sacred image. And hence they dreaded no evil so much as the loss of this invaluable representation of the deity.

But previously to the building of Solomon's Temple, pillars had not fallen into disuse; they were erected in places where devotion was offered, and were sometimes considered as talismans for the preservation of the sacred edifice. Various were the forms which these pillars had assumed amongst the scattered tribes and people which migration had dispersed over the face of the globe. But at this period they had become cylindrical; and a superb specimen of the application of pillars in the construction of temples and palaces, had been exhibited by the Tyrian

[13] Gen. xxviii. 18.
[14] Euseb. præp. evan. l. 1. Clem. Alex. Protrept.—Chrysost. Serm. 12.
[15] Strabo. Geogr. l. 17.

Masons at Gaza, in the Temple of Dagon, which owed its stability to the support it received from two columns of great elegance and beauty.

Pillars or obelisks were often used to commemorate remarkable events in the private annals of nations. The wisdom of Solomon, therefore, induced him to construct a pair of commemorative pillars, and to place them at the entrance of the porch, for a reason which will shortly appear. He called their names Jachin and Boaz, which signified strength and erection; and their union, Stability. The right hand pillar was named after Jachin, the son of Simeon, and that on the left from Boaz, the great grandfather of David. Our traditions say that Hiram gave a name to one pillar, and Solomon to the other. Boaz referred to the Sun, because he rejoiceth as a *strong* man to run his course; and Jachin to the Moon, because it was predicted of Solomon, that in his kingdom, peace and righteousness should flourish so long as the sun and moon endure. Hence, as the kingdom was now permanently established, this wise and pious monarch designed these two pillars as a testimony of his firm conviction that it would continue in prosperity so long as his successors should perform the will and obey the commands of Him who delivered their ancestors from the miseries of Egyptian bondage.

These pillars were made of cast brass, and were the production of Hiram Abiff, who taxed his ingenuity in their construction and symbolical adornment. Their style, like that of the temple itself, was after Egyptian models, being of the usual proportion of five and a half diameters high. The basis was Wisdom, the shaft Strength, and the capital Beauty. Ancient tradition says, that the shafts were covered with astronomical and masonic figures, characters, and calculations; and the hollow space in the interior served as archives of Masonry, and to hold the constitutional records. Each had "a vase rising from the cylindrical shaft, ornamented with lotus flowers. The bottom of the vase was partly hidden by the flowers; the belly of it was overlaid with network, ornamented by seven wreaths—the Hebrew number of happiness."[16] They were further adorned with chapiters of five cubits

[16] Bardwell's Temples. p. 85.

in height; enriched with network, chains, lilies, and pomegranates; emblematical of unity, fortitude, peace, and plenty. They had a double row of the latter, each containing a hundred pomegranates; and on the summit were placed two spherical balls, to represent the earth and heavens, as symbols of the universality of Masonry. It is difficult, say the lectures, at this distance of time, to state the precise ornaments and combinations of these emblems. But our traditions give us to understand that the chapiters respectively represented the whole system of creation, celestial and terrestrial. This conjecture is founded upon the symbolical reference of these ornaments; which, how descriptive soever they may be of the union, the strength, the peace, and plenty which the people of Israel enjoyed under the mild sway of that wisest and best of kings—are emblems of far more extensive signification. The network refers to the strong and beautiful texture of the universe. The chains denote the orbits which the planetary bodies describe round the sun, and their revolutions on their several axes. The opening flowers point out the mild irradiation of the fixed stars; and the pomegranate was invariably used throughout all antiquity to denote the secret power by which the works of nature were originated and matured.

These two sublime columns were further intended to commemorate the awful pillar of a cloud and a fire, by which the Divine Presence was exemplified, when he inflicted wrath on the Egyptian host, and gave freedom and salvation to the house of Jacob, by the destruction of Pharaoh and his army in the Red Sea at a moment when the Israelites deemed themselves out of the reach of mercy. This was a noble instance of zeal and gratitude to the Disposer of all events, and worthy the wisdom of our illustrious Grand Master. He consulted equally the glory of God, and the benefit of his subjects, when he placed these remarkable obelisks in this conspicuous situation. The Israelites were thus furnished with an opportunity of recalling to their remembrance this great event in their history, whenever they entered into the house of God to worship. Thus their faith was strengthened, and their confidence increased in Jehovah their almighty deliverer.

These two noble pillars were of such vital importance

to the support and admiration of the temple, that at its destruction by Nebuchadnezzar, the Lord is represented by a magnificent figure, as standing in all his majesty upon the altar, and commanding his angel to strike the caphtors, chapiters, or heads of these pillars, to ensure the ruin not only of the pillars and porch, or the temple itself, or even all Jerusalem, but of the entire nation and polity of the Jews. Hence, as the erection of these pillars is recorded in scripture as an eminent proof of the magnitude and splendour of Solomon's empire, as well as of the wisdom, strength, and beauty of the three united Grand Masters; so was their destruction typical of the ruin of the Jewish state, which received a temporary annihilation of seventy years when this temple was destroyed for their sin in neglecting to keep holy the sabbatical year, and was finally abolished and the people dispersed over the face of the globe, at the final destruction of Herod's temple by the Romans.[17]

A secret apartment was constructed at the western extremity of the Temple, as a depository for the ark of the covenant, illuminated by the glory of God. No unhallowed steps were permitted to tread its sacred pavement; and even the High Priest, after many ceremonial purifications—humble and unshod—was only allowed to enter this Holy place on the great day of annual expiation. Small were its dimensions, but costly were its ornaments, and taste and genius were displayed in lavish profusion.

> Of riches much, but more of wisdom see,
> Proportioned workmanship and masonry.

Some idea may be formed of the riches of this temple from the fact, that the gold used in decorating the Holy place alone, amounted to six hundred talents;[18] which is equal to £4,320,000 of our money. The room was a perfect cube of thirty feet only, wainscotted with cedar overlaid with plates of gold, and decorated with precious stones, amongst which the topaz[19] was most abundant;

[17] Antiq. Mas. p. 357, with authorities. [18] 2 Chron. iii. 8.

[19] The old Lectures of Masonry contained a legend about the topaz; but I am unacquainted with the authority on which it was introduced. It was as follows: About four years before the Temple at Jerusalem was commenced, Hiram Abiff, the Grand Architect of Tyre, purchased

and it emblematically signified SEEK AND YE SHALL FIND. Here were also a profusion of emeralds, sapphires, and garnets, as symbols of Faith, Hope, and Charity. The ceiling was gloriously enriched; and in the middle of its square surface a circle was inscribed—symbolical of Him whose centre is everywhere, and whose circum ference is nowhere—adorned with gems of various colours, each invested with a mystical signification; and all concurring to elucidate that sublime inscription which masonic tradition informs us was embroidered amongst the cherubim, on the veil of blue, purple, and scarlet,[20] which concealed the glories of the adytum from the profane gaze of the multitude. The interpretation was—I AM THAT I AM—PAST, PRESENT, AND TO COME—THE BEGINNING, THE END, THE FIRST AND THE LAST—MORTAL MAN CANNOT COMPREHEND MY INFINITE PERFECTIONS; and its symbol was depicted on the ceiling of the apartment. The entrance door was in the east. It was composed of olive wood covered with purple, hyacinth, crimson and gold, to represent the four elements; and enriched with palm trees, open flowers and cherubim, all in embossed gold.

————————behold
What massy stores of burnished gold,
  Yet richer is our art;
Not all the orient gems that shine,
Nor treasures of rich Ophir's mine,
  Excel the Mason's art. *Weekes.*

from some Arabian merchants for the use of the palace, a quantity of curious stones and shells; and upon enquiring, found that chance had produced them; for some Arabian Trogolodites having been cast away upon an island in the Red Sea, about three hundred furlongs from the coast, lost their ship, and were much distressed for want of provisions and other necessaries. At length, in digging up certain roots which promised to alleviate their hunger, they discovered an abundance of curious shells and precious stones. This event was considered of such importance by the king, that he deputed Hiram Abiff, accompanied by a considerable number of workmen, to explore the island in question for the purpose of ascertaining the truth of these representations; and in a few days he had the good fortune to find the TOPAZ in great abundance; and it became a general article of traffic with the Tyrian merchants. It s mentioned by the Prophet Ezekiel as an enrichment of the Tyrian monarch's throne.

[20] Or rather azure, purple, and crimson. The original word for the former is Teheleth, which is translated *hyacinthum*, in reference to the precious stone called by that name; which, like the sapphire, was anciently believed, according to the testimony of Oleaster, Tostatus,

How was the Deity represented in this gorgeous temple, since statues and images were forbidden? By his own direction the Israelites placed in their Tabernacles an Ark or Coffer, as a symbol or representative of the Divine Presence. Is this, then, to be considered an imitation of the rites and practices of the heathen? By no means. It is rather a reproof of their degeneracy This splendid box was placed in the sanctuary on a rough stone pedestal[21] to point out the inefficiency of visible objects of worship. And for the same reason the Deity assumed the appearance of a shapeless cloud whenever he condescended to visit his people; and in this form, which was incapable of being imitated with an idolatrous intention, the Divine glory overshadowed the ark both in the tabernacle and in the temple.

Lyranus, and other learned men, to be of the colour of a clear serene sky. The second is Argaman, which signifies purple; being derived from Ragam, or prince, who was distinguished by his purple robes; and the latter Tolaghath shani. The first word means a worm, as Psalm xxii. 6. and has been translated by the word *coccinum*, from *cocus*, which means either scarlet or crimson; and shani is derived from shanals to double. Hence the phrase means the crimson colour twice dyed.

[21] There exist among Masons many legends respecting the origin and powers attached to the stone on which the ark of the covenant was placed. It was termed the Stone of Foundation. These traditions, though full of Rabbinical fancies, (vid. Mishna in Yoma, and Buxtorf de Arca. c. 22.) are not uninteresting. As traditions of great antiquity, they merit a brief and passing notice. It was called the stone of Adam; and its progress is traced through Seth, Enoch, and Noah, to Abraham and Isaac, who used it as an altar for sacrifice. It is said to be the stone on which Jacob rested when he was favoured with his sublime vision of the Ladder. It was carried into Egypt and placed in the sepulchre of Joseph, with whose bones it travelled over the Red Sea, and found its way into the hands of Moses, who used it successfully on various occasions; and at length it became the resting place for the ark of the covenant during the wanderings in the wilderness, and in the promised land until the time of David. It retained the same honourable place in the Sanctum Sanctorum of Solomon; was found in the temples of Zerubbabel and Herod; although the ark of the covenant was missing after the Babylonish captivity; and remained in the foundations after Titus had destroyed the temple, to resist the impious attempt of Julian the apostate to frustrate our Saviour's prophecy, by emitting flames of fire which scattered and destroyed the workmen. On this stone was engraven that awful Name which none but Royal Arch Masons know, and is depicted in our Chapters by the Equilateral Triangle, the Circle, and the Double Cube. But this remarkable stone had a still more extensive reference, which endears it to the Christian Mason, and invests the legend with a portion of sublimity. It was emblematical of the Messiah—Jesus Christ, the chief corner stone of man's immortality; who was triumphant

The ark was made of Shittim wood, but was covered over inside and out, with pure gold. This wood possessed the properties of smoothness, hardness, and durability; it was not subject to rottenness or decay; and by its fragrance resisted the attacks of worms and insects. Our traditions say, that it was taken from the Burning Bush, which had been already consecrated by the awful presence of God. It remained uninjured by time, from its construction in the wilderness till the Babylonish captivity—a period of nearly one thousand years; and there are those who believe that it is still concealed in the bowels of the earth waiting for the final restoration of the people of God.

The most holy appendage to the ark was its lid or cover, called the Mercy Seat. This was composed of solid gold, four inches in thickness, and bore on its upper surface two golden cherubim face to face; which, with outspread wings, appeared to embrace the whole area of the lid, forming, as it were, a splendid chariot, on which the Shekinah rested, when the ark was in its place within the Holy of Holies.

From this sacred utensil the Oracles issued audibly whenever it was deemed necessary to consult the Deity on any public emergency. Christian writers have discovered many symbolical meanings in the Propitiatory and Mercy Seat. The cherubim were considered as emblems of God's universal presence as the moral governor of the universe. Their faces were turned towards the Mercy Seat in admiration of the promised Redemption of man, and that they might speedily ascertain the Divine will and pleasure; and towards each other, to denote concord and harmony. Their wings were displayed, not only from a principle of reverence for the awful majesty of God, but also to point out the alacrity by which his commissions were executed. United with the propitiatory, they denoted the ascending and descending angels at the nativity of Christ, to apprise mankind of the benefits re-

in his warfare with sin, death, and hell; and worked out the redemption of mankind by an expiatory sacrifice. From this reference arose the Rabbinical fable, that Jesus Christ stole this Sacred Name from the Stone of Foundation, and by the use of it worked all his miracles. Vid. Toledoth Jesu. p. 6. Raymund. Pugio Fidei. p. 2. c. 8. Buxtorf. Lex. Rab. p. 2541.

sulting from his divine mission; and in mutually beholding each other, they displayed their joint consent in performing the will of God. These are a few of the most rational interpretations with which conjecture has invested this holy appendage to Jewish worship. But according to the doctrine contained in the old Lectures of Masonry, it was principally intended by the wisdom and mercy of God, to preserve his people from falling into the error, so common at that early period, of violating the second commandment. When they came out of Egypt, they had adopted the idolatrous custom of carrying about "the tabernacles of Moloch and Chiun their images; *the star* of their god Remphan, which they made to themselves."[22] To supersede the necessity of this abomination, therefore, God condescended to give them a tabernacle of their own, attended by a glorious Shekinah instead of a star, and furnished with every requisite for the celebration of a pompous ceremonial worship. And how were these gracious purposes accomplished? Not certainly in accordance with the means used for their purification. The people were wedded to error—they loved darkness rather than Light—they cherished the Spurious Freemasonry of their heathen neighbours to such an extent, that at one unhappy period of their history, there were only seven thousand persons amongst all the tribes of Israel who had not embraced it.[23]

The Ark was placed in this sacred depository that the Israelites might know, with absolute certainty, where to offer up their sacrifices; for, where the ark was, there was also the glory of the Lord. As God intended to establish a peculiar system of worship, so he appointed one certain place where external rites should be performed; and, to secure their observance with decency, sanctity, and reverence, he condescended personally to superintend it, by a visible emanation of His glory, whom the heavens cannot contain, seated between the cherubim of the Mercy Seat, or lid of the ark,[24] as a symbol of the Divine presence. And here the High Priest made his annual atonement for the people. Hence it was accounted so sacred that none

[22] Compare Amos v. 26. with Acts vii. 43. [23] 1 Kings xix. 18.

[24] Exod. xl. 34. Thus Calvin said:—" Præsentiam gratiæ voluit visibile symbolo testari.

were permitted to see it but the High Priest, and he only once a year, after much ritual purification. "The author of the book Cozri justly saith, that the ark, with the mercy seat and cherubim, were the foundation, root, heart, and marrow of the whole temple, and all the Levitical worship therein performed. And, therefore, had there nothing else of the first temple been wanting in the second but the ark only, this alone would have been reason enough for the old men to have wept, when they remembered the first temple in which it was; and also for the saying of Haggai, that the second temple was as nothing in comparison of the first; so great a part had it in the glory of this temple, as long as it remained in it."[25]

Is it asked, what became of the tabernacle of Moses when the temple was completed, and the ark removed into the Sanctum Sanctorum? The enquiry is very natural, and I will endeavour to answer it. The middle chambers of each story over the porch of the temple—which it will be recollected was of greater altitude than most of our English church steeples, being one hundred and eighty feet high—were appropriated as depositories of such parts of the tabernacle as were not introduced into the temple worship, viz., the golden candlesticks, the altar of incense, the curtains, &c. All these chambers were without light, except the upper story, that the holy paraphernalia might not be subject to profane inspection. The contents of the middle chamber of the upper story were the most sacred; and our traditions say, that King Solomon rewarded so many of the 80,000 Fellow Crafts as embraced the Jewish faith, with the privilege of admission into this sacellum; and every brother who has been passed to that degree, is acquainted with its furniture and contents.

Some faint idea of the splendour attending the services of the temple, may be formed from an enumeration of the appendages to divine worship which the munificence of Solomon induced him to consecrate to that purpose. These are, according to Josephus, a table constructed wholly of pure gold for the shew-bread, while the other tables contained 20,000 golden vessels, and 40,000 ves-

[25] Prid. Con. vol. 1. p. 147.

sels of silver. There were 12,000 candlesticks, many of them being of gold; 80,000 wine cups, and 10,000 goblets of gold. 20,000 goblets of silver; 20,000 golden and 40,000 silver measures; 80,000 dishes for the altar, of gold, and 160,000 of silver; 20,000 golden, and 50,000 silver censers. The priestly habiliments were equally profuse and magnificent. There were 1000 pontificial robes, with ephods and suits of precious stones; with 10,000 silken, and 10,000 purple vestments for the priests. Solomon also provided 200,000 trumpets, with 200,000 silver stoles for the Levites, and 400,000 musical instruments formed of gold and silver. The estimate of the cost of all these georgeous utensils, robes, &c. exceeds our comprehension. The expense was necessarily prodigious; but the resources of our Grand Master appear to have been inexhaustible. This was a proud era in the Jewish history; and if their monarchs had not proved worthless, they might have remained a great and mighty nation to the end of time.

On a view of this magnificent edifice, thus finished, furnished and decorated, what sublime ideas arise in our minds. It was—to use the language which Professor Green applies to a Christian cathedral—it was an architectural *word* for the Omnipresence of God.

Amongst such a vast concourse of people as were assembled together at the construction of this edifice, it is natural to expect every variety of propensities both good and evil. Accordingly, our traditions furnish instances both amongst the Apprentices and Craftsmen, of treachery—violation of sacred pledges—and the commission of actual crime. But nothing could escape the wisdom and vigilance of the Grand Masters, and their subordinate officers; and as we have seen rewards distributed to meritorious workmen; so strict justice was executed on offenders. . These instances, some of which have been thought worthy of preservation in the ineffable Degrees, were not numerous; for the brethren became fortified against evil by the Lectures of their Masters and Wardens; and their hearts, imbued with the mild spirit of philanthropy and kindness, were open to the impressions of Truth and Brotherly Love. From the above causes, however, the connection of the Widow's Son with the building of the temple was endeared to the two monarchs; and, to preserve and consecrate his memory, a new arrangement of discipline was adopted; and a legend incorporated into the system, which served to promote a similar object with the fabulous narrative used in the spurious initiations, viz., to inculcate and impress on the candidate's mind, the doctrine of a resurrection and a future state. Indeed, the respect which both the Grand Masters entertained for their useful ally was euthusiastic and overwhelming; and they acceded, on many occasions, to his wishes, in points unconnected with the profession of which he was so bright an ornament. Thus he prevailed on the King of Tyre to issue a proclamation, forbidding his subjects to offer children in sacrifice to their god Moloch or Cronus.

And how were his services requited? Not merely by honours and distinctions, but by a reward which exceeded, in his estimation, all earthly compensations. He demanded of Solomon the hand of Adoniram's sister in marriage. His request was granted, and honoured by the two kings with a public celebration. The legend of his death it will be unnecessary to repeat; but there are some circumstances connected with it, which may be interesting. His illustrious consort, whose memory is dear to every true Mason, was so sincerely attached to him, that at his death she became inconsolable; and refusing to be comforted, she spent the greater part of her time in lamentation and mourning over the tomb which contained his venerated ashes. The monument erected to his memory was peculiarly splendid; having been curiously constructed of black and white marble, from plans furnished by the Grand Warden on the purest masonic principles; and occupied an honourable situation in the private garden belonging to the royal palace.[26]

Th' associate band in solemn state
The awful loss deplor'd;
And Wisdom mourn'd the ruthless fate,
That whelm'd the mystic Word.

[26] "The burial place called the sepulchres of the kings of the house of David, was a very sumptuous and stately thing. It lies now without the walls of Jerusalem, but, as it is supposed, was formerly within them, before that city was destroyed by the Romans. It consists of a large court of about one hundred and twenty feet square, with a gallery or cloister on the left hand; which court and gallery, with the pillars that

His afflicted widow pined away in retirement at his sepulchre; until one evening, as she was returning from the performance of her melancholy duty, along the terrace from the gate Shallecheth to the royal palace, where probably she had apartments, overcome by the intensity of her feelings, she precipitated herself from the arched causeway which overhung the valley of Moriah, and perished in the dreadful abyss. To perpetuate the recollection of these distressing circumstances, the Israelitish and Tyrian monarchs erected three brazen statues; one at Jerusalem, another at Joppa, and a third at Tyre; the former of which was carried in triumph to Rome by Titus, after the final destruction of Herod's temple; and the latter shared in the demolition of Tyre by Alexander the Great.

The principles of Masonry thus cemented and exemplified in the experience derived from the erection of this magnificent temple was propagated throughout the world. "Many of Solomon's Masons, before he died, began to travel, and carried with them their skill and taste in architecture, with the secrets of the fraternity, into Asia, Africa, and also into Europe; for the old constitutions affirm that one called Ninus, who had been at the building of Solomon's Temple, carried the art into Germany and Gaul. In many places, being highly esteemed, they obtained special privileges; and because they taught their liberal art only to the free-born, they were called Free Masons; constituting Lodges in the places where they built stately piles, by the encouragement of the great and wealthy, who soon requested to be accepted as members of their Lodges, and Brothers of the craft; till by merit those Free and Accepted Masons came to be Masters and Wardens. Even princes and potentates

supported it, were cut out of the solid marble rock. At the end of the gallery there is a narrow passage, through which there is an entrance into a large room or hall, of about twenty-four feet square; within which are several lesser rooms one within another, with stone doors opening into them; all which rooms, with the great room, were likewise cut out of the rock. In the sides of those lesser rooms are several niches, in which the corpses of the deceased kings were deposited in stone coffins. It seems to have been the work of King Solomon; for it could not have been made without vast expense; and it is the only true remainder of old Jerusalem which is now to be seen in that place." (Prid. Con. vol 1. p. 27. from Maundrell, p. 76.)

became Grand Masters, each in his own dominions, in imitation of King Solomon, whose memory, as a Mason, has been duly revered, and will be till architectures hall be consumed in the general conflagration."[27]

Such were the results of the union of Speculative and Operative Masonry at the building of this noble edifice. It was symbolized in the temple itself, which was a place for the worship of all nations;—universal as the attributes of him in whose honour it was erected. Here was a Sanctum Sanctorum for the residence of the Divinity; a holy place or sanctuary for the priests; a portico and courts for the Jewish people; and a court for the Gentiles; besides innumerable apartments for the accommodation of all. Unfortunately, the Light of Speculative Masonry became obscured and almost extinguished by Jewish apostacy, added to the meretricious attractions of the spurious system, before their total punishment by the captivity of Babylon; when the temple was razed to its foundations; and Light, or the Shekinah of God, withdrawn for ever.

Where is this gorgeous temple now? Where the altars and cherubim and vessels of silver and gold? Where are the palaces of the Jewish monarchs;—where the cities, and gardens, and vineyards of Palestine? All vanished from the face of the earth. The rich and prolific soil of Judea—the land of milk and honey—is a barren waste, unfit for the abode of man. The rock on which the temple was built presents its bare breast to every storm, and appears, in its utter desolation, to lament the downfall of its glories.

> The Niobe of nations! There she stands,
> Childless and crownless, in her voiceless woe;
> An empty urn within her withered hands,
> Whose holy dust was scattered long ago.
>
> *Byron.*

[27] Noorth. Const. p. 31.

LECTURE X.

ON THE FORM AND DISPOSITION OF A MASONS' LODGE

Come all ye gentle springs that move
  And animate the human mind,
And by your energy improve
  The social bond by which we're join'd.
The Sacred Lodge, of care devoid,
  From haggard malice always free,
Shall by your aid be still employ'd
  In social love and harmony.

Gavin Wilson.

A LODGE OF MASONS consists of a certain number of Brethren who are assembled together to expatiate on the mysteries of the craft; having the Holy Bible open on the Pedestal to teach them the sacred principles of religion and justice; on which rest those two expressive emblems the Square and Compass, to remind them of the duties they owe to society and to themselves; the Book of Constitutions, where they may study the general statutes of Masonry; the Bye-Laws, to point out their duty as members of an individual Lodge; and the Warrant, by virtue of which, having been issued by the Grand Lodge, and enrolled in the archives of the Province where it is situated, at the general quarter sessions of the peace, the Brethren meet to transact the business of Masonry.

The Form of the Lodge is an oblong square, situated due East and West; supported by three pillars, and standing on holy ground. Its dimensions are unlimited, and its covering no less than the spangled canopy of heaven. To this object the Mason's mind is continually directed; and in those blessed regions he hopes at last to arrive by the aid of the theological ladder, which Jacob in his vision beheld reaching from earth to heaven; the three principal rounds of which admonish us to have faith in God, hope in immortality, and charity to all mankind.

From these general principles it appears that a Masons' lodge is a microcosm or miniature world, over which the glory in the centre sheds its refulgent rays, like the sun in the firmament, to enlighten the Brethren in the paths of virtue and science. In the Lodge, the practice of social and moral virtue is as essential towards the Brethren, and invested with the same degree of approbation or censure, as the performance of our public duties as Christians and citizens of the world at large. Hence arises the propriety of that sublime recommendation in the charge which is delivered to an Entered Apprentice at his initiation, to practise "the important duties he owes to God, to his neighbour, and to himself. To God, by never mentioning his name but with that awe and reverence with are due from the creature to the Creator, by imploring his aid, on all lawful undertakings, and by looking up to him in every emergency for comfort and support. To his neighbour, by acting with him upon the square; by rendering him every kind office which justice or mercy may require; by relieving his distresses, and soothing his affliction; and by doing to him as, in similar cases, he would wish to be done to. And to himself, by such a prudent and well regulated course of discipline, as may best conduce to the preservation of his corporeal and mental faculties in their fullest energy; thereby enabling him to exert the talents wherewith God has blessed him, as well to his glory as to the welfare of his fellow-creatures."

A Mason sitting in his Lodge, surrounded by the characteristic symbols which are distributed on all sides, feels that he is a member of the universal lodge of nature; created by the Author and Source of *Light* and redeemed by divine love or *Charity*. He seriously reflects on the incumbent duties that bind him to practise the permanent virtue and morality which these emblems embody and recommend; in the hope that when he is finaly summoned to give up his accounts, he may he transferred from his lodge on earth to the Grand Temple above; there to enjoy for ever the bright system of Freemasonry in its perfect and glorified state of ineffable Light. unbounded Charity, and undisturbed Peace.

I now proceed to consider in detail the characteristic principles which prevail in the form and disposition of our Lodges.

1. They are formed in upper chambers, and carefully guarded by tyled doors and drawn swords. The highest of hills and the lowest of valleys are situations the least exposed to unauthorized intrusion. Thus Masons are said to meet in these situations to commemorate a remarkable custom of the ancient Jews in the building of their temples, schools, and synagogues; and as by the Jewish law, whenever ten of them assembled together for that purpose, they proceeded to work; so it was with our ancient brethren, who formed themselves into a Lodge whenever ten Operative Masons were assembled, consisting of the Master, two Wardens, and seven Fellow Crafts.

Such places were always accounted holy; and the spirit of God was thought to repose on the highest hills. Thus the Deity appeared to Abraham on Mount Moriah; to Moses on Mount Sinai and Pisgah; whose cemetery was in the valley; and was constantly present on the former mountain after the building of the temple. The final Grand Lodge which shall be holden on earth will be convened in the valley of Jehoshaphat, or Judgment; when the captivities of Judah and Jerusalem shall be restored, and all nations gathered together into one fold under one shepherd.

This belief appears to have been confirmed by the Almighty himself; for he said to the prophet Ezekiel "upon the top of the mountain, the whole limit thereof, round about, shall be most holy." For the same reason the nations by which the Jews were surrounded sacrificed on the summit of high hills. Generally before the erection of temples, the *celestial* deities were worshipped on mounds, and the *terrestial* ones in valleys. At a later period we find Christian churches placed on eminences wherever it was practicable.

In such situations, therefore, our ancient brethren opened their Lodges; and tradition says that, on this principle, the oldest Lodge in England was held in a crypt beneath the foundations of York Cathedral. Such precautions, in those early times, were esteemed necessary for the preservation of that secrecy by which our institution has ever been distinguished, and which constitutes its essence and pride. This is, indeed, the characteristic by which its benefits are preserved and transmitted to posterity. Deprived of its secrecy, Freemasonry would long since have been lost to mankind. Like the glorious Gospel, it is a mystery which hath been hidden from the foundation of the world.[1] Our Saviour expressly assigns this reason for the mysterious allegories or parables in which his instruction was so frequently imbedded, "that the people who heard him might not understand the valuable truths which he privately expounded to his disciples."[2] Thus we follow the example of the Great Architect of the Universe, who concealeth from mankind the secret mysteries of his providence. And, as our lectures very sublimely teach, "the wisest of men cannot penetrate into the arcana of heaven, nor can they divine to-day what to-morrow may bring forth."

If we consider secrecy as an abstract principle, a series of weighty evidence might be adduced to prove that it is one of the praiseworthy virtues which man, in his present state, is bound, not only to estimate very highly, but to practise in his commerce with society, if he would execute the duties of his station with credit to himself, and advantage to the community at large. In all ranks of life the duty remains the same. The apprentice must keep his master's secrets; the master must take care of his own. Is an individual impannelled on a Jury of his country? His deliberations are conducted in private, and must not be divulged. If a statesman were to betray the secrets of his cabinet, public business could not be carried on, and the most ruinous effects would soon appear. What would be the consequence were a sentinel to communicate to the enemy that secret pass-word by which his post is guarded? The same principle pervades the policy of every institution under heaven.

Nor is secrecy a novel doctrine. A regard for this virtue has been peculiar to every nation and people of the world from the earliest times on record. The Egyptians venerated it so highly as to veil all their religion and politics under its impenetrable mask: and their great goddess, Isis, had this inscription attached to her altars,

[1] Eph. iii. 9. [2] Mark iv. 11, 12

"I am all that is, has been, or shall be; and no mortal can remove the veil that covers me." Pythagoras also not only enjoined upon his disciples a silence of five years' continuance, in his exoteric degree, but bound them under the most solemn obligations to a perpetual secrecy respecting the peculiar mysteries of the institution when advanced to the higher grade of the esoteric or acroatic degree. And Iamblichus says,[3] their peculiar secrets and doctrines were forbidden to be committed to writing, and were preserved by memory only. The Master's lectures were heard only within the walls; and, if the brethren were desirous of communicating with each other in public, they used Signs and Tokens, which were intelligible only to themselves. We are told by one of the ancient fathers of Christianity that "their phlosophers had sublime notions of the divine nature, which they kept secret and never discovered to the people but under the veil of fables and allegories. All the Eastern nations, the Persians, the Indians, the Syrians, concealed secret mysteries under hieroglyphical symbols and parables. The wise men of all those religions knew the sense and true meaning of them, whilst the vulgar and uninitiated went no further than the outward and visible symbol, and so discerned only the bark by which they were covered."[4]

The Spurious Freemasonry was entirely founded on silence and secrecy; and no candidate could be admitted to participate in the privileges which it was supposed to convey, without having first given an unequivocal proof of his taciturnity by a long and severe probation. A terrible instance of the consequences which attended a violation of this principle has been handed down to us in the story of Hipparchus, a Pythagorean, who, "having out of spleen and resentment violated and broke through the several engagements of the society, was held in the utmost detestation, expelled from the school, as a most infamous and abandoned person; and, as he was esteemed dead to the principles of virtue and philosophy, they had a tomb erected for him, according to their custom, as though he had been naturally dead. The shame and disgrace that justly attended so great a breach of truth and

[3] Vit. Pyth. c. 17. [4] Orig. cont. Cels. l. 1. p. 11.

fidelity, drove the unhappy wretch to such despair that he proved his own executioner; and so abhorred was even his memory, that he was denied the rites and ceremonies of burial used to the dead in those times; instead of which *his body was suffered to lie upon the sands of the sea shore* in the isle of Samos, to be devoured by rapacious animals."[5]

It is unnecessary to extend this subject. Solomon, our Grand Master, and the wisest of men, brands those with dishonesty who cannot keep a secret.[5] Society is founded on the principle of mutual dependance and mutual aid. Each state, community, family, and individual, is possessed of secrets whose disclosure would be personally injurious, without conveying a corresponding benefit to the public; and though private feelings or interests ought to yield, if placed in competition with the general good, yet, in all cases, where the advantage is equivocal, it is the wisest and best policy to withhold the information. On this principle Freemasonry disseminates its benefits in the tyled recesses of the Lodge. They are open to the ingenuous and candid enquirer, if he seek them by the legitimate process; while they are carefully concealed from those who might use them improperly, or convert them to purposes which would prove injurious to society. The good and worthy candidate is received with open arms; but to the vicious and dissolute the tyler is instructed to oppose the point of his naked sword.

But, says the sceptic, where is the necessity of secrecy now, when you confess that the darkness of error is past, and the true Light shineth? If your Institutionbe laudable as you describe it, why not reveal it for the benefit of mankind? I should as soon look for a star to fall from the firmament of heaven, as for a caviller against this divine science to be satisfied with even a mathematical demonstration. The benefits of Masonry can only be enjoyed by their union with secrecy. Lay its peculiar mysteries open to the world and the charm would cease to operate. They resemble the Sybil's leaves—exhibiting to the uninitiated merely the appearance of a series of naked and disjointed facts; while to the well-instructed brother they constitute a wise and connected system

[5] Calcott, p. 32.

which conveys essential assistance towards the consummation of human happiness. If publicly disseminated, they would become familiar as the growth of a plant; and, like that incomprehensible phenomenon, would be neglected and perhaps despised. At the Reformation of our church, nothing could exceed the curiosity of mankind to read and investigate the golden stores contained in the Holy Bible, which had been as a sealed book for many centuries. Yet, though it contains secrets of far greater importance than those of Freemasonry—curiosity being gratified, the passion subsided; and it is regarded by the mass of mankind with as much indifference as though it contained nothing affecting their temporal or eternal welfare. So Masonry, were its privileges thrown open to the world, would probably be neglected, because the stimulus would be wanting from which it derives its popularity and interest. But its secrets are open to the inspection of the worthy and the good in every class of mankind. The page is displayed before them; and if they refuse to read, it is too much to hear them complain of ignorance, or to speak evil of a science which they want the inclination or the capacity to understand.

2. The form and extent of the Lodge considered.

The form of a Masons' Lodge possesses nothing in common with the caverns of initiation into the Spurious Freemasonry, although its professors, like ourselves, used many astronomical symbols; and considered the cave as an emblem of the universe. *It was circular* or domed, in reference to the solar worship; and all its enrichments partook of the same character, and were conducted by corresponding machinery. Our Lodges, on the contrary, are *angular;* ample in their dimensions, and extensive in their reference. We may indeed say, in the expressive language of Zophar, the friend of Job. "*It is as high as heaven;* what canst thou do? *Deeper than hell;* what canst thou know? The measure therefore is *longer than the earth and broader than the sea.*" And what can more strongly express, or more strikingly demonstrate an idea of universality? What can produce upon the Mason's mind a more forcible impression, that his benevolence should know no bounds, save that of prudence? Josephus asserts "that the proportions of the measures of the tabernacle proved it to be an imitation of the system of the world."[6] In like manner a Craft Masons' Lodge, with its three chief degrees —with its science and its morals—the system and polity of its government—its constitutions and its sacred symbols, arranged in due form and order—is a perfect world in itself; excluding every thing which might interfere with the general harmony and brotherly love that form its great and peculiar characteristics.

That the extent of the Lodge may be more clearly typified in the mind of a well instructed brother, a symbol of the All-seeing Eye of God is placed in some conspicuous situation; that the idea of his universal presence and divine inspection may never for a moment be absent from his recollection. And while the great luminaries of heaven, those living proofs of God's eternal power and goodness, overshadow the holy place where he is seated, he is impressed with reverence and devotion to the Being whom the heaven of heavens cannot contain.

By this disposition of the Lodge we are admonished that our thoughts and affections, in one glorious strain of uninterrupted praise, ought always to flow spontaneously from the heart; under the assured conviction that wherever we may be—in the temple or in the closet—in the field or in the vineyard—still we are before the altar of our God—still the protecting arm is over us. "He shall defend us under his wings, and we shall be safe under his feathers; his faithfulness and truth shall be our shield and buckler."

3. The ground of a Masons' Lodge is holy.

We now approach a subject of grave and serious consideration. If there be found in the world a single spot of earth which the Deity appears to have marked with greater care, and to have consecrated with more than ordinary solemnity;—should we discover a single holy place where he himself delighted to dwell—that spot of earth is an emblem of the floor of a Masons' Lodge. There we may reasonably expect to find the Light of Truth—there we may hope to be exempt from the intrusion of those wordly passions which agitate our nature amidst the cares, and troubles, and jealousies of this transitory life. Should this floor happen to be covered

[6] Jos. Ant. Jud. l. c. 7.

with a mosaic pavement, surrounded by its beautiful tesselated border, we find no difficulty in appreciating its moral reference. We know that though we are not free from the calamities of life; yet there is a method by which adversity may be lightened, and pain deprived of its sting. When our steps tread amidst the chequered scenes of good and evil with which this uncertain world abounds; if our cup teem with affliction and sorrow, we are taught by our emblematical floorcloth, not to grieve as if we stood alone in misery, for it is the lot of our species; not to sink into despondency; because sorrow is allotted to us as a corrective and purifier; that presumption may be subdued, and the intrusions of doubt or infidelity suppressed in the bud. Affliction constitutes an essential part of the system of providence; and it is by the operation of occasional losses and disappointments—so teaches the masonic pavement—that the greatest measure of general happiness is secured and distributed by a wise and beneficent Creator, who "does not afflict willingly, nor grieve the children of men."

If we look abroad we shall find that divine *mercy* in the distribution of good is the prevailing sentiment. Some, indeed, are oppressed by sickness, but more enjoy their health; a few perhaps are mourning, but numbers happily rejoice; a sight of pain is occasionally presented to our eyes, but generally we see nothing but ease and comfort. Thus the checquered scenes of life are usually bright and cheerful, though at times obscured by an accidental shadow. Clouds and darkness are the portion of vice only, while virtue is enlightened with the sunshine of peace.

We further learn from the beautiful groundwork of our Lodge, the precariousness and uncertainty of our tenure in this life; whence arises the duty of "rejoicing with those who do rejoice, and weeping with those who weep;" or, in other words, congratulating the happy, and compassionating the distressed. The latter, however, is more in unison with the benevolent lessons of Freemasonry. It is inculcated on the principle before us. How diversified soever men may be with respect to rank, or talent, or wealth, in this transitory life, the time will soon arrive when all these accidental distinctions will cease, and be effectually levelled by death. And though splendid monuments and pompous epitaphs may be the heralds of riches and power, yet it is virtue alone which ennobles the mind, and will procure lasting distinction when the grave gives up its dead. From this consideration we are taught in the old Lectures, "to conduct ourselves, in our commerce with the world, according to the dictates of right reason; to cultivate harmony; to maintain charity, and live in unity and brotherly love."

4. A few reasons to shew the propriety and wisdom of placing our Lodges due East and West.

This was a disposition which universally accompanied the practice of religion in all nations, and has been thought to have originated from the rising and setting of the sun, and the origin and propagation of human learning and science. But there are other reasons for this custom which appear to be equally worthy of our consideration. The garden of Eden was placed in the East, and our first parents expelled towards the West. The Ark of Enoch was placed due East and West, as also were the tabernacle and temple of the Jews. If we view with the eye of philosophy and religion the beautiful works of the creation, and all things therein contained—the heavens declaring the glory of God, and the firmament shewing his handiwork—it becomes an incumbent duty upon his creatures to bow with reverence and humility before the great Creator, who has never, from the earliest period of time, left himself without a living witness amongst men. In the first ages of the world, Abel offered a more acceptable sacrifice than his brother Cain—Noah was a just and upright man—Jacob wrestled with an angel, and obtained a blessing for himself and his posterity. But we do not find any records of a temple peculiarly set apart for divine worship, till after the deliverance of the children of Israel from their Egyptian bondage; which it pleased the Lord to accomplish with a high hand and a stretched out arm, under the conduct of his faithful servant Moses. As this chosen people were destined to inherit the promised land, and to become a great and mighty nation, God gave them a series of laws and revelations for their moral and religious guidance; and as a repository for these invaluable documents, as well as a place for the solemnization of divine worship, Moses was commanded to erect a tent or tabernacle in the wilderness, which he placed due East and West, in commemoration of that great and mighty wind which first blew East and then West, by which their happy deliverance was effected, and Pharoah and his host destroyed in his attempt to follow them through the passages of the Red Sea. As this tabernacle was intended as a temporary substitute for a more permanent building, constructed on the same model, and placed in the same situation with respect to the cardinal points of the compass, when his people should have obtained peaceable possession of the land of Canaan; it may be justly inferred that the practice was sanctioned by the Divinity.[7]

Heathen temples were, in like manner, placed due East and West; and the statues being deposited at the West end, the people, during their devotions, stood with their faces towards that quarter.[8] Judah, the most distinguished of the tribes, had the eastern part of the camp assigned to him, as the station of honour. The Gospel was first published in the East, and afterwards spread over the western parts of the globe. Christian Churches and Masonic Lodges are built due East and West, and the eastern part in each is considered the most sacred. Interments of the dead are still conducted on a similar principle.

Throughout the works of nature the same system is visible; and, therefore, its origin must be ascribed to the Creator of all things. The sun, that great source of light and heat, created for the benefit and convenience of man, rises in the East to open the day—gains his meridian in the South, to point out the necessity of a brief cessation from our daily employments, that we may be invigorated by rest and refreshment—and retires to the West to close the labours of the day. From these remarkable appearances in the heavens, the ancient inhabitants of the world considered the East to be the face of the earth, and the West its back.

An objection has been taken to the above arrangement, by considering that the changes occasioned by the precession of the equinoxes have somewhat altered the position of ancient buildings; and that, if the eastern and western points are to be determined by the rising and

[7] Ezek. xxiv. 2. [8] Porph. de ant. Nympharum.

setting of the sun, a system of uniformity would appear necessary throughout the whole course of time; as these edifices, therefore, are at variance with the points thus ascertained, the position is not correctly exemplified, and the theory, of course, falls to the ground. It will be seen at once that this objection, though often urged, is so replete with fallacy and subterfuge, as scarcely to need a formal refutation. The terms East and West have been honoured with peculiar notice ever since the world began; and it is from the uniform practice of our ancient brethren that we retain a regard for these points in all our ceremonies.

In the early times of Christianity, this practice was observed with reverence. There was, however, this material variation from the ancient system, that while both Jews and Heathens worshipped with their faces towards the West, in which quarter the adyta were placed, the Christians reversed the custom. Our Saviour is denominated by St. Luke "ORIENS;" and therefore the Christian converts worshipped, and covenanted with Christ, with their faces to the East, and they were taught to abjure Satan towards the West.[9] Origen,[10] who flourished about the middle of the third century, *announces* the fact, though he assigns no reason for it. His words are: "In Ecclesiasticis observationibus sunt nonnulla hujusmodi quæ omnibus quidem facere necesse est, nec tamen ratio, eorum omnibus patet; nam quod genuæ flectimus, orantes; et quod ex omnibus cœli plagis, *ad solam orientis partem conversi*, orationem fundimus, non facile cuiquam puto ratione compertum." Epiphanius says that it was the error of Elaxus to forbid his followers to pray towards the East;[11] and Prochorus adds, that St. John the Evangelist used always to pray with his face in that direction.[12]

The reasons which have been assigned for this custom are derived, as I have already observed, from the creation; the garden of Eden being placed in the East, and man expelled towards the West; wherefore Christians pray, says Basil,[13] looking towards the East, in earnest expectation of a better country,[14] i. e. Paradise. Clement of

[9] Ambrose. Dion. Areop.
[10] Orig. in lib. Num. Hom. 5.
[11] Epiph. adv. Oss.
[12] Proch. in vit. S. John, c. 5.
[13] Basil de. S. Sancto. c. 27.
[14] Ezek. xliii. 2.

Alexandria refers it to another cause. The East, he says is, as it were, the birth of the day, and from thence the light springeth; therefore we pray towards the East.[15] Again, the custom has been referred to the crucifixion; for, as the Redeemer was sacrificed with his face towards the West, Christians, during their devotions, ought to look towards Him from whom they expect salvation. And it has also been considered to have respect to the general judgment, because the angels revealed to the disciples who were witnesses of Christ's ascension *towards the East*, that "the same Jesus which is taken up from you into heaven, shall so come, *in like manner*, as you have seen him go into heaven." And indeed the very same thing had been already communicated to them by Christ himself, in these remarkable words, "As the lightning cometh *out of the East*, and shineth even unto the West, *so shall also* the coming of the Son of Man be."

5. Remarks on the Pillars which support the Lodge.

Our Lodges are supported by three pillars called Wisdom, Strength, and Beauty; which have been adopted as the basis of the system; because without wisdom to contrive, strength to support, and beauty to adorn, no architecture can be considered perfect. Wisdom contrived the temple at Jerusalem; Strength supported the design with materials and men; and Beauty adorned it with a profusion of curious workmanship in timber, jewelry, and the precious metals.

Amongst the primitive professors of this holy science, the creation of the world out of Chaos formed a sublime subject of disquisition, in which were displayed those three prominent attributes of the Deity—Wisdom, Strength, and Beauty. Wisdom was exemplified in the formation of our planet, and its attendant orbs. Strength, in the nice adjustment of the balance by which they are mutually supported in their rapid and complicated evolutions:

For ever singing as they shine,
The hand that made us is divine.

And Beauty, in the entire arrangement, as well as in the natural decorations with which the parts are so profusely adorned. Gradually were the effects displayed. Order

[15] Clem. Strom. vii. p. 520.

succeeded Chaos. Darkness vanished before the blessed radiance of light. The sea became dry land. Water, earth, and air, teemed with their myriads of inhabitants. And last of all, man, the crown and glory of the creation, appeared in the image of God—erect in stature; "infinite in faculties;" having "dominion over the fish of the sea, and over every living thing that moveth upon the earth."

Thus Wisdom, Strength, and Beauty were triumphant; and "God saw every thing that he had made, and behold it was very good." The concave vault of heaven, like a superb coronet, spangled with brilliant gems, equally with the gaudy scenery which is spread in such rich profusion over the face of nature, proclaim, as with the voice of angels, the existence of these grand masonic pillars at that period to *contrive*, to *support*, and to *adorn* the august bodies which occupy the regions of universal space.

In a masonic Lodge these pillars are represented by three principal officers, whose duty in governing the brethren is expressed in the symbols which are suspended at their breasts. But when the Lodge is harmoniously constructed, these duties are not onerous; and if exercised in the spirit of genuine Masonry, they constitute the links which connect the members in an unbroken chain of brotherly love.

And here I may, with great propriety, offer a few suggestions to these officers on the efficacious discharge of their several duties, that pleasure and profit may mutually result. First, let them set a good example of regularity and decorum in their own conduct, both in the Lodge and in the world. Order is heaven's first law. It constitutes the beauty and stability of the masonic system. Let them open the Lodge punctually at the prescribed hour—work the lectures diligently and scientifically, during the time of labour; and if the Junior Warden's call be heard, let not refreshment be extended beyond the moderate bounds which decency prescribes. When the sun sets, let the Senior Warden be ready to perform his duty at the command of the Worshipful Master, and see that none go away dissatisfied, or unimproved in virtue and science.

The W. M. should always bear in his memory, that to

him the brethren look for instruction—on him depend the welfare and success—the credit and popularity of the community. His situation, as the chief pillar of the Lodge, is most important; and if he fail in the satisfactory discharge of its duties, he inflicts a fatal blow, not only on the Lodge, which will be the first victim of an ill-placed confidence, but on the order of Freemasonry itself, which will suffer in public estimation, should its principal officer prove incompetent to the high office he has undertaken; should fail through inattention, neglect, or incapacity, to improve the brethren in wisdom and knowledge; or to vindicate and defend the purity of the order against the attacks and surmises of those who ridicule or condemn it, simply because they do not understand its object, and are incapable of comprehending its beauty and utility.

There is one point in the management of a Lodge, which requires not only great tact, but true firmness of mind in the Worshipful Master and his officers. I mean in those unhappy cases where disputes and divisions prevail amongst the brethren. On such occasions, a regard for the purity of Freemasonry, and its reputation in the Lodge over which he presides, makes it necessary that the Worshipful Master should act promptly and decisively; nor must he, under any circumstances, shrink from the performance of a positive duty, for the surest method of obtaining at once the approbation of the brethren and of his own conscience, is to discharge his duty punctually, faithfully, and impartially.

Freemasonry is a system of peace, order, and harmony. The elements of dispute and division are not found in any of its institutes. The brethren meet on the level and part on the square. The utmost extent of fraternal affection which can subsist between man and man, is supposed to be displayed between the brethren of a masonic Lodge. It is enjoined equally in the ancient Charges, the Constitutions, and the Lectures; and the world at large, amidst all their cavils and objections on other points, are inclined to give us credit for our brotherly love.

From these considerations, the Master will use his influence and authority to convince his masonic companions of the necessity—so far as regards the interests of the Craft in general—so far as regards the welfare of the Lodge—so far as regards their own peace, or the happiness of their brethren—of preserving the unity of the spirit in the bond of peace. In all cases it is is more honourable to unite in the principle of conceding points of minor importance, than to foment disputes that may involve consequences which it is impossible to foresee, and frequently impracticable to remedy. On all occasions he ought to possess sufficient knowledge of human nature to prevail on the brethren to be unanimous in their conclusions, however their opinions may vary in detail; for it is the safest, wisest, and best policy to submit cheerfully and implicitly to the decision of a majority, in the assured belief that such a decision has the greatest chance to be correct.

A portion of responsibility, although in an inferior degree, is incurred by the representatives of Strength and Beauty. If they conscientiously perform their allotted tasks, the Master will not only be assisted and encouraged, but, in a manner compelled to execute his office, at least creditably, if not beneficially. He will escape censure, if he do not merit praise. Prompted by the *equal* measures of the one, and the *integrity* of the other, he may be induced to govern his Lodge on the principles of *morality* and *justice;* even should higher incentives be absent from his bosom—even though a love of the science should have waxed cold, and he should have coveted this high office merely to enjoy its honours and its power.

It is devoutly to be wished that improper motives might never induce a Mason to aspire to an official situation in the Lodge. From such an unnatural ambition evil is sure to proceed. If unqualified, office is rather a disgrace than an honour, because it is impossible, under such circumstances, to conceal ignorance, or to throw a veil over imperfection. And an exhibition of incapacity, in those who are expected to instruct the ignorant and lead the anxious enquirer to a knowledge of the truth, excites no feeling but pity and contempt. While, on the other hand, when the Master's chair is filled with ability and talent, respect and approbation are ensured; the words of sound doctrine fall, like the dew of heaven, from the lips of such an instructor, and are eagerly imbibed by the gratified hearers; improvement in masonic knowledge rapidly augments, the pupils emulate the Master's accomplishments, and the triumph of virtue and science becomes visible to the world, although mankind are ignorant how the noble attainment has been acquired. So truly is it said, that "the Light shineth in darkness, but the darkness comprehendeth it not."

6. The cloudy canopy illustrated.

In all communications which the Creator has been graciously pleased to make with the creature, he has been enveloped in a cloud.[16] Hence our Lodge is figuratively said to be covered with the clouds of heaven, because a cloud is the acknowledged emblem of that glorious Being, whose all-seeing eye inspects our actions, and whose aid we implore in all our undertakings. In the early history of the Jewish nation, we find God appearing in a cloud, because, as he himself declared by his prophet Moses, the people saw no manner of similitude on the day that the Lord spake unto them in Horeb out of the midst of the fire;[17] for he would not shew himself to them under any specific figure, lest they should make an idol of the same form, and worship it.[18] But the appearance of the Lord in a cloud had been adopted from the earliest times,—in the garden of Eden,[19]—at the sacrifice of Abraham,[20]—at the Burning Bush,[21]—at the deliverance of the Children of Israel from their Egyptian bondage it was most remarkable; for at that period the cloud directed them through the Red Sea, and attended them during their journeyings in the wilderness, and was intended as a visible manifestation of the Divine presence, and a token that Jehovah[22] was at hand to render them

[16] Consult Lev. xvi. 2.; Lam. iii. 44.; and Ps. civ. 1, 2, 3.

[17] Deut. iv. 15.

[18] Cat. ex. Decr. Conc. Trid. p. 394. See also Syn. Nic. 2. act. 3. p 184. a Theod. Patr. Hierosol.

[19] Gen. iii. 24. compared with Ezek. i. 4. [20] Gen. xv. 17.

[21] Ex. iii. 2. "There is a convent and church on Mount Sinai, according to Pococke; and a chapel on Horeb, called the Chapel of the Bush, which they say grew where a white murble slab is now placed under the altar; into which no one enters without first *taking off his shoes*." (Desc. of the East. vol. 1. p. 150.)

[22] In this instance the Deity is said to be in the cloud, under the name of Jehovah; and was none other than the Redeemer of mankind, who is the same yesterday, to-day, and for ever. The pillar of a cloud which preceded the Israelites on the above occasion, is said by ancient writers to represent Christ in many respects. He is the sacred pillar that sup-

assistance in all cases of difficulty and danger. Again, the Deity was shrouded in a cloud over the tabernacle; and at that sublime period when the law was delivered to Moses;—at the dedication also of Solomon's Temple —and when God discomfited the idols of Egypt.[23] This was the Divine Shekinah vouchsafed to the prophet Isaiah; and declared by St. John to be the actual glory of Jesus Christ the Saviour of mankind.[24] And we may consider further, that his human body was the ark of the Christian covenant, over which the Shekinah appeared in the cave at Bethlehem in the form of a supernatural star in the East; which hence is placed in the centre of our Lodges; again, at his baptism by St. John, as a celestial dove surrounded by a shining cloud of glory; and again, at his transfiguration and ascension, when a cloud at length received him, and he returned to his seat in heaven, which is also in a cloud; there to remain as our intercessor till the day of Judgment, when he shall again appear in a cloud to pass the final sentence on mankind.

The cloudy canopy, then, is a symbol of heaven. There our thoughts and affections centre, while we are engaged in the moral and scientific investigations which constitute the business of the Lodge. The central Star illuminates this picture of the firmament; and opens to the contemplative eye, the regions of everlasting space, accessible by a Ladder placed on the Holy Volume, containing staves or rounds, innumerable to fill up the intervals of those Three Great Steps by which the Mason hopes to ascend to the blessed regions of eternal day. And when he is enabled to achieve the third and last step, which constitutes the summit of the ladder, he figuratively enters into "a house not made with hands, eternal in the heavens.' veiled from mortal eye by the starry firmament, and symbolized on the Tracing Board by Seven Stars surrounding the silver queen of night.

orts his church; he guides us to eternal life, as to the promised land; or he is the way, the truth, and the life; he opens to us the way of the Red Sea, i. e. by baptism dyed red in his blood. Thus Rupertus says, Aperit nobis viam maris rubei, id est, gratiam baptismi sanguine suo rubentis." He is both a pillar of fire and of a cloud; or in other words both God and man; and Isaiah plainly says, that Christ is the covering cloud by which we are sheltered from the heat and storms of temptation.

[23] Isai. xix. 1.

[24] John xii. 41.

A right application of the several clauses contained in this Lecture, cannot fail to convince the unprejudiced enquirer, not only of the harmonious proportions of a Masons' Lodge, but also of the order and beauty arising from the general principles of the institution. Here we see Wisdom standing in the East to observe the rising of the sun, that he may commence the labour of instructing and improving the brethren in morals and science; Strength in the opposite quarter to support, by virtue of his influence, the lessons which Wisdom imparts; and when the setting sun proclaims the approach of night, to close the Lodge by command, after seeing that every brother has his due; and Beauty in the South, to mark the sun at his meridian, that the workmen may enjoy a just proportion of rest from their labours. To perfect the arrangement, the efficiency of these three Pillars is augmented by subordinate officers, ready to disseminate their commands amongst the brethren, and to see that they are punctually obeyed; while an attentive band stand round in respectful silence, clothed in the badge of innocence, to the honour and antiquity of which the aristocratic orders of the Golden Fleece and Roman Eagle afford no parallel. Inspired by the great moral truths which form the subject of the Master's lecture—

We cheerfully labour in hill or in dale;
At Moriah's fam'd mount, or Jehoshaphat's vale,
And whene'er 'tis High Twelve with due order regale.

No noise, no disorder, no riot we know,
But strictest decorum and harmony show;
Whilst the Graces on each do their favours bestow.

While the sea ebbs and flows, or the stars shed their light,
'Till all nature dissolve like the visions of night;
So long will true brothers in friendship unite.

Foote.

LECTURE XI.

ON THE CEREMONIES OF OPENING, CLOSING, LABOUR, AND REFRESHMENT.

Sweet fellowship from envy free,
Friendly converse of brotherhood;
The Lodge's lasting cement be,
Which has for ages firmly stood.
A Lodge thus built, for ages past
Has lasted, and shall ever last.

Masonic Song.

THE rites and ceremonies of Freemasonry form the distinctive peculiarity by which it is separated from every other institution. In their nature they are simple—in their end instructive. They excite a very high degree of curiosity and surprise in a newly initiated brother, and create an earnest desire to investigate their meaning, and to become acquainted with their object and design. It requires, however, both serious application, and untiring diligence, to ascertain the precise nature of every ceremony which our ancient brethren saw reason to adopt in the formation of an exclusive system, which was to pass through the world, unconnected with the religion or politics of all times, and of every people amongst whom it should flourish and increase. But the assiduous Mason, with the assistance of an intelligent Master in the chair, will not fail to apply every ordinance of the Craft to his own personal advantage.

In this Lecture we approach a subject of overwhelming interest to the Free and Accepted Mason. While expatiating on the routine business of Masonry, as transacted within the tyled recesses of the Lodge, I hope to make myself intelligible to the brethren, without drawing aside the veil which conceals hidden things from the gaze of uninitiated persons.

OPENING.

The first business which occupies the brethren at their stated meetings is, what is technically called Opening the Lodge. It is a solemn and imposing rite, and strongly fixes the attention of every serious Mason. At the well known signal, every officer repairs to his station, and the brethren prepare to execute, with alacrity, the orders of the Master, in silence and submission. The ceremony is then commenced with that venerable simplicity which always characterises the business of Masonry; and forms an interesting introduction to the fascinating exercise of its duties. This beautiful spectacle has been the subject of just and merited panegyric. In the excellent forms prescribed by our ancestors, the brethren are reminded of their dependance on the Almighty Architect of the Universe for every blessing they enjoy. A regular series of ancient landmarks are rehearsed, without a knowledge of which, no person can esteem himself a Mason, or be admitted into a strange Lodge.

These general heads are of the utmost importance, and cannot be dispensed with, but at the hazard of subverting the foundation, and destroying the beneficent principles of Masonry. Every officer is made acquainted with his duty, and seriously impressed with the importance attached to his situation. It is impossible for a Mason to be inattentive to these sublime transactions; and while his heart glows with the sacred fire of benevolence to his species, and overflows with gratitude to the great Author of his being, his devotion is excited by a short and fervent prayer, breathed in the true spirit of masonic philanthropy. The eye is directed to that lucid object which forms the central point of every Mason's hope; and the mind derives life and vigour from those luminous beams which irradiate the operations, and form the celestial covering of every masonic Lodge.

LABOUR.

The true intention of the Speculative Mason's labour, is the exercise of the faculties, and the improvement of the mind. By attaining perfection in this noble art, we hope to construct an edifice which shall be durable as the heavens—lasting as eternity; whence we may arrive, when our masonic course is terminated by death, at "a building not made with hands, eternal in the heavens." The Master, assisted by the Senior Warden, lays the chief corner stone of a beautiful fabric, to which every brother, according to his ability, cheerfully contributes his active co-operation. As the work advances, a regular series of illustrations are furnished by the Master, or by brethren duly qualified to instruct; which contain the strongest incentives to virtue and morality; while the mind inperceptibly imbibes a rational system of ethics, calculated to expand the faculties, and progressively to advance the diligent enquirer to a reliance on a superior power for consolation, when the world refuses the balm of comfort to assuage the sorrows incident to mortality.

All the illustrations of Masonry, whether symbolical or preceptive, whether legendary or scientific, tend to improve the mind and consecrate the affections to virtue and morality. If we consider the system as a whole, or its constituent parts in detail, all and each proclaim and inculcate the sacred duties which we owe to God, our neighbour, and ourselves; and it is the habitual practice of those duties which constitutes the character of a good and worthy Mason. In this bond, Masons are linked together by the strongest ties and obligations; and the chain of social relations cannot be broken by time, distance, or calamity.

On these considerations, the POINTS of Masonry have a most important reference. The practice of Brotherly Love, Relief, and Truth, forms the basis of our temporal felicity. We are instructed by the Chief Point to be contented with the station assigned to us by a benevolent providence, to cultivate peace and tranquillity, and to be ever ready to communicate the same measure of happiness to others, which animates our own bosoms. There are many ways of exciting sensations of happiness in the heart of our brother. And principally by courtesy and kindness. When the desire of inspiring feelings of pure delight is perfectly sincere—when love is without dissimulation—success is certain. On the state and construction of our own mind, depend, in a great measure, the friendship and good-will of those amongst whom we live. If we be distant and reserved, cold or ceremonious, the example will have its effect on our friends; and a free and social intercourse will be obstructed by suspicion and distrust.

Harshness of manner and of language, can never succeed in securing respect or eliciting gratitude, even for actual benefits. Men are apt to indulge a morbid disposition to imagine themselves slighted or despised; for, in the very lowest stations of life, individuals may be found who are so exceedingly sensitive, that an ungracious word—nay, even the tone of voice in which kind expressions are uttered, or the look by which they are accompanied, will be more than sufficient to counterbalance the presumed obligation arising out of a benefit conferred. While, on the contrary, an open and generous carriage, gracious looks, and kind and gentle language, accompanying acts of courtesy and beneficence, cannot fail to inspire a reciprocal confidence, which will be equally beneficial to the giver and to the receiver, and while we thus convey happiness to others, its peace is abundantly returned into our own bosoms.

The Principal Point of Masonry is three-fold, and comprises the exalted virtues of Brotherly Love, Relief, and Truth. Brotherly Love is the bond by which Masons are united, without reference to those artificial distinctions which exist amongst mankind, and separate them into an infinite diversity of grades and classes, each urging its peculiar claim to notice. This virtue is so natural to the human heart, that it has always been *professed*, even amidst the pollutions of the Spurious Freemasonry, and the debasement of ignorance and barbarism. If we search the annals of powerful states and empires, or penetrate the wilds and deserts of savage nations, where religion is unknown, we shall find the philosopher and the barbarian alike boasting of the practice of brotherly love. But in their estimation, what was it? I am afraid it was only another name for some undefined feeling nearly allied to hatred. Brotherly Love, based on the principles of a false faith, would be incapable of comprehending the nature of the bright system from which it was copied. The adherents of a Spurious Freemasonry rejected the doctrine of Brotherly

Love, as a sentiment which included all created beings within its limits; and confining it simply to their own immediate connections, esteemed the rest of the world as natural and hereditary foes. It was deemed a lawful point of honour to sweep away, with "the besom of destruction," all who were opposed to the interest or ambition of individuals, and thus this heavenly virtue was sacrificed at the unholy shrine of superstition and impiety.

Such was Brotherly Love under the domination of Spurious Freemasonry. "Famine and pestilence were not more terrible scourges to mankind than a people who were proverbial for this virtue. The proud and boasted principle of friendship, so liberally praised and complimented by pagan philosophy and legislation, had carried destruction and death over half the world; disturbed the tranquillity of harmless provinces, and defaced and depopulated the garden of God. It has been remarked, and I think with much justice, than in proportion to the enthusiasm to which Brotherly Love or Friendship has been carried, has been the virulence of that enmity amongst mankind, by which it has been accompanied. Such is man in a state of nature. Within a particular circle he has been a friend and a brother; without that circle, an enemy, a destroyer, a fury, and a fiend And then, when most applauded and adored within the contracted sphere of his friendship, most detested and execrated without it;—then when his statues have been rising fastest round him; and the cast brass receiving the history of his honours with busiest industry—then has been the moment when the curses of mankind have been poured, in the most copious shower, upon his head."[1]

This prostitution of a most amiable quality of the mind, for which reason afforded no remedy, was corrected by revelation. The Redeemer, knowing that such a principle had produced a mass of evil amongst mankind, determined to exhibit Brotherly Love in an amiable point of view, that the nations of the earth might form an universal brotherhood. His admonitions were, therefore principally directed to this point: "If ye love them,' said he, "which love you, what reward have ye? Do not

[1] Fawcet.

even the publicans the same? But I say unto you, bless them that curse you, do good to them that hate you, and pray for them which despitefully use you and persecute you." With the same intention he answered the question, who is my neighbour? by relating the parable of the ood Samaritan; which so impressed the enquirer, that e saw, without a comment, that the general relationship of man is not dissolved by distance, climate, form, or language; but all the world are brothers; and that the hand of mercy ought to be extended to the destitute stranger, as well as to an intimate friend or relation. Nay, the stranger, the fatherless, and the widow, however diversified by nation, birth, or colour, are superior objects of man's benevolence. And this is precisely the view of Brotherly Love which is taken by our excellent institution. It inculcates love to all mankind, but more particularly to a brother Mason, as a certain indication of uprightness, which is symbolized amongst us by the moveable Jewel which has been assigned to the Junior Warden.

Brotherly Love must be pure both in profession and practice; unwarped by prejudice; unabated amidst calumny, slander, and detraction; filling the heart with pious fervour and holy resolutions; exalting it from earth to heaven; from a perishable mortality to a celestial intercourse with the Source and Essence of love; ennobling the nature of man by the practice of his earthly Freemasonry, till it conducts him to the eternal Grand Lodge, where the celestial system of Light shall confer upon him perfect wisdom and perfect happiness.

Such is the nature of Brotherly Love, as inculcated in a masonic Lodge. Whoever is included in this bond, the same we acknowledge as a brother. We look not at his politics—we enquire not into his religious creed—his riches are dross—his climate or colour perfectly indifferent;—although we know not the country whence he comes, and are totally ignorant of the language which he speaks—if he employ the universal language of Masonry—if he display the Sign and Token of his profession, his faith becomes intelligible, and we fold him to our hearts as a brother. Is he in sorrow? We will bind up his wounds. Is his heart lacerated and bleeding? We will pour in the oil and wine of kindness and sympathy. Is a worthy brother in pecuniary difficulties? We will relieve his wants and restore his comforts. If he have talent, we will honour it;—if he have none, he is still our brother. Is he a good and virtuous man? We will rejoice at it. Is he immoral? We will draw a veil over his faults, by adopting that distinguishing virtue of our science, which is symbolized by a non-metallic key. For if he have faults—surely he has some virtues; and these we are bound to esteem, let his errors be what they may. This is a lesson which Freemasonry teaches. Charity and Brotherly Love is the foundation and cape stone, the glory and cement of our ancient and honourable institution.

If these principles be strictly inculcated in our Lodges, Freemasonry will become—what it ought ever to be—a beatific vision, leading, through its connection with Christianity, to a Grand Lodge in the skies, where the just exist in perfect bliss to all eternity; where they will be for ever happy with God the Great Architect of the Universe, and dwell to all eternity in the celestial bowers of peace and Brotherly Love.

Relief is the next tenet of our profession. This virtue has been already partially illustrated;[2] but I cannot refrain from adding an extract from that beautiful Lecture which Jesus Christ delivered to his Apostles when he sent them out to evangelize the people. "Heal the sick; cleanse the lepers; raise the dead; cast out devils. Freely ye have received, freely give. Provide neither gold, nor silver, nor brass in your purses; nor scrip for your journey, neither two coats, neither shoes, nor yet staves; for the workman is worthy of his meat. And into whatsoever city or town ye shall enter, enquire who in it is worthy; and there abide till ye go thence. And when ye come into an house, salute it. And whosoever shall give to drink, unto one of these little ones, a cup of cold water only in the name of a disciple, verily I say unto you, he shall in no wise lose his reward."

Applied to Freemasonry, Relief forms a branch of charity, actually emanating from brotherly love. It wa this absorbing characteristic, at the revival of Free masonry, about the beginning of the eighteenth century,

[2] Vid. Lect. 2.

which elevated the science to a distinguished rank in England, and induced the formation of Lodges in every part of the world. This emanation of the Deity advanced the claims of Freemasonry to the favourable consideration of mankind, by the noble institutions which practically exemplified its theories and doctrines. These institutions placed Freemasonry on the broad and permanent basis of public utility, without any reference to the genial and beneficial tendency of the rites and ceremonies, morals and science, which are practised and enforced in the tyled recesses of the Lodge.

The widow's tear—the orphan's cry—
All wants—our ready hands supply,
As far as power is given.
The naked clothe—the prisoner free—
These are thy works sweet Charity,
Revealed to us from Heaven.

It was requisite that Freemasonry should assume a high position amongst the institutions of the country, at a time when, by the re-establishment of its Grand Lodge on a firm basis, public attention was called to the order, and its general utility excited discussion amongst scientific and thinking men. About this period the Duke of Buccleugh proposed the establishment of a general fund of benevolence for the relief of distressed Masons. Local funds of the same description had been long before in active operation amongst the private lodges; but a central fund appeared to promise a more extended usefulness; and its formation placed Freemasonry before the public eye in a new and amiable form. It was soon followed by the establishment of those noble foundations for the children of indigent Brethren, or orphans; one of which sprung from the practical benevolence of the Chevalier Ruspini, and was brought to perfection under the patronage of the Duchess of Cumberland; and the other was subsequently formed under the name of the Royal Masonic Institution for clothing, educating, and apprenticing the sons of worthy deceased Freemasons; both of which are still in active and beneficial operation.

Other institutions, which exemplify the nature of masonic benevolence, have, from time to time, made their appearance amongst us, and are matured by the efficient support of our opulent and wealthy Brethren; for it is by the union of active zeal, with talent and riches, that great results are generally accomplished. In the present age, the benevolence of the masonic system has been still more strikingly developed. An asylum for aged and decayed Freemasons of good character, and an annuity system for their permanent relief, have been recently projected. The former is in active operation; and there is no doubt but the latter will be extensively supported by the wealthy members of the craft. These charities are jewels of inestimable value in the masonic crown, which emanate from a practical exercise of the best feelings of the human heart; and advantageously display the beauty of the system to which they are attached.

TRUTH is an attribute which involves the peace and welfare of civil society. It has been asserted that the word Truth is the third person singular of the verb *Trow;* and that it was formerly written troweth, trowth, or troth, meaning that one troweth, thinketh, or believeth. However this may be, Truth is essential to the Free and Accepted Mason, and forms a constituent part of the wisdom which is the object of his search, while investigating the principles of the Science; and if he expect to derive any advantage from his masonic studies, he will make the sacred dictates of truth the guide and director of all his actions. If the foundation be thus firm and secure, the superstructure can never be shaken. Pure thoughts, holy desires, and upright actions will clear the way for placid contentment, and the happiness which proceeds from rectitude of intention. To be good men and true is one of the first lessons we are taught in Masonry. On this theme we expatiate, and by its dictates endeavour to regulate our conduct. Hence, while under the influence of this principle, hypocrisy and deceit are unknown amongst us; sincerity and plain dealing are our distinguishing characteristics; whilst the heart and the tongue unite in promoting each other's welfare, and rejoicing in each other's prosperity.

THE POINT WITHIN A CIRCLE occupies a conspicuous situation on the Tracing Board of an Entered Apprentice. And deservedly; for it embodies a series of useful lessons, which, if reduced to practice in our commerce with the world, cannot fail to make us wiser and better. This significant emblem takes its origin from the garden of

Eden, which was circular—the trees of life and knowledge being placed in the centre, symbolical of the divine Omnipresence, the centre being everywhere, and the circumference no where. The perpendicular parallel lines, represented by these two trees, signified *justice* and *mercy*, which were practically exemplified at the unhappy fall of our first parents.[3]

The primitive explanation of this symbol did not differ very widely from the elucidation still used in the lectures of Masonry. The circle referred to *eternity*, and the point to *time;* for the purpose of shewing that time was only a point compared with eternity, and equidistant from all parts of its infinitely extended circumference; because eternity occupied the same indefinite space before the creation of our system, as it will do when it is reduced to its primitive nothing.

The application of the circle and perpendicular parallel lines amongst us, refers to the duty of circumscribing our wishes and actions within such prudent limits as to escape the severity of God's *justice* untempered by *mercy*. To speak in the technical language of the old lectures, the point represents an individual Brother; and the circle, the boundary line of his duty to God and man; beyond which he is enjoined never to suffer his passions, prejudices, or interests to betray him. The circle is supported by two perpendicular parallels lines, representing the two St. Johns,[4] who where perfect parallel in Masonry. On the vertex rests the Book of the Holy Law, which points out the whole duty of Man, and supports the theological Ladder, the top of which reaches to the heavens. In going round this circle, we must necessarily touch on these two lines, as well as on the sacred volume; and while a Mason keeps himself thus circumscribed, it is impossible that he can materially err.

The ORIGINAL SIGNS of Masonry are quadruple, and taken from the perfect square or cube which is constructed of four principles, viz., a point, a line, a superficies, and a solid; referring to the four elements.[5] In the true

[3] See Signs and Symbols, Lect. 9.

[4] The union Lectures have rejected this interpretation, and substituted Moses and Solomon; but I must confess that I prefer the prior arrangement.

[5] The Greeks had a very extraordinary compound hieroglyphic to

Freemasonry this is denominated Tetragrammaton; and in the Spurious system, Tetractys; both referring to the ineffable Name of the Deity. A cube was considered the most perfect of all figures; and therefore the Holy of Holies in the Temple, constructed for the peculiar dwelling place of the Most High, was of that form; and the altars of all nations were a cube either single or double. The Name, however, is expressed in masonic hieroglyphics by four distinct geometrical emblems, as well as by a single quadrilateral figure, viz., an equilateral triangle, a circle, a square, and a double cube. The triangle represents eternity, science, and power. The circle, God's Omnipresence. The square, perfection of happiness, and equal justice. Thus the Pythagoreans said, that the tetrad was the first number evenly even, which is a property of Justice; for, being quadrate, it divides into equals, and is itself equal.[6] Pythagoras gave this reason for likening the gods to a square, because he believed that quadrangular figures represented the divine essence; signifying pure and immaculate order; for, said he, "rectitude imitateth inflexibility; equality, firm power; for, motion proceedeth from inequality, and rest from equality. The gods, therefore, who are authors in all things of firm consistence, and pure, incontaminate order, and inevitable power, are not improperly represented by the figure of a square."[7]

These principles being established, the propriety of our Four original Signs will be apparent. They are represented by the tassels which decorate the angles of our Entered Apprentice Tracing Board; and refer equally to the four rivers of Paradise, and the four Cardinal Virtues. To illustrate this in a manner which may be intelligible to the Brethren, I would observe, that the palate and throat being the chief seat of irregular appetites, we are instructed by the first Sign to avoid temptation by a proper restraint on our passions; that we

represent the four elements. Juno was depicted as being suspended from the clouds by a chain fastened round her waist; at the upper end of which is a large ring held by the hand of Jupiter, while heavy stones were bound to her feet; and in this situation she hangs over the waters of the sea. Juno herself represented the *air;* her chain the *fire;* and the weights *water* and *earth.*

[6] Alex. Aphrod. Metaph. 5. [7] Stanl. Hist. Phil. vol. 3. p. 75.

may be *temperate* in all our indulgences, and never exceed the boundary line of decency and decorum, under the *penalty* of disobedience, or the violation of those engagements which, as Masons, we have voluntarily assumed.

The breast being the abode of Fortitude, we are taught by the second Sign to suppress the risings of apprehension and discontent; and to endure, with patience, the attacks of adversity or distress, pain or disappointment, rather than induce, by a weak and temporizing compliance with the persuasions of friends, or the denunciations of enemies, the bitter stings of remorse which must inevitably result from a betrayal of the secrets with which we have been intrusted on the faith of a solemn obligation.

The third Sign contains a lesson equally striking and useful. Prudence is the wisdom of the heart, and prompts cool and deliberate actions. Amidst all the various and chequered scenes which are incident to human nature, consideration and reflection will enable us to avoid the snares with which we are continually beset. Temptation may be powerful and overwhelming—trouble may assail us on every side—despondency may add the weight of its terrors to crown the attack upon our integrity with success; yet with the aid of this powerful Sign, we may, by the exercise of Prudence, overcome them all, and rise triumphant from the ordeal, like silver seven times tried in the fire.

The fourth Sign recommends integrity of principle, by referring to our first appearance on the sacred floor of the Lodge—well and worthily recommended—regularly proposed and approved—freeborn, of mature age, sound judgment, and strict morality; or, in other words, the symbol of a just and upright man. It denotes, therefore, the duty of universal Justice and good-will amongst mankind; and points to that golden rule of our own scriptures—do unto others as you would have them do to you.

It appears, therefore, that the virtues which proceed from these characteristic Signs, are Temperance, Fortitude, Prudence, and Justice. From the Master's chair, these sublime and useful qualities are recommended and eulogised in beautiful and impressive language, that the judgment may be enlightened and the heart improved.

Thus restrained by the salutary efficacy of Temperance, strengthened in our minds by the influence of Fortitude, instructed by Prudence, and guided by Justice into the path of piety and peace, we may pass through this world with the firmness of a rock on the sea-shore, unshaken in mind, from the security of our foundation, though storms and tempests eternally operate to undermine our virtue.

Such dissertations constitute the delightful Labours of the brethren when assembled in a closely tyled Lodge. An ardent desire exists in every breast to improve the intellectual faculties, and make a proficiency in that sublime knowledge which is allied to virtue ; and links devotional feelings to a correct estimate of our own hearts. The Spurious Freemasonry possessed some rudiments of this virtue ; and the inscription, KNOW THYSELF, appeared on the portal of Apollo's temple ; snd was ascribed to his oracle at Delphi. It was, indeed, a precept which attained great celebrity amongst the philosophers of antiquity. But, being applied to an unimportant purpose, it became useless in producing even the happiness of this world, much less of that which is to come. Masonry teaches us to know ourselves, by communicating the nature of our moral situation, and uniting this knowledge with our respective duties to God and our neighbour. Of these requisites to human or divine happiness, the Spurious Freemasons were lamentably ignorant.

To accomplish the important task of self-knowledge with perfect success, our sublime science instructs us to abstract ourselves from the world, and to consider our situation as free and responsible agents, by adverting to the purity of the science of Light, as practised by our first parents in the garden of Eden before their unhappy fall. Comparing this state of perfection with our proneness to indulge in such pursuits as nature rather than grace would suggest, we lament the melancholy defection from primitive innocence which sin has introduced, and endeavour to recover it by a conformity with the eternal laws of righteousness laid down in the Book which covers the pedestal of our Lodges; by examining the grounds and reasons of our faith, and making them the guide and directors of our actions. It is by virtue of such a process that the Labour of Freemasonry is converted to a good account; and the genial affections thus excited in the heart, produce the fruits of virtue, humility, and obedience.

The Labour of Masonry ripens the faculties and quickens them into action. Many a Brother, who has sustained a subordinate part on the great theatre of the world, has had his dormant powers called into operation in a masonic Lodge; and abilities have been elicited where they were not previously supposed to exist. Instances of this kind are frequent amongst us, and our social meetings have thus been elevated into an arena for the exercise and improvement of talent, which would otherwise have remained for ever inactive. The magic touch of Freemasonry has given the first impulse to a just and honourable exertion, whose fruits, applied in accordance with the precepts of the Craft, have excited distinction, honour, and reward. We have reason, therefore, to be proud of an institution which is capable of producing these blooming fruits. And it is owing to the unexampled discipline of the Order, that such inherent excellence is permitted to display its powers. Here native modesty is encouraged, genius fostered, and intellect improved. The discussions of masonic labour afford ample scope for every diversity of talent; and that man's mind must be constructed in an extraordinary mould, which can find nothing in the lectures of Freemasonry to excite attention, or to interest and improve the moral faculties of his nature. The philosophy of Freemasonry has, for its basis, the strong pillar of Truth; and its superstructure is the glory of God. In our moral or scientific, technical or ceremonial pursuits, there is always something which cannot fail to attract the notice, and captivate the affections of every initiated candidate, if his heart be susceptible of beneficent impressions. I have myself initiated many persons who were very unpromising, and yet Freemasonry has touched and enlightened them, and genial fruits, both as Masons and men, have been the happy consequence. Nor am I saying too much when I affirm, that these results, in a greater or less degree, will always accompany initiation, where a Lodge is conducted with talent and discretion, and the Landmarks of the Order carefully preserved and inflexibly maintained.

Much, however, depends on the chief officer in the

East. It is his province to nurture and teach the budding genius to expand. The labour of Masonry is in his hands, and it is his duty to lead the brethren, by degrees and prudently, into all the depths of masonic research. For this purpose he must judiciously appropriate the several portions of his work to the capacities of the brethren. The Apprentice cannot be expected to perorm the business of the Fellow Craft or the Master Mason; and, even in each class, much discrimination is necessary, when mental improvement is the object, and spiritual illumination the grand design. The Tracing Board lies before him, teeming with such moral plans and excellent sketches, that, were we conversant therein, and adherent thereto, it would bring us to a building not made with hands, eternal in the heavens. From this abundant store, the worthy Master selects his materials with judgment, and applies them in the true spirit of universal Masonry, to the edification of his hearers. He expatiates with eloquence and truth on the objects within his view. He traces the rough ashler through all its various forms, till, under the workmanship of the expert Fellow Crafts, it assumes the square die, or cube highly wrought and polished, and incapable of trial and proof, except by the square of God's word, and the unerring compass of an irreproachable conscience.

Above all, the expert Master carefully avoids the frequent repetition of dry technicalities and monotonous forms of speech. Desirable as an uniform mode of working may be, the language may be varied, though the ancient Landmarks ought to be carefully preserved. Our ceremonies and discipline, science and morals, our symbols, tokens, and machinery, are so various and diffusive, that no Master of a Lodge can be at a loss for a subject of instruction, which would edify the brethren and augment the interest that warms and animates them, amidst the miscellaneous topics which our authorised ectures afford.

Twelve monthly lectures would complete the Master's vear; and the punctuality of their delivery would ensure a full and regular attendance of members, increase the popularity and strength of the Lodge, and, by a natural consequence, ensure the efficacy of the order, in promoting amongst mankind the moral blessings of peace, harmony, and brotherly love.

REFRESHMENT.

When the Lodge is called from Labour to Refreshment, the brethren enjoy the blessings of social harmony, without that confusion and irregularity which usually characterize all other assemblies. Each brother strives to convey and receive pleasure, and all attempts at sarcasm are promptly discountenanced. In these hours it is that the true Mason will carefully place those guards over the external avenues of his conduct which may contribute to maintain the sovereignty of reason. If these barriers be removed, and Masonry be made subservient to intemperance or excess, the duties of the Craft become neglected, and the noblest faculties of the mind enslaved. To this cause the contempt and odium which are often reflected on the institution may be truly attributed. He who is possessed of a laudable ambition to practise Freemasonry in its purity, and to enter into an exemplification of its true nature and design, will consider these hours as subordinate to the business of the Lodge, and calculated to no other end than to enliven the mind, and to add a cheerful lustre to the grave pursuits enjoined by the immemorial usages of the Craft.

CLOSING.

In the performance of a ceremony so solemn and momentous as the closing of a Masons' Lodge, every member has a lively interest. At the usual report, preceded by an enquiry involving the best interests of Masonry, the brethren are again reminded what is the chief care of a Mason. The avenues to the Lodge are carefully inspected by the meridian officer, whose knowledge and fidelity have entitled him to the confidence of the brethren, and after he has publicly proclaimed the security of the Lodge, the business of closing proceeds. The particular duties of the leaders of the respective bands of craftsmen are rehearsed. At the command of the Worshipful Master, the Senior Warden performs his duty, after seeing that the brethren have received their due proportion of masonic instruction and improvement; and the whole concludes with an impressive address to the brethren on their respective duties as men and Masons, when pursuing their accustomed avocations in the world; and with a fervent petition to the Deity supplicating his blessings on the fraternity, wheresoever dispersed under the wide canopy of heaven.

Such is the high ground which Masonry assumes from the extreme purity of the system. We are bound, therefore, to reflect that as our station is exalted, so ought our conduct to be exemplary; for the world regards us with a scrutinizing eye; and, which is of more consequence, we are under the constant inspection of the All-Seeing Eye of God. If we would adorn the system which is our pride and boast, nay, if we would not expose it to contempt, we must discharge the relative and social duties of life with a precision at least equal to the most virtuous of our fellow-men; for, as the science we profess may be ornamented by our rectitude of demeanour, so will it infallibly be disgraced, should we be found deficient in any of the obligations which are incumbent on us, in our respective characters of husband and father, citizen and subject, neighbour and friend.

I address myself plainly to the brethren at large on the subject of morals, because Freemasonry is defined as "a beautiful system of morality, veiled in allegory, and illustrated by symbols." It is indeed a system which is, or ought to be, the guardian of every virtue. I am anxious, therefore, for the extension of its principles. I would have every good man become a Mason, from a selemn conviction of its purity, and its decided influence over the moral character of its members, evinced by their propriety of conduct, their industry, sobriety, and public usefulness. I would have their Faith, and Hope, and Charity, like the pentalpha, or triple triangle of Masonry,[8] mutually assist each other, and combine to sup-

[8] Stukeley, in his Itinerary, (vol. i. p. 148.) has the following curious remark on this figure. "One would be apt to suspect that they (the Druids) had a regard to the sacred symbol and mystical character of medicine, which, in ancient times, was thought of no inconsiderable virtue; this is a pentagonal figure formed from a triple triangle, called by the name of *Hygeia*, because it may be resolved into the Greek letters that compose the word. The Pythagoreans used it among their disciples as a mystical symbol denoting *health;* and the cabalistic Jews and Arabians had the same fancy. It is the pentalpha, or pentagrammon, among the

port the rectitude of their professions; and I anticipate that the day is not far distant when Lodges shall be formed in every important town; and the members increase in ample proportion, as mankind behold the fraternity to be wiser and better than those who have not had the advantage of masonic teaching.

With these hopes and anticipations before me, can I be too strenuous in recommending the Free and Accepted Mason to let his light shine before men, that they may glorify the Father which is in heaven? Shall I omit a single opportunity of furthering the interests of Masonry, by raising my voice against the indiscretion of those who are satisfied with a mere profession of masonic zeal, without uniting with it the practice of masonic virtue? No, my brethren in the mystic tie, let it not be said by the uninitiated, that you are deficient in those practical characteristics of the Order, which, when firmly and systematically adhered to, cannot fail to distinguish you from the rest of mankind. And do not forget, that while you cultivate the perfection of your fraternal duties, you will, at the same time, improve in Christian ethics, you will fear God and love your neighbour, you will grow in grace and in the knowledge of that pure system of religion which is cemented by the blood of an atoning Saviour, and, if you persevere to the end, you will receive the reward of your faith, even the salvation of your souls.

Egyptians; the mark of prosperity. Antiochus Soter, going to fight against the Galatians, was advised in a dream to bear this sign upon his banner, whence he obtained a signal victory."

LECTURE XII.

THE BEAUTIES OF FREEMASONRY EXEMPLIFIED; AND ITS PECULIAR CEREMONIES AND OBSERVANCES SHEWN TO BE JUDICIOUSLY SELECTED, RATIONALLY MAINTAINED, AND HIGHLY ADVANTAGEOUS TO THE INSTITUTION GENERALLY, AND TO EVERY BROTHER IN PARTICULAR WHO IS WELL VERSED IN THEIR MORAL AND SYMBOLICAL REFERENCE.

Thy plants are an orchard of pomegranates with pleasant fruits; camphire, with spikenard;
Spikenard with saffron; calamus and cinnamon, with all trees of frankincense; myrrh and aloes, with all the chief spices;
A fountain of gardens, a well of living waters, and streams from Lebanon.

Sol. Song. iv. 13, 14, 15.

THE system of Freemasonry as now practised, combines the Speculative and Operative divisions, as they were reunited at the building of King Solomon's Temple. By the latter I would not be understood to mean the mechanical business of a bricklayer or a mason, but the study of the liberal sciences, including geometry and architecture. The morality of the First Degree, blended with the science and doctrines developed in the Second and Third, constitute the peculiarity, as well as the perfection of the system. If Freemasonry were merely an institution for the propagation of moral truth, it must ong ago have yielded to a superior teacher—the pulpit Had it been confined exclusively to science, a commoL ʟiterary Society would have answered all its purposes. It is the *dulce et utile* mixed together—it is the beauty of the arrangement that convinces the understanding and fascinates the heart.

The hours of labour are marked by pursuits which dignify and adorn the mind. The W. M. expatiates with clearness and perspicuity on the beauties of geometry, astronomy, and other liberal arts and sciences, with their reference and application to the designs of Providence in the creation of man. The imagination luxuriates on his Lecture, and the heart is improved, while the ideas expand under a course of training which blends amusement with instruction; and all his illustrations tend to inculcate a knowledge of those three great branches of masonic morality and true religion—the duties we owe to God, our neighbour, and ourselves.

In the hours of Refreshment, science is not abandoned. Music and poetry take the lead and contribute their aid to enliven the graver pursuits of our more serious hours.

Our excellent and lamented Brother Preston, (whom I always quote with pleasure, because he was one of my first instructors in the science of Freemasonry,) with equal brevity and truth, thus delineates the design of our lectures. Of the First he says: "In this lecture Virtue is painted in the most beautiful colours, and the duties of morality are strictly enforced. Here we are taught such wise and useful lessons as prepare the mind for a regular advancement in the principles of knowledge and philosophy; and these are imprinted on the memory by lively and sensible images, well calculated to influence our conduct in the proper discharge of the duties of social life. The Second Degree extends the plan, and comprehends a more diffusive system of knowledge. Practice and theory are united to qualify the industrious Mason to share the pleasures which an advancement in the art necessarily affords. Listening with attention to the opinions of experienced men on important subjects, the mind of the Craftsman is gradually familiarized to useful instruction; and he is soon enabled to investigate truths of the utmost concern in the general transactions of life." Of the Third, he says, that "In twelve sections, of which this lecture consists, every circumstance that respects government and system, ancient lore and deep research, curious invention and ingenious discovery, is collected and accurately traced. To a complete knowledge of this Lecture few attain; but it is an infallible truth, that he who acquires by merit the mark of pre-eminence to which this degree entitles him, receives a reward which amply compensates for all his past diligence and assiduity."

From these general remarks let us take a brief view of some of the beauties of the Order; for the impossibility of noticing every point, part, and secret by which we are distinguished, will be apparent from the preceding observations.

The ceremonies of Freemasonry are numerous and significant; although, if considered abstractedly, they are of little value, except as they contribute their aid to impress upon the mind a rich series of scientific beauties and moral truths. And I will undertake to affirm, that the system of Freemasonry, complicated as it is throughout the whole routine of its consecutive Degrees, and abounding with appropriate ceremonies, does not contain a single rite that is barren of intellectual improvement; and they all bear a reference to similar usages contained in the Holy Book that has been revealed from heaven.

Out of the numerous and fruitful store of rites and observances contained in this noble system, I shall select a few for illustration; that every enquirer may be informed of the source whence they are derived, and convinced that they have been conceived in a spirit of universal benevolence, and are practised with the design of making us wiser and better men.

1. Brief sketch of the three principal Steps or Degrees.

Like all other sciences, Freemasonry is progressive, and can only be acquired by time, patience, and a sedulous application to elementary principles, as a preparation for the higher and more abstruse points of doctrine, which convey pre-eminence in the superior Degrees. And that no mistake may arise respecting the qualification of candidates, tests have been instituted, to mark at every step their progress in the preliminary Degrees, before they be admitted to a more exalted place in the Lodge.

The Three Degrees of Masonry, as they were probably arranged by the Grand Masters at the building of the Temple, might bear a general reference to the three

Orders of the Jewish Priesthood, an arrangement which has also been introduced into the Christian Church. Indeed, this number was universally adopted in every ancient system. Even the Spurious Freemasonry had the same number of Steps. The first consisted of probation, purification, and expiation. The second was called the Lesser Mysteries, into which the candidate *passed* by solemn ceremonies; and also to the third, after a long period of additional trial, which was denominated the Greater Mysteries. These consisted of fearful rites, introductory to a full revelation of all the ineffable doctrines, which he was bound, under an obligation and heavy penalties, never to reveal.

The Essenes who preserved the true Freemasonry from extinction in the dark ages, which preceded the advent of Christ, admitted only three degrees; and the probationary term extended to one whole year. If, during this period, the candidate gave satisfactory proofs of his temperance, fortitude, prudence, and justice, he was accepted, and received the first Step or Degree; in which noviciate he remained another year before he was passed to the Second Step; and it was not until the expiration of three years that he was admitted to a full participation in the secrets and benefits of the society. And even here the utmost precaution was used. The candidate was previously bound by the most solemn vows to keep inviolably secret the mysteries of his Order, and to act upon and abide by the ancient usages and established customs of the fraternity. The Brethren distinguished each other, in darkness and in light, by signs and tokens. The most profound silence was imposed at their assemblies; the Lecturer only expounding the tenets of their creed, which were enfolded in a series of allegorical symbols, the rest listening with a grave and solemn attention.

In every civil institution the progress to rank, honour, and distinction, is, in like manner, graduated and slow. In the church, the bar, the army, and navy, and all other social establishments, the candidate for fame must toil through a weary probation, and be content with a slow passage through many preliminary steps, before he can hope to attain the object of his ambition. It is the same in Freemasonry. It has several degrees, which are not communicated indiscriminately, but are conferred on candidates according to merit and ability.

The very first step taken by a candidate on entering a Masons' Lodge, teaches him the pernicious tendency of deism and infidelity; and shows him that the foundation on which Masonry rests, is the belief and acknowledgment of a Supreme Being, the Creator and Governor of the world; accompanied by a confession that in Him alone a sure confidence can be safely placed to protect his steps in all the dangers and difficulties he may be called on to encounter in his progress through the mazes of good and evil with which this world abounds; assured that if his faith be firmly grounded in that Supreme Being, he can certainly have nothing to fear. In connection with this faith, the First Degree of Masonry teaches him that his actions must be squared by the precepts contained in the Holy Bible, the constant study of which is strongly recommended. It goes on to enforce the practice of the three duties of morality—to God, his neighbour, and himself. It reminds him of the value of time, by an emblem which points out the division of the day into twenty-four equal parts; and the absolute necessity of regularly appropriating certain portions of it to the purposes of labour, rest, and the worship of his Maker, is forcibly impressed upon his mind. It teaches him the Three Theological and the Four Cardinal virtues; connected with which, it points out to him the necessity of cultivating Brotherly Love, the cape stone, the glory, and the cement of the Institution; it incites him to the duty of relieving the necessities of others, with the superfluities of his own substance; and in all places, and on all occasions, to adhere strictly to truth, as one great and effectual means of pleasing God. These are all emanations of the faith which the Candidate professes at his first admission. We have Three Luminaries in our Lodges;—and what do they point out? They refer to the three precepts of Micah the prophet; that, as Masons we ought to do justly in every transaction of life; to love mercy, and to walk humbly with our God. We are clothed in white, as emblematical of the innocence and integrity which ought always to distinguish a Free and Accepted Mason. Our Jewels have all a moral tendency; and there is not a figure, letter, or character in Masonry but points out some moral or theological duty.

If we pass on to the Second Degree, the first object that strikes us is the symbol of an eternal and self-existent Deity, who will reward or punish us everlastingly, according to our works. In this degree we are solemnly reminded that the All-Seeing Eye of Providence observes our actions, and notes every improper word or thought to produce against us at the day of Judgment. The Star of this Degree points to that supernatural appearance in the heavens which directed the wise men of the East to the place where the Incarnate God was prepared to receive the rich tokens of their adoration.

When the veil of the Third Degree is raised, we are presented with a series of historical facts and ceremonies which illustrate many passages in the Jewish scriptures, and refer to the fundamental truths of our holy religion. It is truly called a sublime degree, for it contains the essence of Purity and Light.

This Degree has a reference to the Christian dispensation, when the day of salvation is more fully revealed; atonement is made for sin; and the Resurrection from the dead plainly communicated and confirmed by the resurrection of Christ from the grave.

The Jewish Law had degenerated into a mass of rottenness and corruption;—piety, which planned the Temple at Jerusalem, was expunged;—the reverence and adoration due to the Divinity, was buried in the filth and rubbish of the world; and religion and morality were scattered to the Four Winds of Heaven. Three Ruffian Nations, from the South, the West, and the East—the Syrians, the Chaldeans, and the Romans—gave in succession this temporary dispensation its death blow; those who sought religion through the wisdom of the ancients were not able to raise her; she eluded their grasp, and their polluted hands were also stretched forth in vain for her restoration. Her Tomb was in the rubbish and filth cast forth from the Temple, and Acacia wove its branches over her monument.[1] In this state of dark-

[1] Freemasonry tells us, in a figure, that the acacian branch shall be severed from its parent stem, and we shall be triumphantly raised from the tomb of transgression, and conveyed by angelic attendants to the

ness and despair, she lay until the Saviour came, instituted the Five Points of Christian Fellowship, and raised her from the dust in which she had been indecently interred, to a more glorious inheritance; to be the means of salvation to generations yet unborn; to unite mankind by the ties of a common Faith and a common Hope, and to produce that perfect and unsullied Charity, which shall have its consummation in glory at the Resurrection of the dead.

2. Freemasonry possesses an universal language. Do you enquire what is its utility? It is for the purpose of enabling a worthy brother in distress to convey his wants and necessities, even though we are ignorant of his vernacular tongue; for thus the stranger and sojourner can freely explain their wishes. Is he surrounded by difficulties? His peculiar distresses are soon made known; and commiseration and relief are promptly administered. By the use of this valuable art we are enabled to hold an intelligible intercourse, and even to maintain a connected conversation with brethren of every clime, and every language. We thus express pleasure and pain, sympathy and disgust, reverence and distress, with many other affections of the mind, even in the most public situations, without attracting notice or exciting curiosity. If a brother, then, should forget himself so far as to be guilty of any public indiscretion, a formidable display of this universal language would restore his recollection and bring him back to virtue. So truly has it been observed, that "however a brother may mistake himself as a man, he has the motive and opportunity of recovery as a Mason."

A knowledge of this invaluable secret—a language of universal application—has saved multitudes of lives in times of war and public discord;—"when shipwreck and misery had overwhelmed them—when robbers had pillaged—when sickness, want, and misery had brought them even to the brink of the grave. In such hard and dismal calamities, the discovery of Masonry has saved them. The discovery of being a brother has stayed the

Grand Lodge above; if we discharge our respective duties here in Faith, and Hope, and Charity, as good Masons and worthy members of the community at large.

savage hand of the conqueror lifted in the field of battle to cut off the captive; has withheld the sword imbrued in carnage and slaughter, and subdued the insolence of triumph, to pay homage to the Craft."[2]

So efficacious is the universal language of Masonry; and to shew that its benefits are not imaginary, I subjoin two anecdotes, out of the stores which every brother would be able to furnish from his own experience; the former communicated to the Freemasons' Quarterly Review (1835. p. 167,) by Brother Leigh, of Taunton; and the latter by an uninitiated individual under the signature of Alpha. (1836. p. 442.)

"During the late war, a small coasting vessel, trading between Plymouth and Hampshire, returning with a cargo to the former, was suddenly surprised in the evening by a French Privateer, who had taken up her position under one of the bold promontories of the Devonshire coast. The crew of the English vessel, being composed of the captain and two or three persons, could make no resistance to a ship of war, and was taken possession of by the enemy. The French officer who performed that duty, in the course of his overhauling the cargo and papers of his prize, discovered a Master Mason's certificate from the Grand Lodge of England. He demanded of the English captain if he were the individual named in it; and, on receiving an answer in the affirmative, the Frenchman observed, that although he was not himself a Mason, this was a circumstance which he knew would very much interest his commander, and that he must, therefore, go aboard the French ship and inform him of it. Having done so, the French Captain now came aboard his prize, and having satisfied himself that his captive was entitled to his fraternal protection, *by the universal language of Masonry*, proposed to him that if he would give him his word as a man of honour and a Mason, that on his return to Plymouth he would use his best exertions to obtain the release of his (the French Captain's) brother, who was then a prisoner of war in Mill prison, Plymouth, he would give him up his vessel, and allow him to proceed on his voyage. The Englishman, happy to be liberated on terms so truly masonic, made the best of his way to

[2] Hutch. p. 186.

Plymouth, in which harbour he in a few hours arrived with his cargo and crew. He immediately went ashore, and having assembled the Masters of the Lodges of that part, communicated to them this extraordinary convention. One of the Masters, happening to be employed at that time by the government in the management and supply of the French prison, lost no time in communicating it to the head department in London, and by the next post received an order to complete with dispatch and fidelity an exchange which the French Brother had commenced with so much generosity and confidence. The French prisoner was shortly conveyed by a flag of truce to the shore of his native land."

Alpha thus relates his adventure :—"In the year 1825, I left England for Bogota, in South America. In journeying with a party consisting of eight persons from Carthagena to a small village, called Baramquilla, situated on the banks of the river Magdalena, we were unable to procure mules to carry us to our destination. Application was made to those persons most likely to supply our wants, without effect; they informed us that several persons had been detained there for the same reasons. The following day we redoubled our search, making very liberal offers for the use of the beasts, but it availed us nought. What to do in this predicament we knew not, we were in a most unhealthy place with a burning sun upon us, and last, though not least, tormented almost to death with musquitoes, without a prospect of being released from these miseries for some weeks. But thanks to Masonry, our troubles were of but short duration, for, in the evening, we chanced to call upon the Alcade of the place, when it was discovered by him that one of our party was a Brother Mason. Judge of our surprise, when he told us that we should all have mules, and be enabled to proceed on our journey the next morning; a promise which he most religiously kept; for, at six o'clock the following day we left the place, with many blessings on the founder of Masonry."

3. We meet on the level and part on the square.

In the open Lodge—Masonry knows no distinctions but those of merit. In the pure language of that sacred volume which is always displayed on the Pedestal, we honour all men, love the brotherhood, fear God, and honour the Queen. The glitter of pomp, the plumage of grandeur, form, however, no passports to especial commendation, except as they are united with moral worth. In our Lodges the rich and the poor meet together. What is their common Charter? The Lord is the maker of them all.[3] It is the mind—the intellect—improved by diligence and industry, that elevates the Free and Accepted Mason to the highest honours of his profession. In the system of Masonry, like that of nature, when the Lodge is open, the badge of innocence assumed, the bond of friendship in active operation, and the Jewel of Equality sparkling in the West; all are on a level;—all are men formed in the image of their Maker. Of noble shape, tall, godlike, and erect. Nature subjects the wealthy to pain, sickness, and death, equally with him who earns his bread by the sweat of his brow. In like manner the Mason, whether rich or poor, is subject to destitution, to helplessness: in both cases, time, in its irresistible progress, brings on the Third Degree—the final catastrophe of life; and Death will have his prey. Sickness approaches without a summons; disease never knocks at the chamber door, or enquires whether he be a welcome guest; death breaks through bolts and bars; he spurns the bribes of the rich, and is deaf to the heart-rending supplications of the poor. Both must repose together on the same lowly bed. The sprig of acacia—that striking emblem of innocence—is rifled from the spot where it grew and flourished, to decorate the crumbling remains of the departed brother; and the draperies of mourning will be alike extended over their place of burial.

From the dust acacias bloom,
High they shoot and flourish free;
Glory's temple is the tomb,
Death is immortality.

With such illustrations in view, Masonry asks the enlightened brother, what is the glory of the world? Is any thing really great, except virtue? Is any thing truly mean and contemptible except vice? "According to the eternal rules of celestial ceremony and precedency," says a celebrated moral writer, "in the sublime and immortal

[3] Prov. xxii. 2.

heraldry of nature and of heaven—Virtue takes place of all things. It is the nobility of angels—it is the majesty of God."[4] "A king in the Lodge, is reminded, that although a crown may adorn the head, or a sceptre the hand, the blood in his veins is derived from the common parent of mankind, and is no better than that of the meanest subject. The statesman, the senator, and the artist, are there taught equally with others, they are, by nature, exposed to infirmity and disease; and, that an unforeseen misfortune, or a disordered frame, may impair their faculties, and level them with the most ignorant of their species. This checks pride, and excites courtesy of behaviour. Men of inferior talents, who are not placed by fortune in such exalted situations, are instructed to regard their superiors with peculiar esteem when they discover them voluntarily divested of the trappings of external grandeur, and condescending, in the badge of innocence and bond of friendship, to trace wisdom and follow virtue, assisted by those who are of a rank beneath them. Virtue is true nobility, and Wisdom is the channel by which virtue is directed and decayed; Wisdom and Virtue alone, mark distinction amongst Masons."

Thus, if Masonry read the rich man a lesson of humility, it teaches also to the poor, obedience and gratitude; while it reminds both of their mortality. It inculcates the necessity of practising Brotherly Love, in our onward march from this world to another and a better. The wealthy and the wise are admonished to use their riches and talents for the purpose of cheering and enlightening the poor and ignorant; knowing that it is to their persevering industry and mechanical knowledge that they are indebted for the elegancies and luxuries of life. And both are admonished to make their accounts perfect by deeds of the purest morality and virtue.

In the mechanism of Masonry, the graduated scale of rank is strictly and immutably observed, and subordination is perfect and complete; for its government is despotic. The Master in the East is absolute in his authority over the Brethren of his Lodge. Yet this does not in the least militate against the doctrine of equality, which is inculcated both by precept and example in all the

[4] Fawcet, vol. i. p. 95.

illustrations of Masonry. For it is an authority founded on brotherly love, and exercised in a spirit of kindness and suavity, which is the more effective, as it brings into operation, both with rulers and brethren, supreme and subordinate, the amiable sympathies which spring from fraternal esteem. If the power vested in the Worshipfu Master be steadily maintained on the judicious principl of *suaviter in modo*, it will be unnecessary to display th sterner featurers of *fortiter in re*. In a word, a Masonic Lodge is governed by love, not by fear. And if, in any instance, this officer should so far forget his Master's obligations, as to exercise the despotic power with which he is undoubtedly invested, tyrannically—the bond of union would be violated—the great principles of Masonry would be scattered to the winds of heaven—and the Lodge, how numerous and respectable soever it might be, would soon cease to exist.

But though Masonry thus inculcates the most impartial equality amongst the brethren, while the Lodge is tyled, and masonic duties are in progress, it yields to every one his proper rank when the Lodge is closed and the Jewels put away. Honour must be given to whom honour is due. Grades of human rank are necessary to support the framework of society; and Masonry, which is Order personified, cements the social system.

> Order is heaven's first law, and this confest,
> Some are and must be greater than the rest. *Pope.*

This is one of the peculiarities of Freemasonry. We meet on the Level and part on the Square. Is it not an amiable regulation? In our intercourse with the world, in the courtesies which we exchange with our species, a worthy Brother Mason is preferred to any other connection. Freemasonry is a science, universal as the Deity we invoke at the very first step of our initiation. It is a chain of affection where the whole brotherhood is linked in the strictest bonds of amity and friendship; and it teaches the incumbent duties which we owe to each other, and to ourselves, in every state of life from the highest to the lowest grades. In whatever station our lot may be cast, whether we move in those magic circles which circumscribe the society of princes, and the great ones of the earth, or whether we occupy the lower, and more retired grades, we have an incumbent duty to perform; and it is on the discharge of that duty, including benevolence and protection on the one hand, and humanity and gratitude on the other, that our future lot will be determined in the day when the Grand Architect of the Universe shall make up his Jewels.

4. The avocations of Masonry are regulated by the mutation of the heavenly bodies.

The Master opens the Lodge at sunrise, with solemn prayer; the Junior Warden calls the men from labour when the sun attains its meridian height; and the Senior Warden closes the Lodge with prayer at sunset; when the labours of our ancient brethren ended. The great luminary of creation rises in the East to open the day, with a mild and genial influence, and all nature rejoices in the appearance of his beams. He gains his meridian in the South, invigorating all things with the perfection of his ripening qualities. With declining strength he sets in the West to close the day, leaving mankind at rest from their labours. This is a type of the three most prominent stages in the life of man, infancy, manhood, and old age. The first characterised by the blush of innocence, pure as the tints which gild the eastern portals of the day. The heart rejoices in the unsuspecting integrity of its own unblemished virtues, nor fears deceit, because it knows no guile. Manhood succeeds; the ripening intellect arrives at the meridian of its powers, while, at the approach of old age, his strength decays, his sun is setting in the West; and, enfeebled by sickness or bodily infirmities, he lingers on till death finally closes his eventful day, and happy is he, if the setting splendours of a virtuous life gild his departing moments with the gentle tints of hope, and close his short career in peace, harmony, and Brotherly Love.[5]

This is the model on which the brethren are admonished in the Lodge to conduct their own private affairs. If the day, like the Lodge, open and close with prayer, the Deity, in all his dispensations, both of mercy and justice, will ever be present to their recollection. And prayer is the key that unlocks the gates of heaven. In this angelic exercise our thoughts and aspirations ascend to

[5] See my Ant. of Mas. p. 35.

the throne of grace; and piety and holiness become habitual to the soul. If we look into the starry firmament, and behold Orion rising in the South, clothed in gigantic majesty,—if we contemplate "the sweet influences" of the Pleiades, Arcturus, and the Wain; what are they but so many speaking evidences of His immortal power and goodness, who contrived, created, and upholds the vast machine of nature? and all those myriads of brilliant orbs that roll over our heads, form a bright blaze of eternal and intelligible Masonry. The heavens declare the glory of God and the firmament sheweth his handiwork. The reflections arising from such contemplations expand the mind, by unfolding the secrets of the skies, which are a sealed book to the ignorant or indifferent observer.

What a range of sublimity does a survey of the heavenly bodies afford? How is the mind lost in the immensity and magnificence displayed in the spacious firmament on high? How do the affections soar beyond the trifling concerns of this short and transitory life—absorbed in the vast idea of Omnipotence?

I have been much pleased with a view of the immensity of the creation, which appears in the "Christian Almanack" for the present year. The writer says: "Some astronomers have computed that there are not less than seventy-five millions of suns in the universe. The fixed stars are all suns, having, like our sun, numerous planets revolving round them. The solar system, or that to which we belong, has about thirty planets, primary and secondary, belonging to it. The circular field of space which it occupies is in diameter three thousand six hundred millions of miles, and that which it controls much greater. The sun which is our nearest neighbour is called Sirius, distant from our sun about twenty-two billions of miles. Now, if all the fixed stars are as distant from each other as Sirius is from our sun, or if our solar system be the average magnitude of all the systems of the seventy-five millions of suns, what imagination can grasp the immensity of creation? Who can survey a plantation containing seventy-five millions of circular fields, each ten billions of miles in diameter? Such, however, is one of the plantations of Him who has measured the waters in the hollow of his hand—meted out the heavens with a span—comprehended the dust of the earth in a measure—and weighed the mountains in scales, and the hills in a balance." This, for a speculation, appears immense, but it forms only a point in the vast idea of universal space, which the human mind is altogether incompetent to grasp; for, who shall attempt to place a limit to the designs of Omnipotence?

The study of this subject, which forms a part of the Fellow Craft's Lecture, prepares the mind for the contemplation of a future world, and elevates our thoughts to the great central emblem, whose sacred initial character, surrounded by a blaze of glory, recals our minds from the work to the Architect, from the science to its mysterious symbols.

And what reference has the situation of the Lodge? Why is it placed due East and West? The tyro in Masonry will answer the question. But this should not only be a station of order and science, but it should also be a station of seriousness and devotion. A Masons' Lodge, should be a Company of Masons, who should behold the rising and setting of the sun with piety, with gratitude, and with devotion! It should be an assembly, where the ignorant are taught Wisdom, where the wanton are taught sobriety, where the dissolute are reclaimed, and where the unruly are influenced to perform all the important duties of religious obedience. As the sun riseth in the East to enlighten the day, so the Master of the Lodge should stand in the East to enlighten with true Wisdom his masonic Companions, and guide all his Fellow Craftsmen to work out their salvation with fear and trembling! As the sun setteth in the West to close the day, so the Wardens of the Lodge should stand in the West to close the labours of the Lodge, and see that none go away, not only not dissatisfied, but also to see that none go away unimproved in moral virtue, and in pious resolutions. This is the perfection of Masonry.[6]

5. The propriety and decorum of processional movements considered.

Processions may be deduced from the highest antiquity. They are the very essence of every ancient institution which has had the most remote alliance with religion, and particularly they form so great a portion of Free-

[6] Inwood's Sermons, p. 66.

masonry, that it could not exist without them. If Freemasonry be considered in all its parts and bearings, from the most simple elements to the highest and most ineffable degrees, this inevitable conclusion will result,—that if Masonry be good for any thing, its excellence is derived, in a great measure, from processional observances. Take away its processions, and obliterate the illustrations con sequent thereon, and where is the system of Freemasonry? Our *public* processions have been instituted for many noble purposes. We visit the house of God in public, to offer up our prayers and praises for mercies and blessings, —we attend in a body, to shew the world our mutual attachment as a band of brothers,—we are arranged in a set form, to exhibit the beauty of our system, constructed on the most harmonious proportions, and modelled into a series of imperceptible grades of rank, which cement and unite us in that indissoluble chain of sincere affection, which is so well understood by Master Masons,—and blend the attributes of equality and subordination in a balance so nice and equable, that the concord between rulers and brethren is never subject to violation, while we meet on the level and part on the square.

But I will bring forward such a cloud of witnesses from the sacred records[7] in favour of this practice, as shall silence all objections to its antiquity and usefulness. To establish the point, I need not mention the solemn procession of Adam and Eve out of Paradise, though it forms a prominent illustration of Royal Arch Masonry. It will be unnecessary to adduce the procession of angels on Jacob's ladder;[8] or that splendid procession, the most numerous, perhaps, ever witnessed in the world, which took place at the deliverance from Egypt, when the people came out with a mighty hand, and were conducted through the wilderness by the rod of Moses.[9] These, however, bear upon the subject, because they are pecu-

[7] The Spurious Freemasonry was all, in like manner, processional; (see my Signs and Symbols, and Hist. Init. passim,) and I name it here, only to shew that as their system was borrowed from the true one, it follows as an inevitable deduction from this general and uniform practice which distinguished the secret rites of all nations,—how widely soever dispersed, or separated from each other by impassable barriers—that our science has always, even from the earliest times, been accompanied by the use of processions.

[8] Gen. xxviii. 12.

[9] This rod, or sceptre, was the visible agent which God thought proper to make use of for the deliverance of his people from captivity; and

liarly connected wilh Freemasonry, and received the sanction of God himself, who attended them in person, enveloped in a cloud of glory.

These processions were accompanied by the banners of the twelve tribes,[10] and many others emblazoned with various devices; and they were conducted on certain prescribed principles, under the immediate direction of God himself.[11]

Look at the procession of David to Mount Moriah, when it pleased the Lord to put a stop to the pestilence which raged amongst his people in consequence of his inadvertently having them numbered;[12] and that most pompous one of Solomon, when his stately temple was dedicated.[13] Look at the Jewish processions generally, and in particular, the triumphal one which preceded the feast of Purim.[14] Contemplate, finally, that grand procession through the streets of Jerusalem, in which the Saviour of mankind was the most prominent character; when the people shouted in strains of gratulation, Hosanna to the Son of David! Blessed is he that cometh in the name of the Lord![15] These are the holy models on

it was emblematical of the united authority which Moses possessed, as king, priest, and prophet. It subsequently became the subject of many Rabbinical fancies. With the Hebrews, the sceptre was always a badge of authority. In Heb. xi. 21. we read that Jacob leaned on the top of his sceptre, or staff, as the patriarch of his race, while he was in the act of blessing the sons of Joseph. And it may be observed, that *virga* is frequently used in scripture for a sceptre. So in the Iliad, book ii.—

" The king of kings his awful figure rais'd,
" High in his hand the golden *sceptre* blaz'd;
" The golden sceptre of celestial frame,
" By Vulcan formed, from Jove to Hermes came."

After which, follows a long list of very important personages, through whose hands the sceptre descended to him; and in a subsequent book of the same Poem, the crier is introduced, placing this sceptre in the hands of Menelaus, and commanding the Greeks to be silent while he spake.

[10] This was a most magnificent spectacle,—if, as some writers think, (viz. Montanus, Simlerus, Theodotion, Junius, and particularly Oleaster,) from the construction of the words *ascenderunt quintati*, that the Israelites marched by five in a rank, *militari ordini*, in battle array; for then, as the whole procession consisted of not much less than two millions of souls, it would have extended nearly a hundred miles in length,—led by Jehovah in a cloud,—attended by the ark of the covenant and tabernacle, —and the whole host overshadowed by numerous banners waving in the air.

[11] The order of this procession may be found in the 10th chapter of the book of Numbers.

[12] 2 Sam. xxiv. 20.

[13] 2 Chron. v.

[14] Esth. vi. 11.

[15] Matt. xxix. 9.

which our processions are founded; and you will, therefore, no longer be inclined to think that such observances are useless, or frivolous, or unnecessary.

Masonic processions are conducted with much greater splendour on the continent than in this country. The superior officers of foreign lodges wear splendid robes of silk and velvet, of the three pure colours, decorated with gold and precious stones. I copy from a ritual of Helvetian ceremonies, in my possession, some other attendant circumstances, which are calculated to swell out the gorgeous magnificence of a masonic procession. "The Great Master walks under a purple, blue, and crimson canopy, with fine linen and bells, and decorated with tassels and fringes; the staves of his canopy are four, or eight, which are borne by Master Masons of the oldest lodge present; on the right hand of the Great Master is a sword-bearer; and on his left hand is a sword-bearer; before the Great Master is a standard, and behind him is a standard. All Masters of lodges present are under blue canopies, each borne by four Master Masons of his own company; the canopies are six feet long, and three feet broad; the staves are six feet long; the framework is of cedar, or pine, or box-wood; the covering hangs down not less than three feet on each side, and in front likewise. In the middle of the procesion is carried the ark, covered over with a veil of blue, purple and crimson, by four of the oldest Masons present.

Such are the ceremonies and observances of Freemasonry. They speak a language to which every brother's heart responds, because they are connected with associations which are highly cherished and prized. These ceremonies cement an attachment to the Craft, which becomes more overwhelming as it is better understood; and as there does not exist a single rite which is barren of instruction, so they are all and each essentially necessary to the perfection of the system. Every increase of knowledge only shews more clearly the necessity of preserving the ancient Landmarks, and of enforcing those technicalities which every true Mason regards with respect and veneration, because they are at once the guardians of our treasures, and the discriminating tokens by which our claims to fraternity are unequivocally substantiated.

COROLLARY.

The above Lectures, it is presumed, will be found to embody much valuable information on every branch which Freemasonry is supposed to embrace. Great pains have been taken in their composition, that the volume may constitute a book of reference worthy the attention of the scientific Mason, as well as of the brother whose talents are more humble and unpresuming. To both, profit and pleasure will mutually result from a careful perusal of its pages. I have been desirous of infusing a taste for the pure Philosophy of Masonry, that it may superinduce the habitual practice of those blooming virtues which its authorized Lectures so strongly recommend.

For this purpose I have defined and illustrated the three great divisions of the science, and traced their existence in every country of the ancient world. I have endeavoured to shew that Light, as our ancient brethren denominated Freemasonry,[1] was a system of primitive devotion, descending from heaven to enlighten and purify humanity;[2] and that the idolatrous mysteries, which were the Spurious Freemasonry of heathen nations, were derived from it. The third and fourth Lectures explain minutely the object, tendency, and result of all these

[1] In the ancient Indian mythology, Light (*Marichi*) was the son of Brahma or Adam; while in Phœnicia, Light, Fire, and Flame are represented as the children of Cain. The designation is still acknowledged in our Masonic custom of dating a document from A∴ L., one meaning of which is *Anno Lucis*.

[2] "Rabbi Hagaon said there are three Lights in God—the Ancient Light or Kadmon; the Pure Light, and the Purified Light. Allix. Judgm. p. 170.

three divisions, and show how they originated, and where they respectively flourished in all their glory, so as to constitute a distinct and influential feature in the civil government of all nations. Having traced the sciences known before the flood, and in particular those of Astronomy, Geometry, and Architecture, which were practised under the idea, if not under the name, of Operative Masonry, by the professors of the Spurious branch of our science; having pointed out how the imitative systems degenerated from the pure principles of primitive Lux, till they substituted the solar and sideral worship for the simple rites enjoined by a common Creator, and the symbol itself was universally adored; having produced some ancient Landmarks of the true system which were preserved in the Spurious Freemasonry, and shewn how they had become perverted from their original design by allegory and mystification; having described this polluted institution to shew that its influence was used for political purposes, to furnish the legislator and magistrate with unlimited power over the public mind, not only from the imposing splendour of its ceremonies, but from the severity of its penalties, and the equivocal nature of its doctrines; I have proceeded to take a review of the symbolical system, which was of such essential service to the Spurious Freemasonry, as to constitute the chief essence of all its mysterious rites and doctrines. The most remarkable emblems were found in the Egyptian, the Pythagorean, and the Druidical mysteries; and these have been copiously illustrated, in order to convey a general idea of the use and application of hieroglyphics in the Gentile world.

The seventh Lecture, therefore, embraces a comprehensive view of the origin and use of symbols, with the intention of pointing out their application alike to the true and the Spurious Freemasonry. Of this kind were the Patriarchal, the Jewish, and the Christian types; many of which have been incorporated into our system of Freemasonry, and constitute a most delightful relief from studies that require a greater portion of serious thought. In a word, the symbolical illustrations of Masonry recommend it strongly to our notice; not merely by the pleasures which result from their acquisition, but from the genuine morality and unsullied benevolence which accompany their elucidation.

An attentive consideration of the progress of Speculative and Operative Masonry, amongst the two grand divisions of men who preserved and who rejected the true faith and worship of God, as delineated in the preceding Lectures, will shew that the distance between them, at one period of the unhappy history of man's apos tacy, was wide as the poles asunder. And the true system of Light will display greater charms from its contrast with the hideous deformity of its spurious rival. For while, as Sir Walter Raleigh justly observes, the apostate race were employed in earthly pursuits, pleasure, and ambition, and in cultivating the arts of music, architecture, agriculture, and the working of metals; the celestial offspring practised the more exalted sciences of divinity, prophecy and astronomy: the children of one beheld the heavens; the children of the other, the earth.

The eighth Lecture records the interesting fact, that Speculative and Operative Masonry, thus marked by broad and distinctive characteristics, made gradual approaches towards each other, as the time drew nigh for the erection of that gorgeous Temple in honour of the true God, which was destined to eclipse, in riches and glory, all the buildings which the pride or vanity of man should induce him to consecrate to deities of his own invention. At that period was consummated the beneficent union of Speculative and Operative Masonry, which produced results that excited the admiration of mankind.

The events which occurred during the progress of this structure, are of such importance to our science—embracing a wide range of ritual observances, and conducing to the enforcement of masonic discipline by precept and example—that I have thought it necessary to devote an especial Lecture to their consideration. The mass of valuable matter which lay before me—the curious documents—the interesting traditions—the significant rites, and the historical associations of that period, so important to the Free and Accepted Mason—were of such vast moment, as to demand an extended illustration; although the suppression of many facts, which could not consistently be submitted to the public eye, was considered indispensable. I have, however, endeavoured to concentrate the principal masonic traditions which have reached our times, respecting the events and traditions of that remarkable epoch; and have recorded, in the ninth Lecture, some circumstances which are known only to few; and which the well-instructed Mason alone will be able to trace through the veil which I have thought it necessary to throw over them.

I hope it will be acknowledged that these two important Lectures contain a fund of information on the subject; and I take credit to myself for having communicated it with such circumspection and care as not to have violated, even in the most remote degree, those injunctions of secrecy which are imposed in our solemn obligations.

The three concluding Lectures are intended to display the beauties of Freemasonry as it is now practised; and I flatter myself that the industrious brother will find there a treasure which will be worthy of his consideration. The forms and ceremonies of the Order are exemplified and defended; nor have their moral and symbolical reference been overlooked.

From the general tenor of these Lectures, we may fairly conclude that Freemasonry is a subject worthy the attention of the Christian and the man of science. It includes a pure system of ethics, and developes the philosophy of mind, at the same time that it recommends and encourages social recreation, to unbend the energies, and recruit exhausted nature after hard and severe application to science. It has ever been my opinion that the philosophy of Masonry is not sufficiently attended to in the generality of our Lodges. And this is not, I am persuaded, owing to remissness or want of talent, but on account of the absence of some adequate and absorbing stimulus. It would, in my opinion, have constituted a most rational and engaging employment, if, added to the routine Lectures, competent brethren, giving due notice, with the approbation of the Chair, were to undertake to illustrate and explain in a familiar manner certain points in our history, doctrines, or discipline, on which the authorized Lectures are silent. It is for want of some such arrangement that so many brethren remain ignorant of the true design of the Order, and of many events, connected with its early history, without a competent knowledge of which, a false estimate is made, and the institution pronounced to be useless in the promotion of any worthy or valuable end.

How often do we hear Masons, many years after their initiation, desire information on subjects, which, under the system I recommend, even a tyro would be capable of furnishing. Brethren, high in rank and office, are often unacquainted with the elementary principles of the Science; and, instead of teaching others, acknowledge with regret that they have themselves much to learn. If a spirit of emulation were once fairly excited in a Lodge of Masons, the most gratifying results would soon appear. A desire to excel would not remain without its fruits; and the brethren would soon be impressed with the idea that it is by the love and cultivation of the philosophy of Freemasonry alone that they can arrive at any true nobleness of character, or real distinction in the science. This process would tend to reform the mind and improve the manners; to change indolence into activity; to teach the ignorant wisdom; to reclaim the dissolute, and to influence the unruly to perform all the duties of social obedience; and if Masonry were thus made subservient to the practice of religion, it would convey peace and comfort in this world, united with the most cheering hopes of happiness in the world to come.

www.ingramcontent.com/pod-product-compliance
Lightning Source LLC
LaVergne TN
LVHW011208110826
845150LV00006B/1368
* 9 7 8 1 4 2 5 5 1 8 2 7 1 *